Gandhi's Free Communication and Free Press

Gandhi's Free Communication and Free Press

Mr Krishnaveer Abhishek Challa

KALPAZ

ISBN: 978-93-5128-167-2

Price : ₹ 790

First Published, 2016

Published by

Kalpaz Publications
C-30, Satyawati Nagar,
Delhi – 110052
E-mail: kalpaz@hotmail.com
Ph.: 9212142040

Printed at: G. Print Process, Delhi

Cataloging in Publication Data—DK
Courtesy: D.K. Agencies (P) Ltd. <docinfo@dkagencies.com>

Challa, Krishnaveer Abhishek, author.
Gandhi's free communication and free press / Mr. Krishnaveer Abhishek Challa.
pages cm
Includes bibliographical references.
ISBN 9789351281672

1. Freedom of the press—India. 2. Communication—India. 3. Government and the press—India. 4. Gandhi, Mahatma, 1869-1948. I. Title.

PN4748.I5C43 2016 DDC 323.4450954 23

Contents

Preface 7
Introduction 9

Unit I

Chapter 1
Freedom of the Press: An Overview 17

Chapter 2
Freedom of the Press and the British Government (1908-1947) 29

Chapter 3
Freedom of the Press and the Indian Government (1948-1988) 47

Chapter 4
Freedom of the Press and Article 19 (a): Case Studies 79

Chapter 5
Freedom of the Press and Press Council of India 93

Chapter 6
Summary and Conclusions 107

Unit II

Chapter 7
Gandhian Journalism 125

Chapter 8
Gandhi's Free Speech 151

Chapter 9
Gandhi's Free Attire 173

Chapter 10
Gandhi's Free Communication Versus Ethics 195

Chapter 11
Gandhi's Free Religion 205

Index 233

Preface

In the contemporary decade of development wherein communication though has touched the abounding heights of technology, still is barred under the clutches of social and political dominance. Journalism, the essential derivative of communication has also been the victim of this chaotic syndrome. Free communication and freedom of press have always been the remedies of the crawling development that has dissolved the country in its propounding commercialisation.

And talking about freedom, the ideology that stands for it, is that of the Mahatma who thundered his agony for his people through his rare *satya* and *ahimsa.* Gandhi saw a free India in his sacrifice that he received with the hope that one day the flag of freedom will flutter the entire world with its aura of liberty. The answers for many of the scenarios questioning freedom can be well dwelled from the life of the Mahatma which is an open purity of inspiration.

'Gandhi's Free Communication and Free Press', sails through the barriers to the liberty of communication and thereby journalism, and presents a Gandhian perspective to bridge the gap between rights and freedom. The struggle for independence in the history has now been transformed into the struggle for free communication as is illustrated in this work.

Various sources including library catalogues, published journals, search engines, trade catalogues, national and general bibliographies have helped us in accomplishing this task. I hope this humble tribute to the Mahatma will serve as a useful work while analysing into the realms of free communication and freedom of press.

Mr Krishnaveer Abhishek Challa

INTRODUCTION:
Knowing the thoughts of the Mahatma on free communication and free press

While seeing the colours of freedom soaring the sky, the thought that resonates over the realms of independence is that of the Mahatma who made it possible to live the dawn of liberty. He freed a country that was brutally bleeding under the clutches of imperialism with his weapons of purity. The saviour of mankind, the leader of a fading country, the father of a fuming nation, Gandhi has always been the flame for free communication. He sprinkled the thoughts of ahimsa over the rooted violence that shed many lives in the name of struggle for freedom.

Mahatma Gandhi was the spark without an ignition that made the world to lean before his thriving thoughts. Today, when the contemporary media scenario bristles with unheard of turmoil- investigative journalism- through all means fair and foul; over-riding role of market forces in the media wherein the "advertorial" and "response" and "response features" edge out editorials, and when the media is trying to project the celebrities and models as the icons of modern society, it would be worth while to revisit Mahatma Gandhi's philosophy and canon of journalism and his contribution as a journalist.

According to Chalapathi Raju, himself an eminent editor, Gandhi was probably the greatest journalist of all time, and the weeklies he ran and edited were probably the greatest weeklies the world has known. He published no advertisement; at the same time he did not want his newspapers to run at a loss. He had gained considerable experience in South Africa, where he had taken over in1904 the editorship of the 'Indian Opinion' and published it in English, Tamil and Gujarati, sometimes running the press himself.

'Young India' and 'Harijan' became powerful vehicles of his views on all subjects. He wrote on all subjects. He wrote simply and clearly but forcefully, with passion and burning indignation. One of the objects of a newspaper, he said. is to understand the popular feeling and give expression to it; another is to arouse among the people certain desirable sentiments, and the third is fearlessly to expose popular defects.

Gandhi's papers published no advertisements. They enjoyed wide circulation. His approach to journalism was totally devoid of ambitions. To him it was not a vocation to earn his livelihood; it was a means to serve the public. In the 'Young India' of 2 July 1925, he wrote: "I have taken up journalism not for its sake but merely as an aid to what I have conceived to be my mission in life. My mission is to teach by example and present under severe restraint the use of the matchless weapon of satyagraha which is a direct corollary of non-violence."

Gandhi looked upon journalism as a means to serve the people. He said in his autobiography: "The sole aim of journalism should be service. The newspaper is a great power, but just as an unchained torrent of water submerges whole countryside and devastates crops, even so an uncontrolled pen serves but to destroy. If the control is from without, it proves more poisonous than want of control. It can be profitable only when exercised from within. If this line of reasoning is correct, how many journals of the world would stand the test? But who would stop those that are useless? And who should be the judge? The useful and the useless must, like good and evil. Go on together, and man must make his choice.

Gandhi was associated with six journals, for two of which he was the editor. His first paper, 'Indian Opinion' was started in South Africa. In order to ventilate the grievances of Indians and mobilise public opinion in their favour, Gandhi started writing and giving interviews to newspapers. He focused on open letters and Letters to Editor, but soon realised that occasional writings and the hospitality of newspapers were inadequate for the political campaign he had launched. He needed a mouthpiece to reach out to the people; so in June 1903 he launched Indian Opinion. It served the purpose of a weekly newsletter which disseminated the news of the week among the Indian community. It became an important instrument of education. Through the columns of the newspaper Gandhi tried to educate the readers about sanitation, self-discipline and good citizenship. How important the journal was to Gandhi is seen from his own statement in his biography? My Experiments with Truth:

"Indian Opinion...was a part of my life. Week after week I poured out my soul in its columns and expounded the principles and practice of satyagraha as I understood it. During 10 years, that is until 1914, excepting the intervals of my enforced rest in prison there was hardly an issue of 'Indian Opinion' without an article from me. I cannot recall a word in these articles set down without thought or deliberation or word of conscious exaggeration, or anything merely to please. Indeed the journal became for me a training in self restraint and for friends a medium through which to keep in touch with my thoughts."

The critics found very little to which they could object. In fact, the tone of 'Indian Opinion' compelled the critics to put a curb on his palm.

Gandhi launched Satyagraha against the Rowalf Act and the massacre in Jallianwala Bagh. He learnt in South Africa how important the press and public opinion could be in politics and had taught himself how to use the written word most effectively.

It will be pertinent to point out as to what Mahatma Gandhi considered to be the role of newspapers. He wrote: In my humble opinion, it is wrong to use a newspaper as a means of earning a living. There are certain spheres of work which are of such consequence and have such bearing on public welfare that to undertake them for earning one's livelihood will defeat the primary aim behind them.

When, further a newspaper is treated as a means of making profits, the result is likely to be serious malpractices. It is not necessary to prove to those who have some experience of journalism that such malpractices do prevail on a large scale. He was of the opinion, 'Newspapers are meant primarily to educate the people. They make the latter familiar with contemporary history. This is a work of no mean responsibility. It is a fact, however, that readers cannot always trust newspapers. Often facts are found to be quite the opposite of what has been reported. If newspapers realised that it was their duty to educate the people, they could not but wait to check a report before publishing it. It is true that often they have to work under difficult conditions. They have to sift the true from the false in a short time and can only guess at the truth. Even then, I am of the opinion that it is better not to publish a report at all if it has not been found possible to verify it.'

The eminent journalist and freedom fighter Salien Chatterjee who covered Mahatma Gandhi, his actions and programmes for a number of years died a few months back. In an article, 'Reporting Mahatma', he had written for the special issue of Vidura on, Gandhi as a Journalist, (Jan-March, 1998) he said:

"I joined journalism in 1942. Reporting Mahatma Gandhi and my tours with him were the best and most memorable period of my journalistic career. Gandhi himself was a journalist. During my tours with him, he often told me how he worked day and night to produce his journal 'Indian Opinion' in Natal, South Africa. He described 'Indian Opinion' as the most useful weapon in his struggle in South Africa. He always stressed the importance of newspapers in educating the people. Gandhi always believed and always emphasised that the sole aim of journalism should be service, service of the people and the country.

In 'Young India' Gandhi once gave a glimpse of the exacting code head set up for himself. "To be true to my faith, I may not write in anger or malice. I may not write idly. I may not write merely to excite passion. The reader can have no idea of the restraint I have to exercise from week to week in the choice of topics and my vocabulary.

It is training for me. It enables me to peek into myself and to make discoveries of my weeknesses. Often my vanity dictates a smart expression or my anger a harsh adjective. It is a terrible or deal but a fine exercise to remove these weeds."

The newspapers should be read for the study of facts. They should not be allowed to kill the habit of independent thinking. - M. K. Gandhi

Mahatma Gandhi's speech during his visit to 'The Hindu' sums up his philosophy and vision of journalism: I have, therefore, never been tired of reiterating to journalists whim I know that journalism should never be prostituted for selfish ends or for the sake of merely earning a livelihood or, worse still, for amassing money. Journalism, to be useful and serviceable to the country, will take its definite, its best for the service of the country and, whatever happens the views of the country irrespective of consequences. I think that we have in our midst the making of newspapers which can do so.

Let us be clear in our minds that-to confine Gandhi to India and to view him as merely the great Indian national leader is to diminish his greatness and personality. Gandhi belonged to the whole world, the humanity at large. The Time magazine, while chronicling the sweeping forces and great events of the twentieth century–catalogued Gandhi as one of the greatest activists–who fought for change from outside the traditional halls of power, who was bound to an abstract vision for which he would pay any price was life. The world that revered few men had revered Gandhi. Although Gandhi died believing his lone voice was unheard- he was mistaken; the power of his message would endure to move men and nations for all times to come.

Unit I

Chapter 1

Freedom of the Press: An Overview

The modern age of communication dates back to the invention of the printing press, this new invention facilitated multiple reproduction of a printed image which resulted in spreading knowledge and ideas through books. The book was invaluable repository of knowledge as well as thoughts in the old civilisations such a Chinese, Indian, Egyptian or Greco-Roman because the book provided an advantage of storing information in a small and durable form (Jowett and O' Donnell, 1992).

The invention of paper replacing the old papyrus helped much in the production of a book. Historically, the paper came into use in China in the first century A.D., in the Arab world in the eighth century, and in Europe in the fourteenth century. The invention of printing press technically evolved in China in the ninth century and then in Europe in the fifteenth century. The Gutenburg invention of printing press in a developed form from the Chinese made possible to produce numerous copies of the same book with little effort.

Books were followed in the seventeenth century by topical pamphlets, and then by newspaper. Some of the early newspapers were found to give information about trade, commodities, shipping movements and the like. They performed an important function of disseminating information (Emery, 1962). In course of time with the development of regular newspaper, the role the newspaper changed. For example, Tom Paine's *Common Sense* gave moral sustenance to the revolt of the American colonies against the British rule. In Latin America, similarly, the content and responsibility of some newspapers was closely connected with the struggle against Spanish domination which was to lead to independence (Many Voices, One World, 1982:7). Thus, the newspapers started taking an active role in the political, economic, social and cultural processes. As a result, the rulers feared that newspapers could endanger their authority. Hence, they started imposing restrictions on expression of ideas and thoughts, particularly through newspapers, books and pamphlets.

The essential demand for free expression and dissemination of thoughts and opinions started in France in 1789. The protagonists for this demand argued that they should have a right to disseminate their views in order to reach the common man. The fight for freedom of expression as well as the freedom of the press was predominantly a battle against authoritarian rulers, who realised that free dissemination of ideas would go against them. However, Britain, the United States and France won the battle for the freedom of the press by the end of eighteenth century (discussed in the following pages). In the nineteenth century and the early years of twentieth century, there was no freedom of the press in nations under autocratic rule such as Russia or the colonial rule such as India.

But, the advent of the press as an essential mass medium and as a pillar of democracy, has engaged the special attention of every Government because the printed world is more powerful than a free speech. Therefore, the printed word has special features, according to Dhavan (1990) who lists them out as follows:

(a) Printed matter records ideas in a permanent form, which speech cannot;

(b) However, large the audience for speech may be, a newspaper or book has a larger circulation than spoken words. Even though in modern times a newspaper has other rivals in the realm of media of expression such as Radio and Television, the morning daily has the widest demand in the world and is the most potent medium of mass communication;

(c) Freedom of the press is an extension of freedom of speech and expression; and

(d) Democracy can endure and thrive not only under the vigilant eye of its legislature but also under the care and guidance of public opinion, and the press is, par excellence, the vehicle through the mandate which public opinion becomes articulate.

In view of these special features, freedom of speech and freedom of the press have been given prominent place in the basic documents of the United Nations and certain other international bodies. The Universal Declaration of Human Rights, 1948, the European Convention on Human Rights, 1950 and the International Covenant on Civil and Political Rights, 1966 recognise the importance of the freedom of expression. All of them declare that everyone should have the right to freedom of opinion and expression without any interference.

Article 19 of the U.N. Declaration reads:

> "Everyone has the right to freedom of opinion and expression, this right includes freedom to hold opinions without interference and seek, receive and impart information of ideas through any medium and regardless of frontiers".

In a democracy, freedom of expression plays an important role as men are entitled to participate in the process of formulation of common decisions. Indeed, freedom of expression is the first condition of liberty; it occupies a preferred position in the hierarchy of liberties giving succor and protection to other liberties. Hence, it is described as the mother of all other liberties. The press as a medium of communication is a modern phenomenon. It has immense power to advance or thwart the progress of civilisation. Its freedom can be used to crate a brave new world or to bring about universal catastrophe.

Communication is the very essence of human life as expressions of thought and ideas are an integral part of the total development of a human personality. Hence, free speech is a basic requirement for human survival in a society. Where men cannot freely convey their thoughts to one another, no freedom is secure and absolute. A free society sustains itself where freedom of expression is paramount. Political philosophers and historians argue that the growth of civilisation is possible only where freedom of speech and expression thrive. Freedom is described as absence of control, interference or restriction. Thus, the freedom of expression has four broad social purposes to serve –(i) it helps an individual to attain self-fulfillment; (ii) it assists in the discovery of truth; (iii) it induces the thought process of an individual to participate in decision making; and (iv) it provides a mechanism by which it is possible to establish a reasonable balance between stability and social change.

The Report of the International Commission for study of communication problems known as 'Many Voices, One World' (1982) emphasised the importance of freedom of speech and press in the preservation of human right in the following terms:

> Freedoms of speech, of the press, of information and of Assembly are vital for the realisation of human rights. Extension of these communication freedoms to a broader individual and collective right to communicate is an evolving principle in the democratisation process. Among the human rights to be emphasised are those of equality for women and between races. Defense of all human rights is one of the media's most vital tasks (p. 265).

The second Press Commission of India (1982) also explained the concept of freedom of the press as follows:

> The expression 'freedom of the press' carries different meanings to different people. Individuals, whether professional journalists or not, assert their right to address the public through the medium of the press. Some people stress the freedom of the editor to decide what shall be published in his paper. Some others emphasise the right of the owners to market their publication (pp. 34-35).

Freedom of the Press in USA and UK:

United States of America: On July 4, 1776, in Philadelphia, the representatives of the American colonies declared their independence by saying that the right of the people to revolt against tyrannical Government. The leaders of this revolt drew their arguments that it was a natural right to fight the Government which was authoritarian (Castberg, 1960). The defence of these arguments was that the British King could rule the people with their free consent. In this case, the King violated the hereditary rights of his American subjects and hence the leaders of the revolt had a constitutional right to revolt against the King (Power, 1992).

With the creation of new nation in the United States of America in 1787, its Constitution contained certain provisions for the protection of individuals from the state. However, some States in the new Union refused to ratify the new Constitution if no addition was made to the Declaration of Rights known as Bill of Rights. In 1789, the United States Congress passed the Ten Amendments known as the Bill of Rights which came into force in 1791. The Bill of Rights gave a formal, constitutional confirmation of the traditionally recognised natural rights. These rights intended to protect freedom of speech. The foremost champion for the Bill of Rights, Thomas Jefferson, the then American President, regarded them as the most fundamental of all rights. The Bill of Rights incorporated into the Constitution of the USA in the First Amendment. The First Amendment declares, "Congress shall make no law respecting an establishment of religion, or prohibiting the free exercise thereof; or abridging the freedom of speech or of the press; or the right of the people peaceably to assemble, and to petition the Government for a redress of grievance". The Constitution did not elaborate what was meant by "Freedom of the Press", but since the U.S. imported the Common law from England, it was natural that the fathers of the Bill of Rights understood it as absence of prior restraint, and what was evident from the very text of the First Amendment which was drafted in the negative sense, as a prohibition upon the Legislative Power (Bhatia, 1997).

Social and economic development in the United States of America in modern times has added a 'positive' content to the initial approach of the press because it means a freedom from control as to what may be published through the press and also from any restriction which may even indirectly hamper that freedom.

In the USA this broader aspect of the freedom of the press has been formulated judicially in these words (Basu, 1986).

> The guarantees of freedom of speech and press were not designed to prevent censorship of the press merely, but any action of the Government by means of which it might prevent such free and general discussion of public matters as seems absolutely essential.

It would positively include the freedom to possess those means equipment which are necessary to achieve the goals for which freedom of the press is required.

This aspect of the freedom of the press was thus expressed by the Commission on Freedom of Press in the USA.

> "The primary suggestion of the term 'freedom' is the negative one, the absence of external interference whether to suppress or to constrain. To be free is essentially to be free from something some arbitrary impediment to action, some dominating power or authority. But since freedom is for action, and action is for an end, the positive kernel of freedom lies in the ability to achieve the end; to be free for some accomplishment. And this implies command of the expression of opinion in all its phases. It is free from the achievement of those goals of press service on which its own ideals and his requirements of the community combine and which existing techniques make possible. For these ends it must have full command of technical resources, financial strength, and reasonable access to sources of information at home and abroad, and the necessary facilities for bringing information to the national market. The press must grow to the measure of this market (pp. 54-55).

In this regard, Minattur (1961: 2-3) aptly summarised the decisions of the US the US Supreme Court as follows:

(i) Freedom of speech and freedom of the press are fundamental personal rights of the citizens:

(ii) The exercise of this freedom is the foundation of free Government by free men;

(iii) The state is foreclosed from assuming a guardianship of the public mind through regulating the press;

(iv) Freedom of the press assumed that the widest possible dissemination of information form diverse and antagonistic source is essential to the welfare of the public; and

Freedom of the press involves the freedom to employ the birth of the press in England, the monarchs adopted violent and repressive measures against the press. Through licensing, censorship and prohibition, attempts were made to crush its freedom. Despite these measures, the absolute power enjoyed by the emperors was challenged. Intellectuals like Milton, John Stuart Mill supported the cause of the press. In his *Areopagitica,* Milton wrote that every free individual should have rights and enjoy the "liberty to know, to utter, and to argue freely according to conscience". In fact, Milton's *Areopagitica* was a protest addressed to the Long Parliament which had taken up licensing, after the abolition of the 'Star Chamber' (Castberg, 1960).

Lacking a written Constitution or an entrenched Bill of Rights, in UK, the concept of freedom of the press, like the wider concept of freedom of expression and liberty, was basically negative. Freedom of the press, in England, means the right to print and publish anything which is not prohibited by law or made offensive, such as sedition, contempt of court, obscenity, defamation or blasphemy.

Freedom of the press in England is the freedom of the press from prior restraint or pre-censorship. This aspect originated out of the historical fact that, there was until 1695, an Annual Licensing Act which prohibited the printing of any literature without licence form the crown or its agent. It was against this system of licensing that the doctrine of freedom of the press was asserted by intellectuals like Milton. As a result of such agitation, the Parliament allowed the Licensing Act to expire and since then no further attempt has been made to introduce any previous restraint on the publication of printed matter (except in the time of war), and by 1784, this was acknowledged by the Courts.

Freedom of the Press and the Indian Scenario

The story of the press and the history of the freedom of press in India have been tales of constant struggle and progressive achievement under the British and the Indian governments. As a whole, the press in India played a decisive role during the British period and fought for freedom of speech and personal liberty (Krishnamurthy, 1966:2). Describing the role of the press during the freedom struggle, Muzumdar (1966: 1016) said. "The press imbued the people with patriotic fervour, indomitable courage and heroic self-sacrifice to an extraordinary degree".

Iyer and Sethi (1966) argued that the freedom of the press is the very basis of democracy. It is one of the great bulwarks of liberty and can never be restrained by despotic governments. Despite governmental suppression, newspapers in India have proved that an ideal newspaperman can exercise a sane and powerful influence upon the people in moulding their opinion and character. The British-Indian Government, from the very beginning attempted to circumscribe the liberty of the press. The British rule from the very inception was lawless, and, rules and ordinances were passed or promulgated to make the press subservient to the wishes of the authorities. The laws affecting the press were many and of a complicated nature. India after becoming a sovereign democratic Republic in 1950 with the adoption of the Constitution recognised freedom of speech and expression as a fundamental right and included it in the Indian Constitution. Article 19(1)(a) states: "All citizens shall have the right to freedom of speech and expression". However, Article 19(2) provided reasonable restrictions in the exercise of freedom of speech and expression in the interest of: (a) sovereignty and integrity of India; (b) the security of the state; (c) friendly relations with foreign states; (d) public order, decency and morality; (e) contempt of court; (f) defamation; and (g) incitements to an offence.

But the Supreme Court of India has recognised the freedom of the press as higher manifestation of freedom of speech and expression (Venkataramaiah, 1989, Bhatia, 1997). Although successive Governments in India since 1947 have made attempts to gas the freedom of press on many occasions, the press has survived such attempts.

A Review of Some Studies

Freedom of the press as a concept has fascinated many research scholars, journalists and legal experts because freedom of the press is the basis for free expression of ideas through mass media channels. These experts have written several books and articles dealing with the freedom of the press to record the historical concept of the freedom of the press in India. Mostly, these books and articles can be broadly categorised into two: (a) historical, and (b) legal.

Researchers who attempted the historical sketch of the press in India focused on the role of the press during freedom struggle or the contemporary issues with specific focus on certain trends. They discussed only the freedom of the press as a concept, but did not elaborate the emergence of the concept in the free and independent India. They include Natarajan (1962), Krishnamurthy (1966), Seshagiri Rao (1968), Mankekar (1973), Nayar (1977), Subramanyam (1984), Parthasaradhy (1991), Padhy (1991, 1994) and Sinha (1994). Most of these books specifically focused on the growth of newspapers in India during the British period and also the repressive methods undertaken by the British Government to suppress the freedom struggle.

As part of the freedom struggle, the British Government enacted laws to curtail the freedom of the press. These historical landmarks were delineated by various authors as mentioned above. Natarajan (1962), however, sketched the growth of newspapers during the British period and the role of newspapers during the freedom struggle. He concluded his study in 1958 by presenting the recommendations of the First Press Commission set up by the Government of India in 1952. Similarly, another study of Krishnamurthy (1966) also elaborately dealt with the growth of newspapers and also the freedom struggle. He focused much on the growth of newspapers and their role during freedom struggle in various regions of the country. He also concluded his study; Subramanyam (1984) also made an elaborate study on the role of newspapers in South India between 1905 and 1932 and only discussed the role of newspapers during freedom struggle. Parthasaradhy (1991) and Padhy (1991) also wrote on the growth of newspapers and occasionally referred to the press laws that were enacted during the British regime. For example, Parthasaradhy in his historical sketch of the press in India wrote one chapter on the press laws in India form the British period to the modern period. Overall, all these books dealt with the historical growth of newspapers and their role in the freedom struggle. But, these books have not focused much on the struggle for freedom of the press in India.

The second category of books and articles dealt with the legal aspects of the freedom of the press and implications of the Court judgements on the freedom of the press. Most of the authors happened to be legal experts in India, they discussed the freedom of the press within the parameters of the Constitution. They elaborated the meaning of Article 19(1)(a) which deals with freedom of speech and expression. Some prominent authors in this category include Ramachandran (1950), Noorani (1970), Sarkar (1975), Dholokia (1980), Sorabjee (1976), Sarkar (1984), Basu (1986), Venkataramaiah (1987), Iyer and Sethi (1996) and Bhatia (1997). Basu (1986) only presented all the Acts that deal with the press, without interpreting them elaborately with reference to contemporary issues. The book has put together all the texts of the Acts for the purpose of an academic text book. In his study, Venkataramaiah (1987) who was the former Chief Justice of India discussed the limits of the freedom of the press as shown in Article 19(2). He defended the reasonable restriction imposed on the freedom of speech and expression. Iyer and Sethi (1996) also dealt with some topics like circulation, pre-censorship and press freedom and Emergency which have affected the freedom of the press in India. Bhatia (1997), however, extensively made a study on the politico-legal aspects of the freedom of the press in the wake of court judgments and press legislation brought out by the successive Governments in India. Her study dealt with only the press legislation and freedom of the press after India attained Independence in 1947.

Contrary to these studies as mentioned above, the presents study makes an attempt to analytically investigate the freedom of the press both historically and legally. Therefore, the objectives of the study are:

(1) to find out the implications of various Acts on the freedom of press in India during the British period as will as independent India;
(2) to study various attempts made by the Central Government to curtail the freedom of the press and its impact on newspapers; and
(3) to find out the role of the Press Council of India in upholding the freedom of the press.

In view of objectives, the present work attempts to study the historical perspective of freedom of the press between 1908 and 1988. The reason for selecting this period is very significant. The British Government in 1908 promulgated Newspapers (Incitements to Offences) Act VII. The purpose of this Act was to curtail the freedom of the press because the newspapers in India were supporting the cause of national movement in driving out the Britishers from India (Krishnamurthy, 1966; Padhy 1991:38). In the modern period, when the Congress Government (1984-89) headed by the late Prime Minister Rajiv Gandhi also brought out a "notorious" Bill (Defamation Bill, 1988) to curb the freedom of the press. As a response to the Bill, newspapers, opposition leaders and lawyers resisted the Bill tooth and nail and forced the Government to withdraw it. The premier national daily, *The Hindu,* in its editorial dated September, 23, 1988, with the Newspaper (Incitements to offences) Act VII of 1908. Thus, the present study has taken into consideration these two landmark years in the history of the press for the purpose of studying the historical developments and also the freedom of the press.

During for the purpose of the study, all newspapers, and periodicals have been considered as press and any attempt to curb their freedom is treated as an onslaught against the freedom of the press. In orders to sketch the history of the freedom of the press and attempts against it, a variety of source material has been used. Books, journals, documents and newspapers have been taken into consideration. However, the researcher has mostly depended on secondary sources such as books and periodicals procured from libraries to study the freedom of the press during the British period. Nevertheless, the role of the newspapers cannot be studied independently on their own unless they are studied along with the political developments in the country. Therefore, the researcher has also presented the historical developments intertwined with the newspapers and their role in political developments. During the British time, the newspapers played a decisive role in molding the opinion of the people as well as the leaders of the country. Thus, the researcher has taken into consideration only historical landmarks that have had an impact on the freedom of the press in India. Since, it is beyond the scope of one researcher to observe and study the minute details of the entire period for want of time and resources.

The present work is organised into six chapters. Chapter II deals with the origin of newspapers in India and various legislations brought out by the British Governments to curb the freedom of the press. This chapter focuses specifically on the freedom of the press and the role of newspapers between 1908 and 1947. Chapter III deals with the freedom of the press and attempts made by the Indian Government during different regimes to curb the freedom of the press between 1948 and 1988. Chapter IV specifically sketches the various court judgments with regard to freedom of the press and interpretations given by the courts in different circumstances. Article 19(1)(a) is the main focus of this chapter. Chapter V discusses the setting up of the Press Council and its role in upholding the freedom of the press in India. Lastly, Chapter VI summarises the study and draws conclusions by offering suggestions.

Chapter 2

Freedom of the Press and the British Government (1908-1947)

The present chapter makes an attempt at examining the freedom of press during the British rule from 1908 to 1947. The press in India faced many problems during the British regime because many curbs were imposing on the freedom of the press or the freedom of expression.

The first newspaper was conceived in India by William Bolts, the author of 'Consideration on Indian Affairs' who planned to start a newspaper in India (Natarajan, 1962; Iyer and Sethi, 1996). In September, 1766, William Bolts pasted a paper on the door of the Council Hall in Calcutta, asking people to avail themselves of newspapers reading at his house. The notice caused great commotion in official circles. His efforts to advance the cause of the freedom of information were nipped in the bud by the Bengal Government which asked him to quit Bengal and proceed to Madras. This incident illustrates the first instance where the Government imposed curbs on the freedom of expression.

The first printed paper in India appeared on January 29, 1780. James Augustus Hicky, the British citizen, published the first paper Bengal Gazette or the Calcutta General Advertiser. The paper, known as Hicky's Gazette, wrote sarcastically against man and affairs, especially against the administration of the East India Company. It took a leading part in writing against Governor – General Warren Hastings. When malicious 'personal attack' was made against

Madame Hasting, the Governor General imposed an order depriving Hicky of the privilege of circulating his newspaper through the General Post Office. The Government action against Hicky, the first full-fledged journalist in India, was the first incident to gag the newspaper. However, the paper continued to fight for the liberty of the press and upheld the freedom of the press as one of the great bulwarks of liberty. Hicky recorded his view of freedom of the press as follows: "The subject should have full liberty to declare his principles and opinions, and every act which tends to coerce that liberty is tyrannical and injurious to the community" (Barns, 1940).

The freedom of the press in India was subjected to many problems even after the Bengal Gazette episode. Various laws, regulations and ordinances to curb the freedom of the press were brought out by the British Government. In 1811, during Lord Minto's tenure, the proprietors of all printing presses in Calcutta and its dependencies were directed to print the names of the printers of all papers printed by them.

In October 1813, Lord Hastings framed rules for the control of printing offices in Calcutta to control writings against the Government. The rules were: (1) the proof sheets of all newspapers, including supplements and all extra publications, be previously sent to the Chief Secretary for revision; (2) all notices, handbills and other ephemeral publications, be in like manners, previously transmitted for the Chief Secretary's revision; and (3) the titles of all original works, proposed to be published be also sent to Chief Secretary for his information, who will thereupon either sanction the publication of them, or require the work itself for inspection as may appear proper.

The rules imposed by Hastings were in force for five years. In 1818, Hastings abolished the "Department of Censor of Newspapers" which was set up earlier and formulated new regulations prohibiting editors of newspapers from publishing any matter relating to:

(1) Animadversions of the measures and proceedings of the Honorable court of Directors or other public authorities in England connected with he Government of India, or disquisitions on political transactions of the local

administration or offensive remarks leveled at public conduct of the members of the council, of judges of the Supreme Court or the lord Bishop of Calcutta;

(2) Discussions having a tendency to create alarm or suspicion among the native population or any intended interferences with their religious opinions or observations;

(3) The republication from English or other newspapers of passages coming under any of the above heads otherwise calculated to affect he British power or regulation in India; and

(4) Private scandals and personal remarks on individuals tending to excite discussion in society.

Consequently, in 1823, an ordinance was issued by the succeeding Governor –General John Adam providing for the licensing of the press under which all the matters printed in a press except commercial matters required a previous licence from the Governor General. Regulations were also framed under this ordinance. The ordinance and existing regulations in British India were replaced by the Press Act, 1835, popularly known as the Metcalfe's Act, which only required the printer and publisher of every newspaper to declare the location of the premises of its publication (Venkataramaiah, 1989).

The attitude of Sir Metcalfe, who was the acting Government – General immediately after the sudden resignation of Lord Bentick, a liberal Governor-General in March 1835 was quite different from his predecessors towards the press. Metcalfe did not like the licensing of the press under the 1823 ordinance. He requested Lord Macaulay, Law Member of the Governor-General-in-Council the Central Government of British Government in India, to prepare a draft Press Bill.

Macaulay's draft bill was opposed by some members of the Council like H.T. Prisep and Lt. Colonel Morison who wanted restrictions imposed on the newspapers published by Indians to continue. However, Metcalfe convinced the members of his council and got the Press Act, 1835 passed. It was hailed as the most liberal Press Act in Indian History (Krishnamurthy, 1966).

Governor-General Lord Canning reintroduced licensing known as the Gagging Act in 1857, the year of the first uprising against imperialism, in respect of all kinds of publications including books and other printed papers. The Indian Penal Code, 1860, made the offences of defamation and obscenity punishable and those provisions were applicable to the press too. The Section 124A which made sedition punishable was included in the code in 1870.

Section, 153A, 153B and 295A which dealt with the offences promoting enmity between different classes, making of imputations or assertions prejudicial to national integration, and outraging religious feelings were subsequently added to the code.

The Press and Registration of Books Act came into force in 1867. This Act which specifically dealt with the press did not in any way control the press. But it only regulated the printing presses and the publication of newspapers and books and provided for the preservation of copies of every book and newspapers printed in India and for registration of such books and newspapers. (This Act is in force even at present in India). It was mainly intended to prevent publication of anonymous literature. Then followed a short-lived legislation–the Vernacular Press Act, 1878 which provided for punishment of those who published seditious writings in newspapers published in Indian languages.

Freedom of the Press and Press Acts

The beginning of the twentieth century in India witnessed a great deal of political and social awakening. This national movement against British rule gained momentum. In order to curb the activities of freedom fighters, the British Government promulgated different Acts to suppress the freedom of expression and freedom of the press. According to Subramanyam (1984) the Government did not have a uniform policy for controlling the press and several experiments were conducted during this period to deal with the press. During the period (1908 to 1931) three important laws and ordinances were brought out the British Government to curb the liberty of the press. These measures were the 1908 Act, the 1910 Act, and the Ordinance of 1930, which later became an Act. Obviously, these attempts of the

Government to stifle the freedom of the national press made the task of the newspapers very hazardous. In fact, the press vigorously fought for freedom for itself even while fighting for the freedom of the country.

The Press Act of 1908

The British Government in 1905 split the Bengal Province into East and West Bengal for the administrative convenience during the tenure of Lord Curzon as Viceroy. On account of this partition, the Government anticipated a series of disturbances in the country. Terrorist action in Bengal, peasant unrest in the Punjab, concern about disaffection in the army and an increasingly extreme voice in some sections of the press led to bringing in legislation, which was thought to be necessary to defend the Government (Israel, 1994).

The political event in 1907 compelled the Government to warn the newspapers against writing. In June 1907, the Government of India framed rules against publishing seditious matters and authorising local governments to institute prosecutions for sedition (Krishnamurthy, 1966). The resolution said: "The Government of India have recently had under their consideration the unbridled licence of certain publications of the press throughout India. They have also considered the deleterious moral effect which such publications are having throughout the country. The Governor-General – in-convinced that such a state of things cannot be allowed to continue and it is, therefore, resolved that in all cases where matter tending to create sedition, ill-will towards government, or ill-feeling between the various races inhabiting India has been published in any newspapers or other publication, local governments and administrations shall be empowered to proceed against those responsible for all such publications under the existing powers of the law".

The year 1907 saw a series of arrests and prosecutions of editors and journalist and confiscation of presses. The editor of Hindustan, Dina Nath was arrested in June, 1907, for ignoring the warning. In July, the editor of Yugantar of Calcutta was prosecuted for sedition and sentenced to a years' imprisonment. The Magistrate ordered the confiscation of the press where the paper was printed. In the same month, the editor of Sonar Bangla of Calcutta was arrested. Later in the month, the police raided the office of *Bande Maṭaram* and the editor, Aurobindo Ghose, was arrested for sedition. The editors of Hindustan and India were sentenced to five year's rigorous imprisonment each (Subramanyam, 1984).

The Indian National Congress which was fighting the British held its meeting at Surat in 1907. There was trouble at the meeting over supporting the British Government on its proposal to have an Indian representative in the Council of Ministers. The session ended with a division among leaders as liberals and nationalists. The liberals were led by Gopalakrishna Gokhale, a prominent leader of the Congress and the Nationalists were led by Bal Gangadhar Tilak. Two newspapers from Maharashtra *viz.*, Kesari and Deshasevak of Nagpur supported Tilak and campaigned in such an effective way that it necessitated the British Government to pass the Newspapers (Incitement to Offences) Act, VII of 1908 (see Appendix-1). This Act empowered the authorities to take judicial action against the editor of any paper which published matter inciting to rebellion (Krishnamurty, 1966: 69). This Act known as the Act of 1908 in Clause 3 (i) states:

> In cases where, upon application made by order or under authority from the local Government, a Magistrate is of opinion that a newspaper printed and published within the Province contains any incitement to murder or to any offence under the Explosives Substances Act, 1908, or to any act of violence, such Magistrate may make a conditional order declaring the printing press used, or intended to be used, for the purpose of printing or publishing such newspaper, or found in or upon the premises where such newspaper is, or at the time of printing of the matter complained of was, printed and all copies of such newspaper, wherever found, to be forfeited to His Majesty, and shall in such order state the material facts and call on all persons concerned to appear before him at a time and place to be fixed by the order, to show cause why the order should not be made absolute.

As a result of this Act, a Magistrate was empowered by conditional order to seize a printing press, if he was convinced that a newspaper printed therein contained any incitement to murder or to an act of violence or to an offence under the Explosive Substances Act. This conditional order could be made absolute either by an ex *parte* decision in an emergency or after hearing evidence from persons concerned against the conditional order. Police sub-inspectors were to carry out the Magistrate's order under warrant and a right of appeal to the High Court lay within 15 days of the order being made absolute. Proceedings under the Act did not save any person from being prosecuted under any other law, and on the order being made absolute the Local Government could annul the declaration by the printer or publisher and prohibit any further declaration in respect of the newspapers or any newspaper which was in substance of the same as the prohibited newspaper. On the charge of violation the Government Order, two editors, Chidambaram Pillai and Subramania Siva were sentenced to six years imprisonment. Editor of Tamil India, Srinivas Iyengar, was deported for five years; the editor and proprietor of Telugu Swaraj were sentenced to nine months imprisonment. In the Central Provinces, editor Hari Kishore was sentenced to five years rigorous imprisonment, and the press was sentenced to five years rigorous imprisonment, and the press was confiscated. In the United Provinces, the editor of the Urdu-i-Moalla was sentenced to two years rigorous imprisonment and a fine of Rs 500 was imposed (Natarajan, 1962: 168). However, the 1908 Act was sparingly used in the Madras Presidency. The incitement to murders and other offences through newspapers was not widely prevalent in South India. Hence, its use against the journals in the Madras Presidency did not arise. It was in 1908 only that G. Harisarvottam Rao, an editor of prominence, was prosecuted and imprisoned for three years for his writings in the Telugu journal, Swaraj, under the provision of the Indian Penal Code. On the day, (July 18, 1908) on which Harisarvothama Rao was arrested at Masulipatnam, Bal Gangadhar Tilak was arrested at Poona for his writings in the Kesari and was later sentenced to six years imprisonment (Subramanyam 1984: 34).

The Press Act of 1910

The British Government was unable to curb the growing hostility against the administration. The Indians were stubborn and uncompromising with the British rule. The press was championing the cause of the national movement. Newspapers with a missionary zeal acted and spread the idea of justice and equality. The press roused the public spirit and asked the people to come forward in opposing the British rule. The authorities termed these ideas as seditious (Krishnamurthy, 1966: 70; Natarajan, 1962; Parthasarathy, 1991; Padhy, 1994; Bhatia, 1997).

It was beyond the reach of the Government to contain this rapid spread of information against the administration. Therefore, the Government thought that a more stringent Act then the earlier one (the 1908 Act) was necessary to curb the expression of ideas through newspaper columns. The Government passed an Act in 1910 by incorporating stringent provisions. The Act, known as Press Act-1 of 1910 included a clause (3)(1) which states:

> Every person keeping a printing press who is required to make a declaration under Section 4 of the Press and Registration of Books Act, 1867, shall, at the time of making the same, deposit with the Magistrate before whom the declaration is made security to such an amount, not being less than five hundred or more then two thousand rupees, in money or the equivalent thereof in securities of the Government of India. Provided that the Magistrate may, if he thinks fit, for special reasons to be recorded by him, dispense with the deposit of any security, or may form time to time cancel or vary any order under this sub-section.

Further, the Act also contained various features which affected the freedom of the Press (See Appendix-2). Clause 4(1) of the Act contained more stringent words to stifle the freedom of expression by the newspapers. This clause also states.

"Whenever it appears to the Local Government that may printing press in respect of which any security has been deposited as required by section 3 is used for the purpose of printing or publishing any newspaper, book or other document containing any words signs or visible representation which are likely or may have a tendency, directly or indirectly, whether by *inference, suggestion, allusion, metaphor, implication or otherwise:*

(a) to incite to murder or to any offence under the Explosive & Substances Act, 1908, or to any act of violence, or

(b) to seduce any officer, soldier or sailor in the Army or Navy of His Majesty from his allegiance or his duty, or

(c) to bring into hatred or contempt His Majesty or the Government established by law in British India or the administration of justice in British India or any Native Prince or Chief under the suzerainty of His Majesty, or any class or section of His Majesty's subjects in British India, or to excite disaffection towards His Majesty or the said Government or any such Prince or Chief, or

(d) to put any person in fear or to cause annoyance to him and thereby induce him to deliver to any person any property or valuable security, or to do any act which he is not legally bound to do, or to omit to do any act which he is legally entitled to do, or

(e) to encourage or incite any person to interfere with the administration of the law or with the maintenance of law and order, or

(f) to convey and thereat of injury to a public servant, or to any person in whom that public servant is believed to be interested, with a view to inducing that public servant to do any act or to forbear or delay to do any act connected with the exercise of his public functions.

The local Government may, by notice writing to the keeper of such printing-press, stating or describing the words, signs or visible representations which in its opinion are of the nature described above, declare the security deposited in respect of such press and all copies of such newspaper, book or other document wherever found to be forfeited to His Majesty.

As a result of these clauses in the Act, many newspapers ceased publication an forfeited their deposits (See Table-1). The *New India* of Annie Besant was an important victim of the demand of the security under the Press Act. When the initial security of Rs 2,000 was forfeited, the paper continued after paying the enhanced security of Rs 10,000 which was also forfeited.

Table-1

Newspapers subjected to harassment by the British Government between 1910 and 1914

Name of the Paper	*Place of Publication*	*Security Demanded Rs*	*Remarks*
1910			
Dharma	Calcutta	2,000	Closed down
Karmayogi	Calcutta	2,000	Closed down
Kal	Poona	5,000	Ceased publication
Rashtramath	Bombay	5,000	Ceased publication
Sakali	Surat	5,000	Ceased publication
Rajasthan	Ahmedabad	1,000	Persecution ended on demand of Security by the Government.
Gujahadi	Bombay	2,500	Ceased publication
Mujahadi	Lahore	2,500	Ceased publication
Desh Sevak	Nagpur	2,500	Ceased publication
Frontier Advoate	Dera Ismail Khan	4,000	Ceased publication
1911			
Daily	Hitavadi Nagpur	5,000	Ceased publication
Almuin	Amritsar	1,500	Ceased publication
Panch Bahadur	Bombay	500	Paid and continued publication
Jhang Sial	Punjab	1,000	Paid and continued publication
Alhuda	Delhi	1,000	Paid and continued publication
1912			
Kesari	Poona	5,000	Deposited as demanded
Kathiawar	Ahmedabad	2,000	Refused the deposit and continued publication; when prosecuted and ordered to pay a fine of Rs.300/-finally closed down
1913-14			
Alhidavar	Delhi	2,000	Paid
Alhi Hadees	Amritsar	2,000	Paid

(*Source:* Krishnamurthy, N., (1966). *Indian Journalism,* Mysore: Mysore University Press, (pp. 70-71).

Similarly, *Andhra Vani, Gnanodava and Brahmananda Asrama Partika,* The *Nationalist* and many other newspapers and periodicals in Andhra region were also closed down. The punitive action of the Government against newspapers for their writings continued. For example, one newspaper *Desamtha* published by a popular Telugu writer and freedom fighter Chilakamarthi Lakshminarasimham from Guntur was about to cease publication. The Government demanded security deposit from the paper for publishing an article allegedly imputing to the Magistracy and Judiciary, partiality toward Europeans in the administrations of criminal justice. Funds were raised from the public to pay the demanded security of Rs 1,000 for the continuance of the journal. An amount of Rs 1, 000 as security was also demanded under the 1910 Press Act from *Andhra Chandrika,* a Telugu paper published from Cuddapah. The security from the paper was demanded as an extra-precautionary measure. The District Collector wrote that the security was demanded from the paper "as it was reported that some of the probable contributors ware not moderate in their views". Later, the paper ceased publication in 1918.

The two newspapers in Bombay which were asked to furnish a security of Rs 5,000 each also closed down. There were cases of papers in other Provinces closed down for their failure to pay security deposit. A statement by the Press Association of India, formed in 1915 to protect the interests of the press, said 22 newspapers between 1910 and 1917 had been asked to furnish security and 18 had shut down. Between 1917 and 1919, 963 newspapers and printing press which had existed before the Press Act of 1910 had been prosecuted under this Act. A bouts 173 new printing press and 129 newspapers had premature death owing to demands of security deposit (Natarajan, 1962; Krishmamurthy, 1966).

The Governments collected about Rs 5 lakhs during the first year of the Press Act through securities and forfeitures. Over 500 publications were prescribed under the Act.

Rowlatt Act

In 1919 the Government passed the Rowlatt Act which gave the executive special powers to deport individuals, to muzzle the press and to set up tribunals to try political offenders. These repressive measures provoked criticism from all over the country. The Telugu press especially *Andhra Patrika* and *Krishna Patrika* protested vehemently against the Act (Ramachandra Rao, 1993: 105).

The Jallianwala Bagh massacre* of 1919 was followed by savage phase of suppression of he press. In Punjab, Kalinath Roy, editor of the *Tirbune,* was sentenced to two years of imprisonment for an editorial entitled "Blazing Indiscretion". B.G. Horiniman, editor of the *Bombay Chronicle* one of those Englishmen who had identified himself with the Indian cause, was another notable victim. The paper published detailed reports of the Punjab horrors. This led to pre-censorship being imposed on it. In protest, the editorial columns were left blank. Eventually Horniman was arrested and deported and the paper itself was forced to close down. It was allowed to reapperar sometime later under strict censorship and on payment of Rs 10, 000 as security deposit. The *Amrita Barzar Patrika* in Calcutta, and the *Hindu* and *Swadesmitran* in Madras were similarly harassed (Jagannathan, 1999: 1230124).

The Government had a rethinking on the Press Act, 1910 since it contained very obnoxious clauses. Both Montagu, the Secretary of State, and Lord Chelmsford, the Viceroy were concerned with the defects in the Press Act, and thought of modifying it to make it less oppressive (Subrahmanyam, 1984).

In 1921, the Government of India appointed a Committee under the chairmanship of Sir Tej Bahadur Sapru, Law Member, to go into the press law and make recommendations. Many leading editors and journalists gave evidence before the committee. Annie Besant, editor of *New India,* told the committee that what could be safely published in Bombay risked forfeiture of security in Madras and the harassed

---

* Jallianwala Bagh Massacre: on 8th April 1919 prohibitory orders served on Gandhi not to enter Delhi or Punjab. Matters came to a crisis on 13 April 1919 when General Dyer ordered the troops to open fire on 20,000 people, who assembled at Jallianwala Bagh (Amritsar) in a prohibited meeting. As the military had blocked the only entrance to the Bagh, the crowd had no way of escape. According to official figures 400 people were killed.

editor had to find out what were the subjects on which the Governor of the stage from where the paper was published was sensitive. And there was no uniformity in the treatment of newspapers. She said the editor of an Anglo-Indian newspaper was allowed to make violent attacks on Indians who advocated reforms which were later made into law. But if an Indian editor replied to the attacks he prosecuted for exciting hatred (Krishnamurthy, 1966; Parthasarathy, 1991).

Thus, the committee recommended the repeal of the Press Acts of 1908 and 1910, the amendment of the Registration of the Press and Books Act, 1867 to enable seizure of seditious literature, to make it obligatory to print the name of the editor in every issue of the paper and to reduce the maximum penalty of imprisonment for violation of the law to six months. The committee said: "More from the platform and through the agency of it inerant propagandists than by the press". The Press Acts of 1908 and 1910 were repealed in 1922 under the Press Law Repeal and Amendment Act, 1922.

Press Ordinance of 1930

The significant event in the history of the press was Mahatma Gandhi taking over *Young India* in 1919 from Jamnadas Dwarakadas of Bombay and also the starting of a Gujarati Weekly *Navjivan* by him. As an editor Gandhi was following strict code of principles in Journalism. He didn't accept advertisements and believed that the newspaper should survive on the revenue from subscribers. The circulation of *Young India* went up to 45, 000 and his articles were very effective. Gandhi wrote three articles in his journal Young India which were thought by the administration as seditious. The first article written in September 1921 was titled Tampering with Loyalty. In the article, Gandhi openly declared that his task was to encourage sedition and to accept the consequences. The second article titled a *puzzle* and its *solution* was published in December, 1921. In the article too, Gandhiji declared, "We want to overthrow the Government. We want to compel its submission to the people's will". The third article, *shaking the manes* was published in February 1922. The publications of these articles were found to be seditious and Gandhiji was prosecuted in March, 1922 and imprisoned for six years.

Between 1920 and 1946, Gandhiji organised major campaigns against alien Government namely, Civil Disobedience Movement, Salt Satyagraha and Quit India Movement. During his time, the national press played a memorable role which was unique in the history of the national movement. The starting of Salt Satyagraha or Civil Disobedience Movement had an adverse impact on the Government. It came down heavily on the press in 1930 when Press Ordinance was issued reviving the provision of the Press Act of 1910.

The Press Ordinance of May, 1930, raised a storm of protest in the country and provided an occasion for the Conference of Indian Editors held under the presidentship of A. Rangaswami Iyengar, Editor of *The Hindu.* Despite protests from Indian editors, the policy of the Government continued to regulate the press and its freedom. In 1931 the Press Emergency Powers Act adopted for only one year to suppress the freedom of the press. The main provisions of this Act, known as The Indian Press (Emergency Powers) Act, 1931, was the repetition of the clause 3(1) of 1910 Act. In addition some more features were added. They were:

1. to seduce any officer, soldier, sailor or airman in the military, naval or air forces of His Majesty or any Policy Officer from his allegiance or his duty, or
2. to bring in to hatred or contempt His Majesty or the Government established by law in British India or the administration of justice in British India or any Indian prince or Chief under the suzerainty of His Majesty, or any class or section of His Majesty's subjects in British India or to excite disaffection towards His Majesty or the said Government or any such Prince or Chief, or
3. to put any person in fear or to cause annoyance to him and thereby induce him to deliver to any person any person any property or valuable security, or to do any act which he is not legally bound to do, or to omit to do any act which he is legally entitled to do, or
4. to encourage or incite any person to interfere with the administration of the law or with the maintenance of law

and order, or to commit any offence, or to refuse or defer payment of any land revenue, tax, rate, cess or other due or amount payable to Government or to any local authority, or any rent of agricultural land or anything recoverable as arrears of or along with such rent, or

5. to induce a public servant or a servant of a local authority to do any act or to forbear or delay to do any act connected with exercise of his public functions or to resign his office, or
6. to promote feelings of enmity or hatred between different classes of His Majesty's subjects, or
7. to prejudice the recruiting of persons to serve in any of His Majesty's forces, or in any police force, or to prejudice the training, discipline or administration of any such force.

The special provision of this Act was seizure of certain documents by the Local Government. Clause 19 this Act states:

> Where any newspaper, book or other document wherever made appears to the Local Government to contain any words, signs or visible representations of the nature described in Section 4, sub-section (1), the Local Government may, by notification in the local office Gazette, stating the grounds of its opinion, declare every copy of the issue of the newspaper, and every copy of such book or other document to be forfeited to His Majesty, and thereupon any police officer may seize the same wherever found in British India, and any Magistrate may be warrant authorise any police-officer not below the rank of sub-Inspector to enter upon and search for the same in any premises where any upon and search for the same in any premises where any copy of such issue or any such book or other document may be or may be reasonably suspected to be.

This Act restricted the publication of exaggerated reports of political events, notices and advertisements of meetings, processions and other activities tending to promote the Civil Disobedience Movement, or of any other matter in furtherance of the ugly incidents for which both the people and the Government were responsible (Krishamurthy, 1966).

Securities were demanded from almost all papers which were pledged to back the Congress Party. *Bombay Chronicle of Bombay* paid Rs 3, 000 and the *Ananda Bazar Patrika of Calcutta* Rs 1,000. The *Free Press* Journal of Bombay and the *Liberty* of Calcutta paid Rs 6,000 each. The Security deposits thus forcibly collected were forfeited. These forfeitures annoyed the press and the public alike. Despite perils, the nationalist press kept the onward march strengthening the Civil Disobedience Movement.

The year 1932 saw two more Acts passed which affected the Indian press. The Criminal Law Amendment Act No. XXIII for "the better control of the press", amended the previous year's Press Act by; (a) embodying all those phrases incorporated in the 1930 ordinance which the Act had originally omitted, and (b) by making the Act permanent. The Foreign Relations Act was the second one aimed at "providing against the publication of statements likely to prejudice friendly relation between His Majesty's Government and the Government of certain foreign states". (Krishnamurthy, 1966: 93).

Throughout the Civil Disobedience Movement, the nationalist press was very active in its support to the freedom cause and was functioning as the true voice of the people.

World War II and the Press

When the World War II broke out in 1939, the Government of India enacted the Defense of India Rules to safeguard the interests of the British and her allies. Rule 41 of the Defence of India Rules provided that:

The Government, for the defence of British India and for the efficient prosecution of was by order addressed to printers and publishers and editors.

(a) required that any matter shall before being published, be submitted for scrutiny to an authority specified;

(b) prohibited or regulated the printing or publishing or the use of any printing press.

The nationalist press was against the War and supported the Gandhiji's Civil Disobedience Movement. In 1940, the Government established the Press Advisory Committee at the centre and the provinces.

A conference of editors from all over India- All India Newspapers Editors' Conference (AINEC) – came into being to meet the extraordinary situation created by the Government of India's order of October 26, 1940, imposing severe restrictions on the press. This order prohibited newspapers from giving expression towards war. The editor's conference always displayed a spirit of accommodation which however, seldom evoked the right response from the Government. Through a resolution, the AINEC declared its uncompromising opposition to pre-censorship of any kind. It demanded freedom fro newspapers to publish objective accounts of incidents connected with the freedom struggle without any previous scrutiny. During this period, a number of newspapers were suppressed. Many suspended their publication as a result of the press restrictions imposed by the Government.

In August, 1942, the Government suspended publication of 96 newspapers and journals, and demanded heavy securities within a period of three weeks following the start of the August Revolution (Krishnamurthy, 1966; Natarajan, 1962 and Parthasaradhy, 1991). The struggle for Indian Independence reached its climax in 1942.

The Quit India Movement forced the Government to issue an order to suppress the activities of the press. According to Natarajan (1962), the restrictions imposed on the newspapers were:

(a) the registration of correspondents;
(b) the limitation on the number of messages regarding disturbances;
(c) prohibition of news regarding acts of sabotage;
(d) limitations on headlines and space given to news of disturbances;
(e) compulsory press advice; and
(f) arbitrary censorship.

On hearing the press restrictions, Gandhi made a statement that it was better not to publish newspapers than to bring them out under all kinds of governmental restrictions.

In another instance, the Government of the Central provinces banned the publication of a protest fast by Professor Bhansali, a respected Gandhian, alleging misbehaviour by the British troops with women in two villages. Even the ban order was not to be published. The ban was ordered without consulting the appropriate bodies including All India Newspaper Editors Conference. With no prospect of the Government relenting, the All India Newspaper Editors Conference decided on a measured response of self-censorship of Government news. It passed a resolution in December that year asking members-papers not to publish Government House circulars (a regular feature those days), announcement of New Year Honours (a matter of some consequence with the new year only days away), speeches of members of the British, Central and provincial Government "except portions thereof which contain decisions and announcements". As a result the *Hindustan Times* had precensorship imposed on it; in Madras, reporters of the *Hindu* were denied facilities (Jagannadham, 1997: 126) but on January 13, the Central Province Government withdrew the ban order and conceded the Professor's demand for an inquiry. Thereupon, the Conferences advised the papers to resume publication. On resumption, the papers published the news of the lifting of the ban, the order for inquiry into allegations of troop misbehaviour and the end of the 63 day-fast by the Professor.

However, the restrictions on the press during the last days of British Government in India did not serve the purpose. In order to arrest the worsening of the situation, the Government armed itself with special powers of imposing pre-censorship and other restrictions which failed totally. At the time of partition the press played a feed role and without caring the restrictions.

It is a great sage of struggle for the Indian press to fight for the freedom of the press. The press fought for it valiantly and retained its independence to fight for the cause of freedom. Nehru (1936) observed: "The question freedom of the press is a vital question and inevitably the brunt of the fight must fall upon the journalists; but the general public must also take their fair share in it."

Chapter 3

Freedom of the Press and the Indian Government (1948-1988)

This chapter presents the evolution of freedom of the press in the post-independent India and the curbs imposed on the press freedom by the Government at the Centre during different periods.

With the declaration of Indian Independence, an interim Government was installed in early 1947. The arbitrary powers being exercised by the British Governments came to an end, and the country's partitions imposed a new emergency and many of the provincial governments promulgated ordinances to contain the rapid deteriorating communal conflicts on account of partition of the country into India and Pakistan. These ordinances were later replaced by Emergency legislation.

Even before India gained Independence in 1947, the Constituent Assembly* had begun its deliberations and adopted the historic Objectives Resolution moved by Pandit Jawaharlal Nehru. This formed the basis not only for the various provisions of the Constitution but its Preamble also. The Assembly declared in the resolution its firm resolve to draw up a constitution guaranteeing, *inter alia,* freedom of thought and expression (Venkataramaiah, 1989:17).

---

* The Constituent Assembly consisting of 299 members representing all provinces in the country was elected by the State legislatures. It held its first sitting on December 9, 1946 and deliberated on drafting the Indian Constitution. The Constituent Assembly was chaired by Dr B.R. Ambedkar.

Draft Constitution and freedom of the press:

Although the Constituent Assembly laid emphasis on the value of fundamental rights, the theory of absolute rights was discarded and there was a consensus on specifying in the Constitution itself the grounds of restriction on the exercise of these rights (Constituent Assembly Debates, Volumes X-XII, pp. 1837-38).

In defense of this argument Chairman of the Constituent Assembly Ambedkar observed:

> It is wrong to say that fundamental rights in America are absolute. The difference between the position under the American Constitution and the Draft Constitution is one form and not of substance. That the fundamental right in America is not absolute rights is beyond dispute. In support of every exception to the fundamental rights set out in the Draft Constitution one can refer to at least one judgements of the United States Supreme Court in judgement in Article 13 of the right requires qualification; it is for the Constitution of all the relevant considerations. All this...is a complete misrepresentation of not a misunderstanding of the American Constitution. The American Constitution does nothing of the kind. Except in one matter, namely, the right of Assembly, the American Constitution does not itself impose any limitations upon the fundamental rights guaranteed to the American Constitution does not itself impose any limitations upon the fundamental rights guaranteed to the American citizens. Nor is it correct to say that the American Constitution levees it to the Congress. The real position is different from what is assumed by the critics. In America, the Fundamental rights as enacted by the Constitution were no doubt absolute. Congress, however, soon found that it was absolutely essential to qualify these fundamental rights by limitations. When the question arose as to the constitutionality of these limitations before the Supreme Court, it was contended that the Constitution gave no power to the United States Congress to impose such limitation; the Supreme Court invented the doctrine of police power and refuted the advocates of absolute fundamental rights by the arguments that every state

> has inherent in it police power which is not required to be conferred on it expressly by the Constitution.
>
> To use the language of the Supreme Court, it said: "That a State in the exercise of its police power may punish those who abuse this freedom by utterances inimical to the public welfare, tending to corrupt public morals, incite to crime or disturb the public, is not open to question…?
>
> What the Draft Constitution has done is that instead of formulating fundamental rights in absolute terms and depending upon our Supreme Court to come to the rescue of Parliament by inventing the doctrine of police power, it permits the Stage directly to impose limitations upon the fundamental rights. There is really no difference in the result. What one does directly the other does indirectly. In both cases, the fundamental rights are not absolute. (Constituent Assembly Debates, Vol. VII, pp.40-41).

The Constituent Assembly and its various committees and sub-committees considered the freedom of speech fairly but the bases of restriction provided on its exercise far outweighed the grounds of restriction in the case of other liberties. The draft Article 13, shaped by the drafting Committee, guaranteed to citizens the right to freedom of speech and expression and permitted the state to make any law relating to libel, slander, defamation, sedition, or any other matter offending against decency or morality or undermining the security or, or tending to overthrow, the state.

In the initial stage of the Constitution-making "public order" as a ground of restriction was suggested by several members but it did not find place in the draft. A member objected to the incorporation of both "public order" and "morality" in the draft article. In his opinion, these expressions were vague and their connotation changed from time to time. In regard to the latter he said that in a land of many religions, with differing conceptions of morality, different customs, usages and ideals, it would be very difficult to ensure unanimity on what constituted morality (Shiva Rao, 1967). Again, the suggestion for explicitly incorporating freedom of the press in the draft was not accepted (Constitution Assembly Debates, Vols. I-IV, pp. 457-68).

This matter came up before the Constituent Assembly during the reading of the Draft Constitution also. Several members vigorously pleaded for such a guarantee in the Constitution. One member said:

> The freedom of the press.. Is one of the items round which the greatest, the bitterest of constitutional struggles have been waged in all constitutions and in all countries where liberal constitutions prevail. They have been attained at considerable sacrifice and suffering. They have now been achieved and enshrined in those countries. Where there are no written Constitutions, they are in the well established conventions or judicial decisions. In those which have written constitutions, they have been expressly included as the freedom of the press. Even the United Nations Charter gives good prominence and special mention of freedom of the press. The press may be liable to abuse; I feel there may have been instances where the press has gone, at least in the mind of the established authority, beyond its legitimate limits. But any curtailment of the liberty of the press is, as one of the present Ministers, who was then a former non-official member, called, a 'black Act' in the last but one session of the legislature when there was an attempt to curtail the liberty of the press under certain circumstances. Freedom of the press is at the being misunderstood, or, at any rate, apt to be regarded as license which you may want to curtail. There are many ways by which laws can be passed or laws can be administered whereby you can regard the liberty as verging upon license an as such to be curtailed. To omit it altogether...would be great blemish which you may maintain by the force of the majority, but which you will never succeed in telling the world as a progressive liberal constitution, if you insist on my amendment being rejected (Constituent Assembly debates, Vol. VII, pp. 716-17).

However, the Assembly though that the freedom of press meant freedom of expression and no specific mention of the same was warranted. Dr Ambedkar again observed:

> The press is merely another way of stating an individual or a citizen. The press has no special rights which are not to be given

> or which are not capacity. The editor of a press or the manager are all citizens and therefore when they choose to write in newspapers, they are merely exercising their right of expression and in my judgement therefore no special mention is necessary of the freedom of the press at all (Constituent Assembly Debates, Vol. VII: 780).

Another member, K.M. Munshi opposed the inclusion of sedition as a ground of restriction. He though that it had been an expression of varying import and created considerable doubt in the minds of not only the members of the Assembly but also of the courts of many counties. He said:

> Its definition has been very simple and given so far back as 1868. It says 'Sedition embraces all those practices whether by word or deed or writing which are calculated to disturb the tranquility of the State and lead ignorant persons to subvert the Government. "But in practice it has had a curious fortune. A hundred and fifty years ago in England, holding a meeting or conduction processions was considered sedition. Even holding an opinion against, which will bring ill-will towards Government, was considered sedition once. Our notorious Section 124-A of Penal Code was sometimes construed so widely that I remember in a case a criticism of a District Magistrate was urged to be covered by Section 124-A. but the public opinion has changed considerably since and now that we have a democratic Government which should be welcome and incitements which would undermine the security or order on which civilised life is based, or which is calculated to overthrow the State.. As a matter of fact the essence of democracy is criticism of Government. The party system which necessarily involves an advocacy of the replacement of one Government by another is its only bulwark; the object therefore of this amendment is to make a distinction between the two positions. (Constituency Assembly Debates, Vol. VII, p. 731).

On the argument of K.M. Munshi, the ground of sedition was dropped.

In the final draft of the Constitution adopted by the Constituent Assembly on November 26, 1949, draft Article 13 became the present Article 19. Article 19(1)(a) guaranteed to every citizen the right to freedom of speech and expression. Article 19(2) provided that the guarantee of this right would not affect the operation of any existing law insofar as it related to, or prevent the state from making any law relating, to, libel, slander, defamation, contempt of court or any matter which offended against decency or morality or which undermined the security of, or tended to overthrow, the state.

Therefore, the framers of the Constitution attached a great value to the freedom of speech and expression in a democratic polity. They enumerated a number of grounds of restriction on the exercise of this right. Again, they clarified that the freedom of the press was covered by the freedom of expression and it would operate on the same wave length as the latter.

When the Constitution of free India was adopted and came into force on January 26, 1950, it was found that the Constitution was vague as regards the freedom of the press (Bhattacharjee, 1972; Ahuja, 1984 329). There were certain judgements by the Supreme Court and High Courts pertaining to Article 19(2) which were amended twice–first time in 1951 and second in 1963 (See Chapter IV for details). Three cases are noteworthy, *viz.*, Romesh Thapar Vs. State of Madras, Brij Bhushan Vs. State of Delhi and the Bharati press for discussion.

In Romesh Thappar case, the Supreme Court struck down as violative of Article 19(1)(a) the Madras Maintenance of Public Order Act, 1949 whose section 9(1A) sought to impose restrictions on the freedom of the press was not against undermining the security of the state or its overthrow but for the wider purpose of security, public safety or the maintenance of public order. In the opinion of the court, the law fell outside the scope of Article 19(2). The Court rejected the contention that insofar as the securing of public safety or the maintenance of public order would include the security of the state; the impugned provision was saved by this clause. The court laid down the following rule:

Where a law purports to authorise the imposition of restrictions on a fundamental right in language wide enough to cover restriction both within and without the limits of constitutionality permissible legislative action affecting such right it is not possible to uphold it even so far as it may be applied within the constitutional limits, as it is not severable. So long as the possibility of its being applied for purposes not sanctioned by the Constitution cannot be ruled out, it must be held to be wholly unconstitutional and void. In other words, clause (2) of Article 19 having allowed the imposition of restrictions on the freedom of speech and expression only in cases where danger to public security is involved, an enactment, which is capable of being applied to cases where no such danger could arise, cannot be held to be constitutional and valid to any extent (AIR, 1950 S.C. 124, 129).

Essentially on the same considerations, the Court also struck down in Brij Bhushan case the East Punjab Public Safety Act, 1949 which, through its Section 7(1)(c), provided for special measures to ensure public safety and the maintenance of public order (AIR 1950 SC, 129,134).

In Bharati Press, the validity of section 4(1)(a) of the Press (Emergency Powers) Act, 1931 was at state. In this case the Government of Bihar issued an order under the Act demanding security from the keeper of the Bharati Press as the press was used for publishing matters in violation of this section which dealt with inciting to or encouraging, or tending to incite to or to encourage, the commission of any offence of murder or any cognisable offence involving violence. The Patna High Court declared the section ultra vires the Constitution as it was worded in general terms and might apply both to aggravated forms of offences like political assassinations as also to ordinary murders or cognisable offences involving violence. In view of Romesh Thappar and Brij Bhushan cases, the court said the impugned provision could not be saved as a permissible legislation under Article 19(2). Therefore, it is obvious that the courts refused to enlarge the scope of Article 19(2) in the matter of the freedom of speech and expression.

This decision did not find favour with the Government. The them Law Minster, Dr. Ambedkar, said in Parliament that their only consequence was to disable the Government to enact a law restricting the freedom of speech and expression in the interest of public order as also a law restraining incitement to violence (Parliamentary Debated Vol. XII, Part II, p. 90).

As a result, Article 19(2) was amended by the Constitution (First Amendment) Act, 1951. the amended article permitted a law insofar as it imposed reasonable restrictions on the freedom of the press in the interest of the security of the state, friendly relations with foreign states, public order, decency or morality, or in relation to contempt of court, defamation or incitement to an offence. Thus, the scope of the restrictive clause was enlarged by the addition of three new grounds *viz.*, friendly relations with foreign states, public order and incitement to an offence. In regard to the first ground, Dr Ambedkar explained that it was imperative to prevent the abuse of the freedom so as not to involve a foreign state in any kind of ignominy. There was no explanation as to why the expressions "libel," "slander" and "tends to overthrow the state" were dropped; but it is clear that "defamation" being a generic term and "libel" and "slander" its offshoots, the latter two were superfluous. Again, the words "tends to overthrow the state" might have been taken as covered by the expression "security of the state". A notable feature of the first amendment was the inclusion of the word reasonable before the word "restrictions". This brought clause (2) in line with clauses (3) to (6).

After this amendment the clause runs as follows:

> Nothing in sub-clause (1) shall affect the operation of any existing law, or prevent the state from making any law, insofar as such law imposes reasonable restrictions on the exercise of the right conferred by the said sub-clause in the interests of the sovereignty and integrity of India, the security of the State, friendly relations with foreign states, public order, decency or morality, or relation to contempt of court, defamation or incitements to an offence.

There is no specific mention of the freedom of the press in Aricle 19(1)(a), but it is the settle view of the Supreme Court that the freedom of speech and expression includes the freedom of the press. However, the freedom of the press is not higher than the freedom of speech and expression of a citizen; no privilege attaches to the press as a distinct from the freedom of the citizen (M.S.M. Sharma Vs. Sri Krishna Sinha, A.I.R. 1959 SC 395 at 402). The judiciary thus supported the stand taken in the speech and expression would cover the freedom of the press also, which is however, no higher than that of the former.

The First Press Commission (1952–54)

The amending of the Constitution was widely opposed by the Press both before and after it was carried out by the Congress Government. The reference to friendly States particularly was objected to on the ground that, if action was to be taken only on representation of a foreign Government, the representation would only come from the non-democratic states which did not understand the workings of a fee press; that, if it was to be taken on its own initiative by the Government of India, it may possibly be in suppression of criticisms of India's foreign policy. Other provisions were attacked on the ground that they vested too much power in the Government. The Press registered its objection, some newspapers suspended publication, and a few more published over their editorials a catch-line of protest drafted by the Editors Conference. Later in the year, the Press (Objectionable Matters) Act provoked greater opposition, and controversy only subsided with announcement in October 1952 of the Press Commission to report comprehensively on questions affecting the Press (Natarajan, 1962: 257-258).

In October 1952, the Government of India appointed a Press Commission to look into the conditions of the press. Justice G.S. Rajadhyaksha was the Chairman of the Commission. The members of the Commission include Dr C.P. Ramaswamy Iyer, Acharya Narendra Deva, Dr Zakir Hussain, Dr V.K.R.V. Rao and Messrs. PH. Patwardhan, T.N. Singh, Jaipal Singh, Jagadish Natarajan, A.R. Bhatt and M. Chalapathi Raju.

The Press Commission which submitted its report in 1954 recommended the establishment of a Press Council with the objective to safeguard the freedom of the press and help the press to maintain its independence. The Commission recommended the setting up of a Registrar at the Centre with State Counterparts. It suggested the setting up of a Press Council under the Chairmanship of a High Court Judge or ex-Judege nominated by the Chief Justice of India with representatives of editors, journalists and proprietors.

The Press Commission recommended emergency legislation for preventing press excesses in preference to incorporation of the provisions of the Press (Objectionable Matter) Act in the Indian Penal Code and the Criminal Procedure Code, because an emergency law is a temporary nature. While it was inclined to retain several of the laws as they were, the Commission favored a change in the law of defamation to afford special facilities of defense to officials. On all these matters of legislation, a minority on the Commission held a different view, pressing for repeal of the Press (Objectionable Matter) Act, a modification of the amended Article 19(2) of the Constitution to remove the reference to friendly relation with foreign states, and a retention of a uniforms defamation law for officials and private citizens (Natarajan, 1962).

The Press Commission at length considered the concept of the freedom of the press and examined whether any of the laws required repeal or amendment, if they were not consistent with the freedom concept. The Commission held that the freedom of the press implied freedom to hold opinion, to receive and to impart information through the printed word without any interference from any public authority. It, however, felt that the rights of individuals had to be harmonised with their duties towards society and some restrictions on fundamental rights and their free exercise was called for. It was, therefore, stated that the concept of freedom 'with responsibility' should not be pushed to a point where the emphasis on the responsibility took the form of negation of freedom itself. Article 19 (2)* of the Constitution was

* Article 19(2) provides reasonable restrictions on the exercise of freedom of speech and expression in the interest of (a) sovereignty and integrity of India; (b) the security of the state; (c) friendly relation with foreign states; (d) public order, decency and morality; (e) contempt of court; (f) defamation and (g) incitement to an offence.

therefore amended by including among permissible restrictions matters relating to: (i) public order, (ii) friendly relations with foreign stages, and (iii) incitement of offence.

Parliamentary Proceeding (Protection of Publication) Act, 1956

The study of the freedom of the press is not comprehensive without mentioning Parliamentary Proceedings (Protection of Publication) Act, 1956. this Act gave ample freedom to the press to report the proceedings of the Parliament (Rajya Sabha and Lok Sabha). The Bill, known as Proceedings of Legislature (Protection of Publication) Bill was introduced by Members of Parliament, Feroze Gandhi in 1956 in order to secure protection to the journalists in reporting the happenings inside the two houses of Parliament. The Act conferred statutory protection to newspapers or broadcasts by Wireless telegraphy of substantially true reports of any proceedings of either houses of parliament. Mr Gandhi made a very strong plea for granting protection to the press and reporting parliamentary proceedings and defended the Bill in the following words: (Lok Sabha Debates, 1956).

> "...These 36 crore people have a right to know what their chosen representatives say and do. Anything that stands in the way must be removed. The extent to which democracy has succeeded can be judged by the extent to which we have successfully compelled the Government to function in full limelight of publicity. The entire machinery of Parliament is geared to that effect. The law of libel or defamation hangs like the Sward of Damocles over the heads of every editor and correspondent and keeps impressing on him how precarious his existence is. Any newspaper which today publishes the proceedings of our legislature does so at considerable risk and throws itself open to both civil a criminal action. The law of libel operates like a kind of silent censor and in a way prevents people from knowing that which they have a right to know".

This Act known as Feroze Gandhi Act provided protection to journalists in filing reports for public good without any malice.

Ironically, when Mrs Indira Gandhi wife of Mr Feroze Gandhi suspended the operation of this Act during emergency (1975-77). (Further details are given in the succeeding pages).

Wars and the Press

During the Sino-Indian War of 1962, Emergency was declared on October 26, 1962. With the promulgation of an Ordinance by the President on the same day, providing defence of India Rules (These rules became an Act in 1962). Since the country was fighting a war with its neighbour, China, the Government of India under Section 3 of the Act prohibited printing or publishing any matter against the defence of India in the newspapers. The Government also imposed rules on the newspapers writing against public safety, maintenance of supply and services to the people (Iyer and Sethi, 1996).

The Government was firm in demanding security and forfeiture of copies of newspapers containing such matters (against the defence of the country). The other severe restrictions imposed on the newspapers were closure of printing presses, or premises used for printing or publishing of newspapers with such reports, prohibition or regulation of the use of the posters, telegraphic or telephone services and censorship of postal articles including letters, postcards, newspapers and censorship material related to specific subjects as mentioned above.

In order to ensure the implementation of these rules, the Government asked All India Newspapers Editors Conference (AINEC) a body of journalists, to set up a committee to advise the Government in dealing with errant newspapers. Another committee consisting of officials from the Government was also set up to screen newspaper reports. Papers with circulation of 10,000 copies and more were dealt by the Central Governments. At the central level a Central Emergency Press Advisory Committee (CEPAC) was set up to look into the reports of big newspapers with more than 10,000 circulations.

Offending newspapers were given a show cause notice and, if necessary, a warning. A warning used to mean an automatic withdrawal of Government advertisements. Besides these two official committees there was the Press Advisory Unit of Press Information Bureau, the Intelligence Bureau also had its cell for screening publications. The number of cases considered by the CEPAC, between 1962 and 1965 were 77, involving 54 papers. Of these, action was recommended in 16 cases. CEPAC recommended prosecution in only one case against the *Chaukhumba,* a Hindi daily published from Indore.

Cases considered by CEPAC included undermining defence preparations, ridiculing the integrity of the Prime Minister; alleged neglect of the army by the Government, inciting one community against the other; stories about recruitment to the Air Force; allegations of bad treatment of jawans; editorials inciting communal hatred; explanation by the editors and publishers usually rested upon three arguments: (i) that of the journalist's right to comment, (ii) that the comment was made in good faith, and (iii) that the facts mentioned were true.

War with Pakistan: Pakistan's unprovoked aggression and declaration of a state or war with India on December 3, 1971, the Central Government declared a national emergency and enacted a Defence of India Act, 1971. Rules were promulgated under the Act some of which had great relevance to the role of the press in furthering the war effort. The spirit of the Defence of India Act, 1971 was similar to the legislation enacted in 1962 to cope with the situation created by the Chinese aggression.

The Union Government appointed a press consultative committee to evolve a code of conduct for observance by editors and correspondents of newspapers and news agencies during emergency 'lest they should by any inadvertent acts of omission and commission prejudice the country's security. (Iyer and Sethi, 1996).

The committee called upon the press to: (a) withhold publication of information considered by the appropriate authorities to be detrimental to national interest; (b) refrain from disseminating directly or indirectly, confidential information that they may collect in the course of their professional duties; (c) avoid re-publication of information and comment prejudicial to the country's interests from foreign and internal sources even for the purpose of criticism and reproduction; and (d) enjoin upon those connected with the press to avoid loose talk, as this is likely to lead to rumours due to the belief among the public that members of the press have access to the sources not generally available to others.

If the press followed these guidelines there was no need for pre-censorship.

In case of doubt, pressmen were advised to refer to the Chief Press Advisor appointed by the Government in Delhi or to the Press Advisors nominated in the State. Thus, the Government imposed restrictions on the freedom of the press.

Freedom of the Press and the Emergency

The years between 1971 and 1977 were turbulent in the history of the freedom of the press in India. But the study of the freedom of the press could not be viewed independently but was intertwined with political developments in the country. Significantly, the ascent of Mrs Indira Gandhi to the pinnacle of political power was very important in this study. Political observers like Mankekar (1977), Nayar (1977), Narasimhan (1977) and Carras (1980) observed that Mrs Gandhi's ambition to retain power led to many undemocratic ways of holding to it. Obviously, important and historical facts compelled Mrs Gandhi to take an extreme step of imposing Emergency on June 25, 1975.

The darkest chapter in the freedom of the press in India occurred during the 19 months period of Emergency. The reasons for the imposition of the Emergency were the events that took place in the country like rebellion in the Congress Party against Mrs Gandhi, the corruption charges against Mrs Gandhi, the growing discontentment, among the people, the political events in Gujarat and Bihar particularly the students agitation, the defeat of the Congress Party in the Gujarat election and the movement of Jaiprakash Narayan (Nayar, 1977).

Commenting on these events, Narasimhan (1977), the chief editor of *Indian Express,* said: "It was not certainly a single act of political aberration by an authoritarian leader entrenched in the seat of power...It was the culmination of a process which had begun in 1973, if not earlier. One of the dominant factors in this process was the emergence of Jaiprakash Narayan into active politics with the name of total revolution".

On June 25, 1975 at 11-45 PM, the President of India issued a proclamation saying "A grave emergency exists where by security of India is threatened by internal disturbance..." The press became the first casualty (Carras, 1980). The President, by an order suspended not only the right to freedom of speech and expression, but also suspended the right of any person to move the court for the enforcement of rights conferred under Article 19* of the Constitution. Not only this, all proceedings pending in courts for the enforcement of these rights were also suspended. The right to freedom of the press which is implicit in the right to freedom of speech and expression in the Constitution was drastically cut. Many opposition leaders including Jaiprakash Narayan and Morarji Desai (who later became Prime Minister of India) were arrested.

On the morning of June 26, 1975, censorship was imposed on all press writings relating to internal situation. *The Hindustan Times* and *The Statesman* had planned supplements to cover the Cabinet meeting which discussed the proclamation of Emergency. By 11 A.M. *The Hindustan Times* supplement was on the streets and the rotary machine in the Statesman was about to be started when a flash message came censoring all news and comments relating to the arrests and internal situation (Nayar, 1977).

---

* Article 19 guarantees fundamental rights to citizens of India such as:

(a) freedom of speech and expression
(b) assemble peaceably and without arms;
(c) to form association or unions;
(d) move freely throughout the territory of India;
(e) reside and settle in any part of the territory of India;
(f) this provision was omitted by the Constitution (44th Amendment) Act, 1978); and
(g) to practice any profession, or to carry on any occupation, trade or business.

All news had to be sent to the Government for scrutiny. *The Statesman* sent its supplement page-proof to the Press Information Bureau (PIB) Office for clearance. But by the time it was returned with the names of the arrested leaders deleted and their pictures removed, the power supply to the office was cut. The supplement could, therefore, not to be printed; the page-proof remained a historic record. Police seized a large number of copies of *The Hindustan Times* supplement from hawkers and delivery vans. *The Motherland* was the only paper to come out with a supplement; its press was later sealed. Despite this, and other stringent measures the news spread like a wildfire crossing the national frontiers.

Pre-Censorship of Newspapers: As a consequence of pre-censorship leading dailies from New Delhi on June 27 appeared with blanks in editorial space. Justifying censorship, Prime Minister Indira Gandhi told the National Union of Journalists that a section of the press was not concerned with the national interests and that it was helping build up vicious atmospheres in the country. It was necessary to prevent incitement to the people to defy laws. The then Minister of State for Information and Broadcasting I.K. Gujral, also criticised the newspapers and said they were becoming 'views papers'. Vidya Charan Shukla, who succeeded Mr Gujral, as Minister, accused newspapers of irresponsible behavior, he said: "For healthy journalism it is necessary that papers should be responsible and accountable". (Iyer and Sethi, 1996).

In protest against the pre-censorship of newspapers, several leading dailies in the country left blank spaces and some other papers published extracts from famous poems of Rabindranath Tagore in the editorials on June 28. shukla convened a meeting of the editors on June 28, 1975 and told them that the Government was not pleased with the editors' performance. He warned them not to leave blank spaces nor quote any passages from Jawaharlal Nehru or Rabindranath Tagore. Criticising the pre-censorship, Narayan (1975:82) said,…it is still doubtful if the Emergency the sweeping arrests the suppression of the press, if these and many other things done since June 26 last, have saved Indian democracy. In a strongly persuaded that these measures have dealt a grievous blow to our democracy from which it will take long to recover".

Foreign correspondents working in New Delhi opposed the new censorship regulations. As a result they were asked to leave the country for defying the censorship guidelines. The international press was against new rules and regulations. Lewis M. Simons of *Washington Post* was expelled on June 30. Kevin Rafferty of *The Financial Times* of London was refused admission in India on July 14 (Narayan, 1975). Peter Hazleburst of *The Times* London and Peter Gill of *Daily Telegraph* and Ms Lorna Jenkins of *Newsweek* were served with deportation orders on July 20, on their refusal to sign an undertaking to observe censorship regulations (Sethi, 1976).

By January 22, 1976, action was taken against 272 newspapers for violating censorship guidelines. This consisted or oral warning, withdrawal of exemptions from pre-censorship, seizure of printing presses, order to make security deposits or in extreme cases prosecution (See Appendix-4 for Censorship Guidelines).

A few journalists who organised protests against censorship or criticised the Government were arrested. K.R. Sunder Rajan of *The Times of India* was arrested in September 1976 in connection with the articles he wrote for American dailies, *The Christian Science Monitor and the Los Angelse Times.*

The Code or Censorship guidelines reveal that almost anything not acceptable to the Government was put in the Code. Nayar (1977) commented, "It was a strange code, more than 3,000 words of exhortation did not once mention freedom of the press". Inrani (1977) also said "the code is a very poorly drafted document which has suddenly appeared on the scene and is being actively promoted as one drafted by the newspaper industry itself. This claim is contrary to the facts".

It was on February 1, 1976 four major news agencies of India namely the Press Trust of India, United News of India, Hindustan Samachar and Samachar Bharati merged into one single integrated news agency called Samachar. The 'voluntary' merger of news agencies took place despite the fact that none of the agencies was willing to merge. It was alleged that Samachar was brought about by successfully intimidating the individual boards of PTI an UNI to opt for voluntary merger (Reddy, 1977).

The way censors functioned came in for scathing criticism in Parliament and outside. The censorship operations lacked objectivity. The worst aspect of censorship was that the use of its power was often at the discretion of minor officials. They even killed stories which obviously did not come under the purview of the censorship. Even the academic journals of the universities had to go for censor's clearance. The result was that a lot of healthy criticism or constructive suggestion was removed. In certain cases the circulation was baned. *The Times Educational Supplement, The Times Higher Education Supplement* and *The Times Literary Supplement* had each been banned twice in September 1976. Fourteen issues of *The Times* were banned in a period of two months (IPI Report, 1976).

Both Mr Mankekar and Mr Kuldip Nayar, editors of repute, have givenj series of instances to show how censorship was used to cover up official embarrassments of various kinds, favour select individuals and expose others. Comment or sometimes 'adverse comment' was banned. Often news and comments on various items were banned by an oral order of the censor. At times only 'Samachar' reports were allowed to be published. Even letters written from jail were subjected to censorship (Nayar, 1977: 41).

Court Cases: Several newspapers in Bombay field write petitions in courts against the orders of the censors and some of them were admitted. The Bombay High Court, in the case of a journal, *Freedom First,* edited by M.R. Masani, struck down the order of Binod Rao, Press Advisor to the Government of Maharashtra, prohibiting publication in the August, 1975 edition of the journal (Narinder, 1976, defined the role of the censor acting under the censorship order and laid down the principles under which an executive action can be challenged.

The court said:

> The role of a censor acting under the censorship order is not to make all newspapers and periodicals trim their sails to one wind or to the along in a single file or to speak in chorus with one voice. He is not meant to make the press an instrument for brainwashing the public; he is appointed the nursemaid of democracy and not its grave digger. Dissent from opinions and the views held by the majority and criticism and disapproval of measures initiated by a party in power make for a healthy political climate, and it is not for the censor to inject into this lifelessness of force conformity. There are permissible limits of dissent and disapproval. The voice of dissent cannot take the form of incitement to the revolutionary or subversive activities, for then instead of serving democracy it would subvert it. It is here that the sensor's real role begins, though it is not for him to stifle all dissent and protest, it is certainly his duty to see that the dissent and protest do not overstep the permissible limits.

In this case, Mr Masani challenged the impugned orders as being beyond the scope and ambit of the censorship order, completely irrational, arbitrary and made without any application of mind. Rao on the other hand, pleaded that the writ petition was not maintainable in view of the proclamation of Emergency and suspension of the fundamental right to speech guaranteed under Article 19(1)(a) of the Constitution.

Rejecting Mr Rao's argument, the Court held that what was suspended under Article 358 of the Constitution on the making of a proclamation of Emergency was not the right under Article 19(1) but the restrictions upon the power of the state to make laws or to take executive action inconsistent with these rights.

In his petition, Mr Massani had not challenged the virus of the censorship order or of Rule 48 of the Defence and Internal Security of Indian Rules or of any provision of any of the rule or any provision of the Defence and Internal Security of India Act.

The Court reject Mr Rao's submission that so long as an executive officer passed an order which purported to be in the exercise of executive power, such an order could not be challenged on any ground whatsoever, but the remedy was merely to make a plea for redress to some higher executive authority.

Suspension of Parliamentary Proceedings Act, 1956: A special session of the Parliament was convened on July 12, 1975 to approve the proclamation of Emergency. The Government of India ordered that the proceedings of this special session of Parliament be not reported to the press. This amounted to the denial of privilege given to the newspapers to report the proceedings of the Parliament under the Parliamentary Proceedings (Protection of Publication) Act, 1956. On July 26, Narayan Ganesh Gorey, the Socialist leader in Rajya Sabha on behalf of the Opposition said that they would boycott the remainder session as a protest against the suspension of the regular Parliamentary rules and the Government's decision to apply the press censorship to the reports of the Parliamentary proceedings.

On December 8, the President in exercise of powers under Article 123 promulgated there ordinances affecting the freedom of the press, namely, the Prevention of Publication (of Objectionable Matter) the Parliamentary Proceedings (Protection of Publication) Act and the Repeal of Press Council Act. Within two months these ordinances were approved by the Parliament. The Prevention of Publication (of objectionable Matter) Act, 1976 empowered the Government to prohibit prejudicial report in the newspapers and to demand and forfeit securities from the keepers of the presses and editors and publishes of objectionable matter. It also empowered the Government to resort to pre-censorship even in normal times. This Act also banned the defamation of the President, the Vice-President the Prime Minister, the Speaker of the Lok Sabha and Governors of the States. The publication of this and other kind of objectionable matters as defined in the Act were punishable with imprisonment for one year or a fine of Rs. 1,000. The Parliamentary Proceedings (Protection of Publication) Act popularly known as Feroze Gandhi Act was also repealed which virtually extended to the newspapers immunities which the Constitution vested in Members of Parliament speaking on the floor of the Parliament.

The Act provided that no person shall be liable to any proceedings civil or criminal, in any court in respect of publication in a newspapers of either Houses unless the publication has been proved to have been made with malice. The Government also abolished the Press Council of India with effect from January 1, 1976. The Annual Report of the Ministry of Information and Broadcasting and 1975-76 said: "The Press Council during the nine years of its existence had failed to curb the tendentious, provocative and unrestrained writings of the press. It was unable to frame a code of conduct for editors and complaints of minor character mostly engaged its attention". The Council was established in 1966 to evolve a code of conduct for press and to uphold the freedom of the press.

With the mounting pressure on Mrs Gandhi to hold elections, Mrs Gandhi declared elections on January 19, 1977. On March 20, 1977 Censorship of Media was lifted. Many people heaved a sigh of relief (Abbas 1978).

Freedom of the Press and Political Parties

In 1977 Lok Sabha elections the issues of the freedom of the press acquired a new dimension. Many political parties pledged themselves to preserve the freedom of the press. This was primarily because never before the press was subjected to so many restrictions as during the emergency. Public sympathy for the defenders of the freedom of the press was clearly visible and, therefore, all parties incorporated a promise to ensure it in their election manifestos. A group of journalists procured over 2,000 signatures from Lok Sabha candidates that they would preserve and fight for the freedom of the press. (Sethi, 1997).

B.G. Verghese, an eminent journalist, who contested from mavelikkara Constituency in Kerala said, "I have entered the election fray primarily to fight for freedom of the press and to put an end to the official violence and indiscipline let loose by the Congress under the cover of emergency" (The Indian Express February 21, 1977).

The abuse of emergency and institutionalisation of it have affected the newspapers and other media. The apparatus of censorship was completely misused throwing to the winds all sorts of freedom of the press.

Mr Verghese narrated several instance of harassment of newspapers and newsmen that refused to obey the rules of the Congress and said that it was really a shame that people were deprived of the privilege of even knowing of development taking place in our country. Public was fed with exaggerated and half true news. The real news was suppressed. Steps like cancellation of advertisements, sealing of press, disconnection of electricity etc., were resorted to for suppressing the newspapers which did not fall in line with the Government. With the formation of Samachar, the Government brought the entire media under control.

In an interview after the elections, Mr Verghese, when asked, 'Can you comment on the swiftness with which the Indian press learned to live with censorship?, he said, "there were some exceptions, but it was an utmost complete capitulation, particularly if you take the larger organs. It was the little journals of opinion, the smaller Indian language papers that adopted the most courageous positions. Big newspapers perhaps felt that they had vested interests keeping alive-they had more to lose. The little papers felt they had little or nothing to lose and were emboldened to strike a blow for what they thought was their fundamental right of expression, whereas the other were more concerned with what they though was their fundamental interest in property-through their proprietors or through losing jobs and partly the general climate of fear. There were number of journalists who felt strongly about this matter but who felt helpless-they were not in charge, it wasn't up to them to determine what went into the paper (Iyer and Sethi, 1996).

Many political parties pledged freedom of the press if they were voted to power in 1977 general elections these parties include Janata Party (Congress-O, Bharateeya Lok Dal, Socialist Party and Jan Sangh), Communist Party of India (Marxist), Congress for

Democracy, Communist Party of India, Akali Dal and Dravida Munnetra Khazagham.

The Janata Party, which came to power, promised to uphold the freedom of the press. The new Government policy in this regard was spelt out by Acting President of India B.D.Jatti in his address to the joint sessions of Parliament on March 28, 1977. he specifically mentioned the repeal of Parliamentary Proceedings Act. The text of his speech contained the following:

> "The Government would also take the following measures. The Prevention of Publication of Objectionable Matters Act will be repealed. The immunity which the press enjoyed in reporting the proceedings of the legislature will be restored. One of the very serious developments in recent past was the erosion of the freedom and impartiality of the media of publicity and information. My Government will take steps to restore to ensure that All India radio, Doordarshan, Films Division and other Government media function in a fair and objective manner.

As promised by the Government, L.K. Advani, the them Information and Broadcasting Minister, introduced two Bills to repeal Prevention of Objectionable Matters Act and Parliamentary Proceedings (Publication) Act. Introducing these two Bills, Advani said:

The basis of democratic Government is the opinion of the people. It is, therefore, of paramount importance that proceedings of Parliament should be communicated to the public. For this purpose the newspapers and the media should be afforded the privilege of publishing substantially true reports of proceedings of Parliament without being exposed to any civil or criminal action. Freedom of the press is necessary for successful functioning of democratic institutions, the Prevention of Objectionable Matters Act is being repealed with this objective in view.

Indian Express, April 13, 1977

One of the most remarkable feature of the Lok Sabha proceedings was that both these Bill were welcomed by the ruling as well as opposition members. The Minister also promised to restore the Press Council of India by bringing an Act.

Second Press Commission (1978-82).

In the two and a half years rule under the Janata Government, many significant things happened as regards the press. The Government reconstituted Press Council and also a Press Commission. The Government set up a second Press Commission on May 18, 1978 under the chairmanship of P.K. Goswami. But the Commission could not finish its task before December 31, 1979. With the coming of the new Government headed by Mrs Indiara Gandhi again in 1980, Goswami and others resigned on January 14, 1980.

The Second Press Commission was reconstituted in April 1980 under the chairmanship of Justice K.K. Mathew. Its terms of reference included: (1) the role of the press in a developing and democratic society; (2) the present constitutional guarantee with regard to freedom of speech and expression; whether this is adequate to ensure freedom of the press, adequacy and efficacy of the laws, rules and regulations for maintaining this freedom; (3) means of safeguarding the independence of the press against economic and political pressures from proprietors and management; (4) role of the press and the responsible it should assume in development policies; (5) ownership patterns, management practices and financial structures of the press; their relation to growth, editorial independence and professional integrity; (6) chain newspapers; links with industry, their effect on competition and on the readers' right to objective news and free comments; and (7) economics to the newspaper industry.

The Second Press Commission in its voluminous report which was placed before Parliament on November 5, 1982, has made as many as 278 recommendations. Through the report is voluminous, the Commission has not adequately dealt with certain important problems affecting the press. The Commission has not also spoken in one voice (Sarkar, 1984: 281).

The Commission consisted of a Chairman and 10 other members. Out of them, 4 members have appended a long joint minute of dissent.

The area of difference is large and the dissenting members do not subscribe to the views expounded and to most of the major recommendations of the Commission. Two other members have also submitted a minute of dissent on certain particular issues. The recommendations of the Commission were not very well received by the Press either. While placing the report before Parliament, the Government did not clearly indicate its reactions to the various recommendations.

The Commission (1982, Vol.1: p.37) which dealt with the freedom of the press, argued that the newspapers had the fundamental right to freedom of expression under Article 19(i)(a), that article did not confer on ordinary citizens any fundamental right to express their views through newspaper. The Commission, therefore, suggested that Article 19(i)(a) should be reviewed so as to permit an ordinary citizen to exercise his fundamental right of freedom of speech and expression through a newspaper. In this regard the argument of the Commission was as follows:

> A newspaper is published for the consumption of the public. The freedom of the consumers or the public to give expression to their views is also equally important. The public has also a right to information. Freedom of expression in its widest amplitude includes the right to information. The public has a right to know the different trends of opinion and views operating in the country. But the newspapers generally refuse to publish news and views which are not to their liking. Everybody cannot afford publication of a newspaper under modern conditions for giving expression to this views which may be of vital interest to the community at large and he loses the opportunity to have his say, unless the Press agrees to publish his views. At present, the Press has unfettered right to decide what to publish and what not to publish. Self-censorship by the Press is as great a menace to the freedom of expression as Government censorship. Our constitutional law has been solicitous in protesting an idea when it comes to the market but has been singularly indifferent in crating opportunities for its expression. A newspaper should give publicity to views which are even hostile to it. (P. 37).

The Commission also said that there was not a reason why the services of the Pres should not be available to citizens for exercise of their fundamental right of freedom of speech and expression on non-discriminatory basis subject, of course, to availability of space and other considerations. A revised, realistic view of Article 19(i)(a) should permit encouragement of expression by providing not only for its protection 'after publication' but also for its 'emergence by publication'.

This recommendation has not found favour with five members Girilal Jain, Rajendra Mathur, S.K, Mukherjee, H.K. Paranjape and Ishrat Ali Siddiqui who have recorded a minute of dissent. However, Sarkar, (1984: 44-45), former Law Secretary, Government of India, pointed out that the recommendations of the Second Press Commission need not be accepted. He put forth the following reasons in defence of his arguments.

"In the first place, though the recommendation may express a noble sentiment, it is not necessary because, as a matter of fact, diverse points of view are already being reflected in the columns of all major newspapers. No newspapers worth the name can afford to shut out important news or views. Even an industrial house owning a newspaper does not willfully prevent the Marxist or leftist point of view from emerging in his paper. Every newspaper has an editorial policy and it has the right to propagate its own views. But no newspaper should be compelled to launch a campaign in favour of ideas it does not believe in, and which its readers may not be prepared to buy".

"Secondly, there are practical difficulties in implementing the recommendation. It will be an open invitation to a large number of persons who are eager to see their names imprint, though what they write many not be worth publishing. Even between scripts which may deserve publication, a choice may have to be made having regard to availability of space and various other considerations. This discretion had to be exercised by the editor, and cannot be left to the Press Council. The Press Council is hardly equipped to decide such issues. Moreover, the Press Council may be flooded with complaints from contributors and it may not be possible for the Press Council to deal with them".

"Thirdly, the recommendation of the Mathew Commission does not fit in with the scheme of Article 19 and cannot be given effect to by an amendment to that Article. It is important to note that freedom of the press guaranteed under Article 19 can be enforced against State action only and not against the action of private citizens. If a person feels aggrieved because a newspaper has refused to publish his views and feels that his right to freedom of expression has been violated by the newspaper, even then, he cannot claim any relief against the newspaper under Article 19. A dispute between a contributor and newspaper is outside the scope of Article 19.

It would not be possible to give effect to the recommendation of the Mathew Commission by amending Article 19 and the recommendation, if accepted, will create more difficulties than solving them. What is really necessary is to create as many forums as may be necessary to give expression to different points of views rather than compelling a newspaper to publish what it does not consider worth publishing".

Freedom of the Press and Defamation Bill, 1988

As discussed in the preceding paged, the governments in power tried to stifle the freedom of expression (freedom of the press) when newspapers exposed the misdeeds of the governments. It is very significant to note that the freedom of the press was affected much during the period when the Congress party headed by Pandit Jjwaharlal Nehru (1947-64), Indiara Gandhi (1969-1977, 1980-84) and Rajiv Gandhi (1984-89). During the time of Rajiv Gandhi, he tried to muzzle the press. The press, particularly, a section of newspapers in the name of investigative journalism brough out many corruption charges against individuals or ministers in Rajiv Gandhi's Cabinet. The cases pertaining to the Bofors Gun deal[1] and West German submarine deal[2] came out accusing the Prime Minister of having received bribes in the deals. Two newspapers which were in the forefront in exposing alleged corrupt deals by the Government were the *Indian Express* and the *Hindu.* The *Statesman* joined them later with the story of kickbacks paid to an Indian by a Japanese firm in a deal with the Oil and Natural Gas Commussion. Day after day, these papers unearthed new material relating to the deals and put the Government and the prime minister in an embarrassing position. A Parliamentary Committee was appointed to go into the Bofors deal and find out the truth about the allegations of kickbacks but its report which cleared the Government of any malpractice was ridiculed and characterised as partisan by the newspapers and opposition parties. And the credibility of the Government continued to be questioned. There were demands that Rajiv Gandhi should resign and opposition parties who were vociferous in this were supported by a section of the press. The phenomenon of trial by the press was witnessed in Indian journalism for the first time on a large scale. (Parthasarathy, 1991; 304).

It was in this context that the Government decided to curb the freedom of the press by introducing the Defamation Bill, 1988 in the Lok Sabha on August 29, 1988 (See Appendix-6).

The Bill aimed at making publication of imputations falsely alleging commission of offences by a person. The Bill also provided punishment in the case of a first offence with imprisonment for a term up to two years or a fine which may extend to Rs. 2, 000 or both and in the case of a second or subsequent offence with imprisonment up to five years or with fine which extend up to Rs. 5, 000 or both.

Where the offence has been committed by publishing an imputation in a newspaper, the court convicting the offender may further order that its judgment shall be published in whole or in part in such newspaper and in such manner as it may specify. The cost of such publication shall be recovered from the convicted person as if it were a fine. The Bill provided that where any matter and which is grossly indecent or scurrilous or is intended for blackmail is published in any newspaper or periodical or circular, the author of such matter the printer, publisher and editor of such newspaper, periodical or circular shall, in the case of first offence, be punishable with fine which may go up to Rs. 2,000 or with both and in the case of a second or subsequent offence, with imprisonment which may extend up to five years and fine which may go up to Rs. 5, 000 or both. When a person pleads unintentional defamation claiming that the objectionable matter was published innocently and makes an offer of amends, the Bill provided that the offer of amends shall be: (a) in writing; (b) expressed to be made for the purposes of the section under which he is charged; (c) affirm that the matter innocently in relation to the party aggrieved; (d) include an offer to publish or join in the publication of a suitable correction of matter complained of an a sufficient apology. The correction and apology shall be published in the same manner and with the same prominence as the matter alleged to be defamatory was published.

Reacting to the Government's attempt to bring in amendments to the Defamation Law in India, newspapers opposed it vehemently. The main objections to the Bill were Sections 8, 12, 13 and 15. *The Statesman* in its editorial, 'Outlawing Democracy?' on September 1, 1988, said":

> ...By trying to suppress public debate that seeks to make the Government accountable for its misdeeds, Mr Rajiv Gandhi had reclaimed the dubious inheritance that the people of India consigned to the dustbin of history in 1977. But some indication of authority's moves and methods can be read into this repugnant measure. By seeking to amend the law whereby the "onus of establishing that the imputation is true and for the public good.. Shall be on the accused", the Government has it be known in no uncertain terms that the official machinery will not be used to bring evidence of political misdemeanors to public attention.

The Inidan Express, also opposed the Bill in its editorial dated September 1, 1988, 'Fight it' said:

> By alleging that its critics had converted the freedom of speech guaranteed by the Constitution into licence, the Government had sought to throttle by intimidation criticism and dissent by saying that it was necessary to shield "the office of the Prime Minister" from being defamed and denigrate. That was during the Emergency. Clearly that restricted protection will not do today.

In the same vein *The Hindu* also wrote an editorial, Withdraw the Defamation Bill", dated September 3, 1988 said:

> The entire Press in India – a many voiced, historically mature and vigorously independent institution for all its shortcomings and superficialities – has been aroused to an intellectual and professional revolt against the thinking, the approach, the content and the timing that has resulted in the Defamation Bill, 1988. It was an insult to the collative intelligence of the press, and to the democratic instincts of the people of India, that the authors of the atrociously draconian and unenlightened attempt to change the law of criminal defamation misjudged the mood as to imaging that they could sneak this in and get away with the coup.

Journalists, politicians and lawyers all over the country opposed the Bill. Journalists in New Delhi held an impressive demonstration on September 5, 1988 and a nationwide newspaper strike was conducted on September 6, 1988 against the Bill. Sensing the mood of the press, the Government called for discussion with prominent editors. But the newspapers refused to hold discussions with the Government. Prime Minister Rajiv Gandhi said the arguments put forward by the press for the withdrawal of the defamation bill were not strong enough and asked the press to come and convince him. (*The Statesman,* September 17, 1988). Reacting to the Prime Minister's announcement that there should be a dialogue on the Bill between the Government and the press, Shourie (1988) wrote an article in *Indian Express* criticising the Prime Minister.

The Government formed a Ministerial Committee to discuss with the press. The Committee held three meeting with the press on September 21, 1988. On September 22, 1988 the Government of India dropped the Defamation Bill.

Mr Rajiv Gandhi made an announcement on the withdrawal of the Bill as follows:

> "A free press is an integral part of the inner strength and dynamism of our democracy. Without a free press, there can be no democracy. The imperishable values of our freedom struggle

have gone into making of the press in India. We uphold this legacy. We shall continue to do so. Our commitment to the freedom of the press is total. We have no intention of curbing, in any way, the freedom of the press.

The Telegraph, September 24, 1988.

Chapter 4

Freedom of the Press and Article 19(a): Case Studies

The press is one of the channels of communication between the Government and the people. As the prime functions of the press are to inform and to educate the people, it should inform the people with correct news and facts because people tend to believe newspaper reports in day to day life. Sometimes, a series of reports about the Government and its functioning will let the people judge about the governance in the country. Because a well-informed citizen is a pre-requisite for democracy, the press must have freedom to write and report about the factual happenings to inform him. Hence, every democratic country ensures freedom of the press.

Freedom of speech presupposes that right conclusions are more likely to be gathered out of many sources because widest possible dissemination of information from as many sources as possible is essential to the welfare of the public. It is the function of the press to disseminate news with as many different facts as possible. Normally, a citizen is dependent on the press for the quality, proportion and extent of his news supply. In such a situation the exclusive and continuous advocacy of one point of view through the medium of a newspaper which holds a monopolistic position is not conducive to the formation of healthy public opinion.

Therefore, the importance of the freedom of the press has been stressed by many people in India on various occasions. In 1950, Pandit

Jawaharlal Nehru said: "I would rather have a completely free press with all the dangers involved in the wrong use of that freedom than a suppressed or regulated press" (Mankekar, 1973). The Second Press Commission (1982:19) commenting on the role of the press observed:

> While the primary function of the press is to provide comprehensive and objective information on all aspects of the country's social, economic, political and cultural life, it has also an educative and mobilising role.

In many cases, the Supreme Court emphasised the great value of the freedom of the press in a democratic society. But at the same time, the Court also endorsed reasonable restrictions imposed by the Constitution in Article 19(2) since freedom of expression or freedom of the press cannot be misused. As observed by the Second Press Commission (1982) that the press had a 'mobilising role', the press cannot take it for granted that it should wrongly misguide or misuse its freedom in disturbing public safety. In this background, Court interpretations assume significance.

The Supreme Court in various cases elaborates and interpreted Article 19(a). Since Article 19(1)(a) does not specifically deal with freedom of the press, the intervention of the courts is necessitated for better understanding of its nature. The cases that came up before the court dealt with: (1) freedom of publication, and (2) freedom of circulation. Thus, this chapter focuses on the important cases that came up before the Supreme Court which has elaborated the concept of the freedom of the press.

Romesh Thapar Vs. State of Madras (1950)

A case dealing with the freedom of the press came up in 1950 in a peculiar situation. Romesh Thapar was a printer, publisher and editor of a weekly journal in English, Cross Roads published from Bombay. The Madras Government banned the magazine from the state by curtailing the circulation of the journal under the Madras Maintenance of Public Order, 1948. the editor filed a case in the Supreme Court in 1950 contesting the Act as contravention to the fundamental right of freedom of expression guaranteed by the Indian Constitution under Article 19(1)(a). However, Madras Government under the Act of 1948 argued that it had the right to impose restriction on the press for the purpose of scrutiny public safety for maintaining public order. Moreover, Article 19(2) states that unless a law restricting freedom of speech an expression is directed solely against the enduring of the security of the state or the overthrow of it such a law cannot fall within the ambit of clause (2).

The Supreme Court in its ruling said freedom of speech and expression included freedom of propagation of ideas and therefore freedom of circulation also was a part of freedom of propagation of ideas. Liberty of circulation is as essential to that freedom as the liberty of publication. The Court emphatically pointed out that without circulation, the publication would be of little value. The imposition of censorship on a journal previous to its publication would amount to an infringement of Article 19(1)(a).

Brij Bhushan Vs. State of Delhi (1950)

In this case too, the same problem of constitutional validity was involved. Brij Bhushan, the petitioner, was the printer and publisher of the English weekly *Organiser* of Delhi which was alleged to have been publishing highly objectionable matter constituting a threat to public law and order. Therefore, the Chief Commissioner of Delhi under the exercise of Section 7(1)(e), East Punjab Public Safety Act, 1949 as extended to Delhi Province, passed an order requiring Brij Bhushan and K.R. Halkani, Editor, to submit for scrutiny, in duplicate the magazine before publication all commercial matter and news and views about Pakistan including photographs and cartoons other to prevent activities prejudicial to the public safety and maintenance of public order.

Brij Bhushan appealed to the Supreme Court against the order of the Commissioner. The Supreme Court held that the imposition of pre-censorship on the journal was undoubtedly a restriction on the liberty of the press which is an essential part of the right to freedom of speech and expression declared by Article 19(1)(a) and struck down the impugned Act, i.e., Section 7(1)(c), East Punjab Public Safety Act, 1949 as void and quashed the order of the Commissioner.

The next important decision in this respect was the State of Bihar Vs. Shailabala Devi. The Supreme Court observed that it was plain that speeches or expressions on the part of an individual which incite or encourage commission of violent crimes, such as murder, cannot but be the matters which would undermine the security of the state and come within the ambit of law sanctioned by Article 19 (2) of the Constitution.

As a result of these decisions, Article 19(2) was amended with retrospective effective from 1950. Therefore the amendment states that the restrictions to be imposed must be reasonable which means that the courts will be entitled to examine whether the restrictions imposed are reasonable or not. The amendments made the categories enumerated in Clause (2) exhaustive. The Constitutional validity of this amendment was upheld by the Courts.

Virendra Vs. State of Punjab (1957)

Virendra, the petitioner was the editor, printer and publisher of two daily newspapers of Jullundhar, the Urdu daily newspapers *Daily Pratap* and Hindi daily newspapers *Vir Arjun.* Since the appointment of the States Reorganisation Commission in December 1953, the Akali Party Punjab started a campaign for the partition of Punjab on communal and linguistic lines. On the other hand, the Hindus were opposed to it and the two newspapers helped in propagating, 'Save Hindi Agitation'. Under such circumstances the Punjab Government passed sections 2 and 3 of the Punjab Special Powers (Press) Act, 1956. Under Section 2(1)(a) it prohibited the printing and publishing of any article, report, news item, and letter of any other material of any character whatsoever relating to or connected to 'Save Hindi Agitation' and under section 3(1) imposed a ban against the entry and the circulation of these two papers published from New Delhi in the Stage of Punjab. Though these two sections of the Act resulted in total curtailment of the freedom of the press, the judiciary in views of the circumstances stuck to the reasonableness of the restrictions under Article 19(1)(a) and 19(1)(g). The Supreme Court upheld the section 2 of the Act for the following reasons: (a) it did specify the specific purposes of the section; (b) it was to be for a limited duration only; and (c) it was liable to be modified or rescinded upon a representation made.

All this was considered as well within the scope of Article 19(2) and Article 19(6). But the Supreme Court did strike down the Section 3 of the Act as it did not provide for the safeguards i.e., (a) there was no time limit for the operation of an order made not, (b) there was any provision for any representation to be made to the State Government.

This shows that sensitivity and responsibility with which the Supreme Court weights the fundamental rights in the prevailing circumstances for justification of restrictions. Moreover, the Supreme Court does not regard prohibition of the press or banning of the entry of newspapers as unconstitutional provided there are reasonable safeguards i.e, the laws or orders of the executive are substantively and procedurally reasonable within the meaning of Article 19(2) and 19(6).

Ramjilal Modi Vs. State of Uttar Pradesh (1957)

This case involves an editor, printer and publisher of a Hindi monthly magazine called *Caurakshak* who was convicted for his article of November 1952 issue in the magazine by the Sessions Judge who acquitted him of the charge under Section 153-A* but convicted him under Section 295-A† and sentenced him to 18 months imprisonment and a fine of Rs. 2,000. The Petitioner filed an appeal

---

* Section 153-A of Indian Penal Code, 1860 deals with punishment for promoting enmity between different groups on grounds of religion, race, place of birth, residence, language, etc., doing acts prejudicial to maintenance of harmony, etc.

† Section 295-A of Indian Penal Code, 1860 deals with imprisonment upto 3 years or fine or both for indulging in deliberate and malicious intention of outraging religious feelings of an class of citizens of India by words, either spoken or written, or signs or by visible representations or otherwise, insults or attempts to insult the religion or the religious beliefs of that class.

to the Allahabad High Court which held that the article was published with the deliberate and malicious intention of outraging the religious feelings of Muslims and the petitioners were guilty under Section 295-A of Indian Penal Code but reduced the punishment of 12 months imprisonment and Rs 250 fine. Then the editor appealed to the Supreme Court challenging the constitutional validity of Section 295-A as it was an infringement over Article 19(1)(a) and was not a law imposing reasonable restrictions under Article 19(2).

The Supreme Court upheld the Section 295-A of Indian penal Code as well within the scope of Article 19(2) and stated that its constitutional validity was beyond question. The Supreme Court also stated that the expression 'in the interest of' occurring in the amended Clause (2) after Romesh Thappar and Brij Bhushan cases instead of 'maintenance of public order' had the effect of making the protection afforded by that very clause wide and the appeal was dismissed.

Express Newspapers Pvt. Ltd., Vs. Union of India (1958)

In this case, the Lt. Government of Delhi alleged that the new Express building was constructed in contravention of Municipal Corporation laws and served a notice for entry and its demolition.

The court held that the impugned notices constituted direct and immediate threat to the freedom of the press and were thus violative of Article 19(1)(a) and are invalid. They intended to silence the voice of *Indian Express*. In this case too, the Supreme Court upheld the argument of the newspaper and struck down the notice the corporation.

Sakal Newspapers Vs. Union of India (1962)

The case filed by the Sakal newspapers of Poona before the Supreme Court formed the basis for clear definition of the freedom of the press by the Supreme Court. The need for filing the petition by the Sakal Newspaper arose when the Government of India passed an order known as Daily Newspaper (Price and Page) Order 1960 under the Section 3 (1) of the Newspapers (Price and Page) Act, 1956. This Act was passed by the Government following the recommendation of the First Press Commission.

The newspaper *Sakal* was started in the year 1932 and it claimed that it had a net circulation of 52,000 copies on week days and 56,000 copies on Sundays in Maharashtra and Karnataka and as such plays a leading part in the dissemination of news and views and in moulding public opinion in matters of pubic interest. The daily edition of the newspaper contains six pages a day for five days in a week and four pages on one day. This edition is priced at 7 NP. The Sunday edition consists of 10 pages and is priced at 12 NP. About 40 percent of the space in the newspapers is taken up by advertisement matter and the rest is devoted to news, articles, features, views, etc. in this case, the *Sakal* papers, the petitioner challenged the constitutional validity of the newspaper (Price and Page) Act, 1956 and the Daily Newspaper (Price and Page) Order, 1960, especially Section 3(1) of the Act, which is its pivotal provision, is held unconstitutional and therefore the Daily Newspaper (Price and Page) Act, 1956, section 3(1), the Central Government passed the Daily Newspaper (Price and Page) Order, 1960 which made the right of a newspaper to publish news and views and to utilize as many pages as it likes dependent upon the price charged to the readers. Prior to the promulgation of the order every newspaper was free to charge whatever price it choose, and thus had a right unhampered by state regulation to publish news and views. This liberty was interfered with by the order which provided for maximum number of pages for the particular price charged. In brief, the effect of the Act and the Order were that:

(a) they regulated the number of pages according to the price charged,

(b) they prescribed the number of supplements to be published, and

(c) they prohibited the publication and sale of newspapers in contravention of any Order made under Section 3 of the Act,

(d) the Act also provided for regulating by an order under Section 3 the sizes and areas of advertising matter in relation to the other matters contained in a newspaper,

(e) they attracted penalties for contravention of either the Act or Order.

The preamble of the Act was to secure to newspapers further opportunities of freedom of expression by preventing unfair competition. This was to be achieved by regulating the price of the newspaper.

The fixation of the minimum price for the number of pages was obviously not for ensuring a reasonable price to the buyers of newspapers but for expressly cutting down the volume of circulation of some newspapers by making the price so unattractively high for a class of its readers as is likely to deter it from purchasing such newspaper;

(1) Raising the price of a newspaper even by a small amount such as one naya paisa in order that its present size is maintained would adversely affect its circulation.

(2) On the other hand, reduction of newspaper would amount to restricting dissemination of news and views thus directly affecting Article 19(1)(a).

(3) Control of Government on the sizes and space of advertisements would also affect freedom of circulation. For if the area for advertisement is curtailed, the price of the newspaper will be forced to go up and thus the circulation will go down.

Thus, from all angles the Act and the order directly affected freedom of the press and its circulation and therefore was struck down. The Supreme Court held that the only restrictions which may be imposed on the rights of an individual under Article 19(1)(a) are those which clause (2) of the Article permits and no other.

The court finally said that Act was good, for, its objective was to give some kind of protection to small or newly started newspapers. But for such an objective the state cannot make in roads on the right of other newspapers which Article 19(1)(a) guarantees to them. There may be other ways of helping them.

The Court observed:

The right to propagate one's ideas is inherent in the conception of freedom of speech and expression. For the purpose of propagating his ideas every citizen has a right to publish them, to disseminate them and to circulate them. He is entitled to do so either by word of mouth or by writing. The right guaranteed thus extends, subject to any law competent under extends, subject to any law competent under Article 19(2), not merely to the matter which he is entitled to circulate, but also to the volume of circulation, in other words, the citizen is entitled to propagate his views and reach any class and number of readers as he chooses subject of course to the limitations permissible under a law competent under Article 19(2).

Bennett Coleman and Co. Ltd., Vs. Union of India (1977)

Bennet and Coleman and Co. Vs. Union of India is a case of great significance in the area of freedom of speech and expression. India faced a shortage of indigenous newsprint in the early 70s. Therefore, newsprint had to be imported from foreign countries. Because of shortage of foreign exchange, quantity of newsprint imported was not adequate to meet all requirements. Some restrictions became necessary on consumption of newsprint. Accordingly, a system of newsprint quota for newspapers was evolved. The actual consumption of newsprint by a newspaper during the year 1970-71 or 1971-72, whichever was less, was taken as the base for sanctioning Government quota of newsprint (Jain, 1987). For dailies with a circulation of up to 100, 000 copies, 10 per cent increase in the basic entitlement was to be granted, but for newspapers with a larer circulation, the increase was to be only 3 per cent. Newspapers with less than 10 pages daily could raise the number of pages by 20 per cent subject to the ceiling of 10. A few more restrictions were imposed on the use of newsprint. The dominant direction of the policy was to curtail the growth of big newspapers which could not increase the number of pages, page area or periodicity by reducing circulation to meet their requirements even within their admissible quota.

The import policy for newsprint for the year April 1972 to March 1973 was challenged by the petitioners, i.e., Bennet and Coleman, the publishers of *The Times of India.* The newsprint policy was impeached as an infringement of fundamental rights to freedom of speech and expression in Article 19(1)(a) and right to quality in Article 14 of the Constitution. The petitioners contended that some provisions of the Newsprint Control Order 1962 were violative of Article 19(1)(a) and Article 14* of the Constitution. The restrictions imposed by the Newsprint Policy were said to infringe the rights of freedom of speech and expression guaranteed in Article 19(1)(a) of the Constitution. First, the policy said no newspaper or new edition could be started by a common ownership unit within the authorise quota of newsprint. Secondly, there was al limitation on the maximum. number of pages to 10. No adjustment was permitted between circulation and the pages so as to increase the pages. Thirdly, no interchangeability was permitted between different paper of common ownership unit and different editions of the same paper. Fourthly, allowance of 20 per cent increase in page level upto a maximum of 10 was given to newspapers with less than 10 pages.

Thus, the Supreme Court held that the newsprint policy for 1972-73 violated Articles 19(1)(a) and 14 of the Constitution. The restrictions by fixing 10 page limit infringe Articles 19(1)(a) and 14 of the Constitution and were, therefore, declared unconstitutional and struck down.

By a majority judgement, the Supreme Court declared "the policy was unconstitutional and felt that the Government could evolve a policy of allotting newsprint on a fair and equitable basis, keeping in view the interests of small, medium and big newspapers, the Government control the growth and circulation of newspapers. In effect, the Court said the newsprint policy became the newspaper control policy. While newsprint quota could be fixed on a reasonable basis, post-quota restrictions could not be imposed. The newspaper should be left free to determine their pages, circulation and new editions within their fixed quota. The policy of limiting all papers whether small or large, or in English or an Indian language, to 10 pages was held to be discriminatory as it treated unequals as

---

* Article 14 of the Indian Constitution states that:

"The state shall not deny to any person equality before the law or the equal protection of laws within the territory of India".

equals. The restrictions imposed cut at the very root of the guaranteed freedom. The press has the right of free propagation and free circulation without any previous restraint on publication".

Indian Express Newspapers (Bombay) Pvt. Ltd., Vs. Union of India (1986)

The Government of India in March, 1981 imposed import duty* on newsprint from abroad in order to get more foreign revenue as the Government wanted to generate more funds to tide over the fiscal deficit in the financial year. *Indian Express,* the country's elite newspaper and several other newspapers filed writ petitions in May, 1981 challenging the constitutional validity of the notifications issued by the Centre imposing specified rates of customs duty and auxiliary duty on imported newsprint drawn by different categories of newspapers from March 1, 1981. The main plea of the petitioners was that the impugned levy of duty on Imported newsprint had the direct effect of crippling the freedom of speech and expression and the carrying on of the business of the publishing newspapers as it had led to an increase in the price of newspapers resulting in reduction of their circulation.

The court accepted the plea of the newspapers but instead of quashing the impugned notifications, it directed the Government to consider within six months the entire question of levy of import duty or auxiliary duty on newsprint with effect from March 1, 1981. If on such reconsideration, the Government decides to modify the levy of the duty, it should take necessary steps to that end. Quashing the impugned notifications would have led to the petitioners paying much higher duty and the result would have been disastrous to them. The Court emphasised that it did not the petitioners had to pay on the newsprint. The court thus rejected the plea of the petitioners that no duty could be levied on the newspaper industry. Having regard to the facilities like telephones, teleprinters, postal, transport and other communication amenities provided by the state at considerable cost

* The Government imposed 10 per cent import duty and 5 per cent ancillary duty on newsprint imported from abroad under the Customs Act, 1962.

to itself, the newspapers "have to bear the common fiscal burden like the others".

However, such a levy was "subject to review by courts in the light of provisions of the Constitution". Underlining the importance of the freedom of the press in democratic society, the court noted that with a view to checking malpractices interfering with the free flow of information, democratic constitutions all the world over, make provisions guaranteeing the freedom of speech and expression and laying down the limits of interference with it. "It is, therefore, the primary duty of all the national courts to uphold the said freedom and invalidate all laws or administrative actions which interfere with it, contrary to the constitutional mandate".

In essence, the two case Romesh Thappar Vs. State of Madras (1950) and Indian Express Newspapers (Bombay) Vs. Union of India (1986) have summarised the concept of freedom of the press as observed by the Supreme Court in its judgements from 1950 to 1986. In the first case, the Supreme Court held that the freedom of speech and expression includes freedom of propagation of ideas and that freedom is ensured by the freedom of circulation. In this case, the Court distinguished between 'public order' and 'public safety' and held that public safety was a part of the wider concept of public order and if it was intended to signify any matter 'public order', it would not have been competent for the Madras Legislature to enact the provision relating to public safety. 'Public Safety' ordinarily means security of the public or their freedom from danger. In that sense, anything which tends to prevent danger to public health may also be regarded as securing public safety. The meaning of the expression must, however, vary according to the context. The Court then rejected the argument that the securing of the public safety or maintenance of public order would include the security of the state which was covered by Article 19 (2). In other words, the Court allowed the imposition of restrictions on the freedom of speech and expression only in cases where danger to the State was involved, an enactment which was capable of being applied to cases where no such danger could arise cannot be held to be constitutional and valid to any extent.

In the other case (Indian Express Vs. Union of India), the Court held that the expression 'freedom of the press' has not been used in Article 19 but it is comprehended within Article 19(1)(a). This expression means a freedom from interference from authority which would have the effect of interference with the content and circulation of newspapers. There cannot be any interference with that freedom in the name of public interest. The purpose of the press is to advance the public interest by publishing facts and opinions without which democratic electorate cannot make responsible judgements. Freedom of the press is the heart of social and political intercourse. It is the primary duty of the Court to uphold the freedom of the press and invalidate al laws or administrative actins which interfere with it contrary to the constitutional mandate.

The freedom of expression has four broad social purposes to serve: (i) it helps an individual to attain self fulfillment, (ii) it assists in the discovery of truth, (iii) it strengthens the capacity of an individual in participating in decision making, and (iv) it provides a balance between stability and social change. All members of the society should be able form their own beliefs and communicate them freely to others.

In sum, the fundamental principle involved here is the people's right to know. Freedom of speech and expression should, therefore, receive a generous support from all those who believe in the participation of people in the administration. It is on account of this special interest which society has in the freedom of speech and expression that the approach of the Government is more cautious concerning the newspapers industry.

Chapter 5

Freedom of the Press and Press Council of India

Press Council plays a vital role in upholding freedom of the press. Several countries like the USA, the UK, and Sweden set up Press councils or Press Regulatory bodies to monitor the freedom of the press all over the world. Sweden was the first country to have set up a Press Council in 1916. Similarly, the United Kingdom also set up a Press Council in 1953 following the recommendations of the First Royal Press Commission Report in 1949. However, the Press Council in the United Kingdom was replaced by the Press Complaints Commission in 1993 on the recommendation of a Committee appointed by the British Government. The need for the Press Complaints Commission (PCC) in the United Kingdom was felt by newspapers because the privacy of individuals was invaded by the tabloid press in Britain. Following the Princess Diana case, the PCA proposed to bring in a new code to prohibit publication of any pictures obtained through persistent pursuit or a result of unlawful behaviour (Davidson, 1997).

The main difference between the Press Council and the Press Complaints Commission was that the Council was responsible for the preservation of the freedom of the press and the press Complaints Commission was expected to ensure a decent standard of conduct by the British newspapers. The Complaints Commission was guided by a Code of conduct (Press Council of India Report 1990: 18).

In the case of United States of America, a National News Council was set up in 1973. The need for this Council was recommended by the Hutchins Commission in 1947 (Bhatia, 1997: 253).

According to McBride Report nearly 50 countries set up Press Councils by 1980. India set up a Press Council in 1965, but the basic difference between Press Council of India and other bodies in other counties is that the Press Council of India is a statutory body and has the powers of a Civil Court and the inquiry by the Council is quasi-judicial.

Set-up of Press Council of India

After the Independence, the Government appointed a Press Commission in 1952 known as First Press Commission with an objective to study the state of Indian Press. The Commission after studying the state of press submitted its report in 1954. in its survey of the press in 1952, the Commission found a lot of perversities which crept into the professions of journalism just to increase the circulation of newspapers. There was yellow journalism, sensationalism, malicious and irresponsible attacks on well-known personalities, objectionable writings, unbridled indecency and vulgarity (Sarkar, 1984: 267, Bhatia 1997: 251 and Dhavan, 1991: 43). Although some press laws were existing at the time of Independence, they were not sufficient to deal with the newspapers. One Act, the Press (Objectionable Matter) Act, 1951* was existing in India. This Act was enacted when Rajagopalachari was the first Home Minister of free India (Bhatia, 1997: 250). The purpose of this enactment was to curb the writings of the press such as encouragement of violence, crime and sabotage and certain other grave offences like publication of matters, scurrilous writings. But this attempt of the Government of bring in

* The Act defined Objectionable Matter as follows: The expression 'Objectionable Matter' means any words, signs or visible representations which are likely to—

(i) incite or encourage any person to resort to violence or sabotage for the purpose of overthrowing or undermining the Government established by Law in India or in any state thereof or its authority in any area; or

(ii) incite or encourage any person to commit murder, sabotage or any offence involving violence; or

(iii) incite or encourage any person to interfere with the supply and distribution of food or other essential commodities or with essential services; or

(iv) seduce any member of any of the armed forces of the Union or of the police forces from his allegiance or his duty, or prejudice the recruitment of persons to serve in any such force; or

(v) promote feelings of enmity or hatred between different sections of the people of India; or which

(vi) are grossly indecent, or are scurrilous or obscene or intended for blackmail?

The Act was opposed by H.N. Kubzru, Opposition Leader, in the Parliament on the ground that it would affect the freedom of the press. But this Act was passed only to be in existence for two years till an alternative mechanism was developed Commenting on this Act, N. Raghunadhan, Senior Editor, *The Hindu,* said: "The Britisher at his worst did not dream of consigning the press perpetually to the status of a prisoner on parole. It was left to the Mahatma Gandhi's understudy to turn Rousseau's dictum upside down and say that the press was everywhere born in chains and in India it must continue to wear a good few of them for its own good. The luxury of a free pres is not for us. Every one of the Home Minister's specious pleas for muzzling the press was in an earlier day denounced by him and his fellow paladins as an affront to common sense and a sin against the light. The sabotage that the August patriots so easily reconciled with their non-violent consciences owed nothing to the instigation of the press; still it did help them to climb to power. And is it not the most natural thing in the world to kick the ladder by which you rose?" (Parthasarthy, 1991).

The First Press Commission in one of its recommendations suggested the setting up of Press Council to look after the profession of journalism in upholding the freedom of the press. It was in this context that the recommendations of the Commission to set up a Press Council to monitor the role of the press became significant. A Press Council Bill was introduced and passed by Rajya Sabha, the House of Elders, following the recommendations of the First Press Commission. With the dissolution of the Lok Sabha in April 1957, the Bill lapsed and Press Council could not be set up immediately. However, on the recommendations of the National Integration Council, a Recommendatory Body to the Government, the Press Council Bill was passed in Parliament in 1965 when Lal Bahadur Sastri was the Prime Minister of India. The first Press Council of India was set up on July 4, 1965, with Justice J. Mudholkar as its Chairman (Parthasaradhi, 1991: 175).

After the first Chairman, the Press Council of India was headed by Justice N. Rajagopala Ayyangar, and (after its revival) by Justice A.N. Grover, Justice A.N. Sen, and Justice R.S. Sarkaria. Besides the Chairman, the Council has 28 other members.

Thirteen of them represent working journalists i.e., six editors of newspapers and remaining seven working journalists other than editors. There are six members from the business and management side of newspapers. There is a member representing the area of news agencies and usually one of general managers, either from PTI or UNI, has been on the Council. There are besides five MPs, three nominated by the Speaker of the Lok Sabha and two by the Chairman of the Rajay Sabha, while there are three other members, each of whom is nominated by the University Grants Commission, representing the field of higher education, one legal luminary chosen by the Bar Council of India and a man of letters nominated by the Sahitya Akademi. All the journalist members and other newspapermen are chosen by their respective associations and nominated by the Chairman (See Appendix-5).

This gives the Press Council a representative character as journalists and mediamen are in large majority. There are also eminent men and women from other walks of life. The concept behind this representation is that peers will judge the functioning of editors and other working journalists, while the presence of the non journalists ensure that the relevant social and other factors would also influence the final assessment of the functioning of newspapers. The Government does not have any role to play in the Council. More transparency has been introduced in the work of the Press Council by throwing open its proceedings of its main committee and the Inquiry Committee to the press.

The Council was unique in having statutory authority. The Press Council Act, 1965, empowered it to summon and enforce attendance of persons and examine them on oath; to require the discovery and production of documents; to receive evidence on affidavits; and to issue commission for the examination of witnesses or documents which were valuable aids in the conduct of investigations. Every inquiry held by the council was deemed to be a judicial proceeding and no suit or other legal proceedings lay against the Council or its members in respect of anything done in good faith. The other functions were the building up of a code of conduct for newspapers, ness agencies and journalists accordance with high professional standards, ensuring on the part of newspapers, etc., the maintenance of high standards of public taste, fostering a due sense of both the rights and responsibilities of citizenship and encouraging the growth of a sense of responsibility and public service among all those engaged in the profession of journalism (Basu, 1986: 76).

The Functions of the Press Council

When an individual, organisation or Government in one's opinion finds anything that is written in newspapers is objectionable, they can complain to the Press Council of India. Normally, the complaints deal with writing that incite communal hatred, indecency and obscenity, journalistic improprieties, articles of character assassination, scandalous reporting and suppression of news. Similarly, a newspaper or an individual working in a newspaper organisation or journalist can also complain to the Press Council when they are intimidated in discharging their journalistic duties. If any complaint is considered serious or grave in nature which is affecting the freedom of the press Council will take up the complaint for inquiry.

Generally, if a complaint is received and the Chairman is convinced that it requires to be looked into (he can reject a complaint), the complaint, along with the accompanying documents, are forwarded to the respondent for his comments. After a reply is received from him, it is supplied to the complainant and the issue is placed before the Inquiry Committee, presided over by the Chairman, for adjudication. Parties are called for oral presentation of facts, arguments and production of evidence, if any, and they can be represented by a legal practitioner or any knowledgeable person as council. This is, of course, not strictly necessary and in a number of cases only the complainant makes an appearance or the respondent. Sometimes not even one of them, and yet justice is ensured. The parties and the counsel are questioned by the Chairman and the members during the inquiry. The Press Council, in any case, has the powers of a civil court for summoning and enforcing the attendance of persons, production of documents and receiving an affidavit.

Since, the Press Council does not have penal powers to impose penalties on a newspaper or an individual, its verdict is not a judicial pronouncement. Hence, many newspapers ignore the admonitions of the Press Council and do not public them in the respective newspapers. Thus, the Press Council is labeled as a "paper tiger" (Bhatia, 1997: 260; Bhatt, 1977). In a classic case, *The Telegraph* of Calcutta although censured by the Press Council of India for its writings against Indian Express, refused to publish the admonition. In such a case what can the Press Council do? Shourie (1990) suggested that then a newspaper which has seemed to depart from the Code does not print the comments regarding departure then alternative is to write about it in some other newspaper or magazine, not just about the original departure from the norm but about the refusal of the paper to carry a comment which recorded that departure. Thus, the latter would bare the paper and the journalists concerned even more than the former.

The Press Council suggested that the Act should be amended to empower it with more powers so as to be more effective and meaningful. The Council is not in favour of imposing sanctions like fines or suspension. Instead it has suggested that the Act should be amended to empower it to recommend to the Central or State Governments or other public bodies etc., for stoppage of issue of advertisements, curtailment of newsprint quota or suspension of confessional rates of postage, for a specified period, in the case of newspapers which have been censured three times. In the case of journalists and editors who are held three times by the Council to have violated the accepted principles of journalistic ethics, the Council desired to have the power to deny facilities of accreditation for a specific period. The Council has urged that its recommendations should be binding on the authorities concerned. That matter was considered by the Second Press Commission (1982) in which majority of the members were of the opinion that the Press Council be given the powers sought by it with the modification that a newspaper would invite sanction if it comes to the adverse notice of the Council three times whether by way of disapproval, warning, admonition or censure. However, three members of the Commission viz., S.G. Jain, S.K. Mukherjee and H.K. Paranjape did not agree that Press Council should be given penal powers (Bhatia, 1997).

However, the statute gives the Press Council only moral authority. Despite demands from time to time that it should acquire 'teeth' both the Government and the council have not found it necessary to amend the law and give the Council legal powers to award punishment. The concept of journalists judging other journalists and, in a manner of speaking, subjecting oneself to 'self-censure' would be defeated if fines and jail terms are handed out. From just 87 complaints received by it in 1979, the first year of its post-Emergency reconstitution the Press Council received as many as 595 complaints by March 31, 1989. this not only indicates that the problems are increasing but also that the complainants the Press, ordinary citizens, organisations and governmental authorities- have abiding faith in the procedures and the capacity of the Press Council to do justice.

The task of the Press Council of India in the 80's became crucial and daunting in the wake of controversial problems in the country. Newspaper organisations and journalists faced threats from militants in Punjab. On the other hand, some language newspapers indulged in communal writing in flaring up communal tensions in the country. The Council looking into the issue of communal writing in late 1980s observed in its annual report (1990-91: 54) "Recognising that the press which enjoys the utmost freedom of expression has a great and vital role to play in educating and moulding public opinion on correct lines in regard to the need for friendly and harmonious relations between the various communities and religious groups forming the fabric of Indian political life and in mirroring the conscience of the best minds of the country to achieve national solidarity, the Press Council of India considers that this object would be defeated, communal peace and harmony disturbed and national unity disrupted if the press does not strictly adhere to proper norms and standards in reporting or commenting on matters which bear on communal relations".

However, in one of the addresses the then Press Council Chairman Sarkaria (1989) said, "The Council functions effectively with the aid and assistance of the Committees constituted by it. The most important of its Committee are Inquiry Committees which hear complaints filed before the Council by individuals/authorities for violation of journalistic ethics and by journalists/editors, for threats or attempts to curb the freedom of the Press, emanating from any source, whether such source is the Government or any authority under it, or the Press barons or others. In case of any interference with the freedom of the Press, the Press Council in appropriate cases even takes *suo motu* action. The Council thus acts as a watchdog of the freedom of the Press. But the other facet of its role, if not more, is equally important to preserve this freedom. This freedom is endangered not only by onslaughts from without, but also from large scale violations of professional ethics from within the press".

Press Council and cases

The adjudications of the council have covered a wide variety of subjects, ranging from communal writings defamation, obscenity and bad taste to investigative journalism, right to privacy, right to reply, pre-publication verification, threat to press freedom, advertisements and press freedom, and impropriety and press freedom. Quite early in its inception, the Council took up, in a *suo motu* action, the question of writings in the press which might exacerbate communal feelings. The cases were dropped but the Press Council observed that restraint by the Press was necessary "during a period when the country is passing through a tense phase resulting from conflict over such sensitive issues as communal rights". The papers involved were the Dainik Jagran and Asli Bharat (Hindi), Current, Free Press Journal and Northern India Patrika (English), Malayala Manoram (Malayalam) and Shri Warsha (Marathi).

Several cases of threats to the freedom of the press have been adjudicated by the Council including those resulting from complaints by the Malayala Monorama against the Kerala Government and against some other state governments, the *Dainik Jonmabhumi* of Jorhat against the Assam Government, and a number of complaints by groups of small newspapers against district or municipal authorities. In several cases the council took *suo motu* action to uphold the freedom of the press like attacks on the Gujarat Samachar in Ahmedabad (1986).

The Council laid down broad general principles in a numbers of cases after inquiry. In a case filed by the *Malayala Monorama,* the Press Council held that an attack on a paper or those connected with it editorially or the management, with the object of pressurising or intimidating them in the matter of the opinion expressed by it, constituted gross interference with the freedom of the press. It expressed the view that raids on newspaper offices by unruly mobs amounted to interference with the freedom of the press. It said that the police ought to have taken suitable precautionary measures.

In another case arising out of a complaint for the Mahajati, a Marathi paper the Press Council decided in 1983 that the implication of an editor in a case fabricated by the police to harass him for this treatment of the news of critical writings amounted to interference in the freedom of the press.

On the subject of advertisements, about which there were numerous complaints from many newspapers, mainly small and medium, the Council held in the case of Tribune (Chandigarh) in 1970 that the giving or with holding of Government advertisements as a lever to influence editorial policy jeopardised the freedom of press. The Government being a trustee of public funds was bound to utilise them without discrimination. In the same case, the Press Council also held that advertisements form any party inclukig the Government cannot be claimed as a matter of right by a newspaper. The Government has; however, to frame objective criteria and advertisements must be placed without taking editorial policy of a paper into consideration. In a 1974 case of the Searchlight and Pradeep papers of Patna, the Council held that if the editor had committed a wrong, or any employee or even the proprietor, the matter should be proceeded against the individual (under the law of the land) but advertisements cannot be withheld (Bhatt, 1997).

On issues affecting propriety and press freedom, the council took the view that it was improper to offer an inducement to a journalist to make him adopt a certain line nor was it proper for the journalist to accept an assignment which would be incompatible with the integrity and dignity of his profession. In 1973, in a case involving a correspondent of the *Hind Samachar,* Urdu daily of Jalandhar, the Council held that asking a correspondent to divulge his source of information was a threat to press freedom. In the late 80s the cattiest and communal issues came to the fore. As a result, the Press Council issues came to the fore. As a result, the Press Council received complaints by members belonging to some organisations. Two such issues illustrate how the Press Council delivered its ruling to uphold the freedom of the press.

Kanshi Ram Issue

The Delhi Edition of Indian express on May 28, 1988 published a news item in the inside page with the following heading **"Kanshi's Presence to Endanger Congress-I"**. The news item contained the following paragraph:

> "Initially Mr. Kanshi Ram had given a green signal to his district party chief Mr Jang Bahadur Patel an advocate belonging to the

Kurmi community, to contest from Allahabad and he filed his nomination also. He himself became inclined when he learnt from 'reliable sources' (Harijan Officers I the top position) that the Congress (I) is not fielding the megastar: but he was in a dilemma for a few days".

Against this news report D.C. Atree complained to the Press Council of India against the use of word 'Harijan' in the news report by alleging that the editor of the newspaper had "deliberately and willfully maligned the Scheduled Caste officers in particular and Scheduled Caste community in general with the intent to degrade them the eyes of their superiors in Government, which could pose a threat to the unity an integrity of the county.

Following the complaint, the Council issued a show-cause notice to the editor of the newspaper to explain the use of the word. The editor replied that the word 'Harijan' had been used by many newspapers in their reporting.

Mr Kanshi Ram had himself used this world on several occasions and had openly talked of Government employees working for him".

The Council constituted an inquiry committee to look into the complaint. The Committee found that there had been no "violation of norms of journalistic ethics in the publication of the news item and in the use of the word Harijan in the impugned write-up. Times have however changed since the days of Mahatma Gandhi who had coined this world to denote the downtrodden and the oppressed. It appeared that the use of the word 'Harijan' now hurts the sentiments of the Scheduled Castes/Tribes. This word has not been used in our Constitution which used the expression Scheduled Castes and Scheduled Tribes".

However, the Committee desired that newspapers should consider whether in the changed circumstances the word 'Harjina' should continue to be used or the world "Scheduled Caste' should be used in the reporting by a newspaper. With these observations the Committee disposed of this complaint.

The Telegraph Case

A news item published in The Telegraph, Calcutta; on April 27, 1988 with the heading **"Islam Gains in Popularity in the US".** One complaint, Chandmal Chopra found the following sentence as objectionable:

> "Since Islam declares that there is no compulsion in religion, the ideal Islamic state is a freedom of ethical ideas where men and women exercise their free will".

He complained to the Council that he "essence was hopelessly wrong because there was no freedom for men and women to exercise their free will in the matter of religion". Following a show cause notice to the paper, editor MJ Akbar in his written statement dated August 20, 1988 submitted that the "same was written by most eminent journalists in the USA who enlightened the public with historical details about the Muslims in the Western Countries".

On consideration of the written statements by both the parties the inquiry committee felt that the "impugned article was published in public interest and with a view to maintaining communal harmony" and had to be welcomed. The committee said, "It cannot go into the merits of the Holy Quran. On the contrary on perusal of the complainant's rejoinder it appeared to the Committee that his letters if published would have given rise to some communal feelings and the editor was perfectly within his rights in not publishing his letters". The committee also found form the record that the complainant had gone to the High Court on same grounds as had been alleged in the impugned news items and his petition was dismissed. In view of it the Committee found no substance in the complaints and dismissed them, upholding the freedom of the press.

The principal objective for the creation of the Press Council in India was (a) to preserve the freedom of the press and (b) to maintain and improve the standards of newspapers and news agencies in India. In its long existence from 1966-1974 under the Press Council Act, 1965 and from 1979 to 1988 under the 1978 Act it dealt with innumerable cases.

From the period 1966 upto the end of 1978, the Council dealt with 389 complaints. This did not include the figures for 1975 which were not available. Of these, 214 were complaints involving freedom of the press, mostly against Central and State Governments and local bodies, alleging discrimination in distribution of advertisements, denial of facilities and harassment.

In the 80's there has been a tremendous increase in the number of complaints before the Press Council. The increase in the complaints against the press does not necessarily denote the newspapers are violating the norms of journalistic ethics with greater frequency than before, as stated by the Annual Report of the Press Council 1991-92. There are other causes which have contributed to this increase. There is phenomenal growth in the number of newspapers/ periodicals published in India i.e., their number has increased to about 28,500 published in 93 languages. Secondly, there is relative increase in the complaints by the press against the Government and/ or its authorities. Thirdly, more and more people from all over India are becoming aware of the Press Council as a forum of easy and inexpensive redress as an alternative to the law courts.

According to the Press Council of India office, New Delhi, the Council has received a total of 595 complaints by the end of March 31, 1989. Out of these cases, the Council has adjudicated 200 cases while dismissing 224 cases for lack of sufficient records (see Table -2 and Diagram-1).

Table -2

Total complaints received and adjudicated by the Press Council of India between 1979 and 1989.

Year	*Received*	*Adjudicated*	*Dismissed*	*Balance*
1979	87	1	33	53
1980	100	29	60	64
1981	224	36	129	123
1982	254	43	167	167
1983	278	47	201	197
1984	286	132	163	188

1985	317	30	247	228
1986	399	162	164	301
1987	361	177	201	284
1988-89	595	200	224	455

Complaints received till the end of March 31, 1989.

Source: Press Council of India Office, New Delhi.

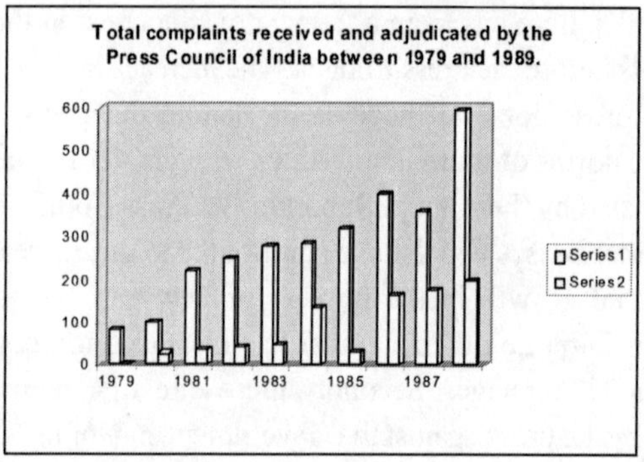

Chapter 6

Summary and Conclusions

The moderns age of communication began with the invention of printing press and paper which facilitated printing of books in multiple reproductions. The preservation of knowledge and ideas in the form of a book was found to be quite useful to the people. As a result, the publication of pamphlets in the beginning and late books helped much in disseminating ideas and thoughts. With the launch of newspapers in the seventeenth century in giving information about trade, commodities, shipping movement and the like there was a significant change in the course of events in the world. For example, the founding of Tom Pain's Common Sense gave moral support to the American colonies against the British rule.

When newspapers started taking an active role in the political, economic, social and cultural processes, the rulers feared that the newspapers would endanger their authority. Hence, they started imposing restrictions on expression of ideas and thoughts. But, people won the right for freedom of expression of thoughts in France in 1789. By the end of eighteenth century, Britian and the United States also won the battle for the freedom of expression *inter alia* freedom of the press.

Since, the printed word became more powerful than a free speech, the international bodies like United Nations recognised freedom of speech as a fundamental right. The United Nations Declaration of Article 19 states:

> Everyone has the right to freedom of opinion and expression, this right includes freedom to hold opinions without interference ad seek, receive and impart information of idess through any medium and regardless of frontiers.

Historians and philosophers argue that the growth of civilisation is possible where freedom of speech and expression thrive. Therefore, in their view the freedom of expression has four broad social purposes to serve:

(1) it helps an individual to attain self-fulfillment;
(2) it assists in the discovery of truth;
(3) it strengthens the capacity of an individual to participate in decision making; and
(4) it provides a mechanism by which it is possible to establish a reasonable balance between the stability and social change.

The story of the press and history of the freedom of the press in India has been a constant struggle under the British and Indian Governments. Newspapers in India fought valiantly to achieve freedom of the press from the British period to the modern period. Therefore, the researcher made an attempt in the present work to examine the freedom beings enjoyed by the press between 1908 and 1988. The objectives of the study are:

(1) to find out the implication of various Government Acts on the freedom of the press in India during the British period as well as independent India;
(2) to study various attempts made by the Central Government in India to curtail freedom of the press and its impact on newspapers; and
(3) to find out the role of the Press Council of India in upholding freedom of the press.

To sketch the historical perspective of the press. The researcher examined various books, journals, documents and newspapers to ascertain the struggle for the freedom of the press in India.

Freedom of the Press and the British Period

Although, the first newspaper was conceived in India by William Bolts, the credit of publishing the first newspaper in India went to James Augustus Hicky. He published the first newspaper, *Bengal Gazette,* on January 29, 1780. The paper made a scathing attack on the Governor General in the beginning and incurred the wrath of the Government. In fact, this was the first incident where the freedom of the press was affected. But, Hicky boldly fought the British Government in upholding the freedom of the press. However, the Government imposed various regulations on the newspaper to curb the freedom of the press and brought out various ordinances and Acts during its regime. The Press Act of 1835, the Gagging Act, 1857 the Press Act, 1878 were the important Acts passed by the British Government during the eighteenth century to deal with books and newspapers.

The beginning of the nineteenth century in India witnessed a great deal of political and social awakening. The National Movement against the British rule gained momentum. In order to curb the activities of freedom fighters, the British Government brought out stringent Acts to suppress the freedom of expression and the freedom of the press.

During the period between 1908 and 1931, two important Acts and Ordinances were brought out by the British Government to stifle the freedom of the national press which was encouraging and supporting the national movement for the freedom of the country from the foreign rule.

The two Acts the Press Act of 1908 and the Indian Press Act of 1910 empowered the local governments to seize any printing press which published a newspaper, supporting the cause of the freedom struggle. As a result of these Acts, several newspapers ceased publication and several journalists were imprisoned. Between 1917 and 1919, 963 newspapers and printing presses were prosecuted for violating the Acts.

The entry of Mahatma Gandhi into the freedom struggle in 1919 changed the political scene. Mahatma Gandhi started writing articles in *Young India* in 1919 criticising the British Government. The movements launched by Mahatma Gandhi against the British rule and the support given by the press to his movements incensed the Government to press an ordinance in 1930. The Press Ordinance of 1930 was very rigorous containing stringent provisions. This Ordinance which became an Act later imposed heavy restrictions on freedom of the Press.

When the World War-II broke out in 1939, the Government of India enacted the Defence of India rules to safeguard the interests of the British and its allies. One of the rules specified that any matter that was printed in the newspapers should be submitted for scrutiny for censorship. Many newspapers opposed professorship and suspended publications.

Describing the struggle made by the press to win freedom of the press, Nehru (1936) said, "the question of freedom of the press is a vital question and inevitably the brunt of the fight must fall upon the journalists."

Freedom of the Press in Free India

With the declaration of Indian Independence, an interim Government was installed in early 1947. the arbitrary powers being exercised by the British Government came to an end. Even before India gained independence, the Constituent assembly had begun its deliberations and adopted the historic Objectives Resolution moved by Pandit Jawaharlal Nehru. This formed the basis for many provisions of the Constitution. The framers of the Constitution in their very first resolution committed themselves to secure the people of India the right to 'freedom of though, expression, belief, faith, etc. the Constituent Assembly Debates reveal that the Constitution makers deliberately did not incorporate the language of the American First Amendment, but nonetheless, retained its spirit while framing the right to freedom of speech and expression. Dr B.R. Ambedkar Chairman of the Constituent Assembly stressed that the freedom of expression includes freedom of the press.

The Constituent Assembly and its various committees and sub-committees considered the freedom of speech fairly but the bases of restriction provided on its exercise far outweighed the grounds of restriction in the case of other liberties. The draft Article 13, which later became Article 19(1)(a) shaped by the Drafting Committee, guaranteed to citizens the right to freedom of speech and expression and permitted the state to make any law relating the libel slander, defamation, sedition, or any other matter offending against decency or morality or undermining the security of, or tending to overthrow, the state.

When the Constitution of free India was adopted and came into force on January 26, 1950, it was found that the Constitution was vague as regards the freedom of the press. There were certain judgements by the Supreme Courts and High Courts pertaining to Section 4(1)(a) of the Press (Emergency Powers) Act, 1931 which enabled the States to prevent encouragements of or incitement to the offence of murder or other congnisable offences. The courts imposed restrictions on the freedom of the press on account of Article 19(2), which empowered the state to impose reasonable restrictions on the freedom of speech and expression. To end the ambiguity, the Government sought to amend Article 19(2) of the Constitution. The Constitution which was adopted by independent India deals with fundamental rights and Article 19 of the Constitution appearing in this part dealing with various rights of freedom of citizens provides in Article 19(1) as follows:

> "All citizens shall have the right to freedom of speech and expression".

Because of this Article, the Constituent Assembly thought that these provisions would guarantee right to freedom of speech *inter alia* freedom of the press, as forming part of freedom of speech and expression. By Section 3 of the Constitution (First Amendment) Act, 1951 the original clause 2 in Article 19 which used to read as follows:

> " Nothing in sub-clause (a) of clause (1) shall affect the operation of any existing law, insofar as it relates to, or prevent the stage

> from making any law relating to libel, slander, defamation, contempt of court or any matter which offends against decency or morality or which undermines the security of, or tends to overthrow, the state".

But as a number of High Court and Supreme Court decisions around 1950-51 went against the Government and editors who wrote provocative articles were left free on the ground that undermining public order was different from undermining the security of the State. Thus, the Government of India amended the cause to read:

> Nothing in sub-clause (a) of clause (1) shall affect the operation of any existing law, or prevent the state from making any law, in so far as such law imposes reasonable restrictions on the exercise of the right in the interests of the security of the state, friendly relations with foreign states, public order, decency, morality, or in relation to contempt of court, defamation or incitement to an offence.

The amending of the Constitution was widely opposed by the press both before and after it was carried out by the Congress Government. The reference to friendly states particularly was objected to on the ground that, if action was to be taken only on representation of a foreign Government, the representation would only come from the non-democratic states which did into understand the workings of a free press; that, if it was to be taken on its own initiative by the Government of India, it may possibly be in suppression of criticisms of India's foreign policy. Other provisions were criticised on the ground that they vested too much power in the Government. The press registered its objection, some newspapers suspended publication, and a few more published over their editorials a catch-line of protest drafted by the Editors Conference. Later in the year, the Press (Objectionable Matters) Act provoked greater opposition, and controversy only subsided with announcement in October 1952 of establishment of the Press Commission to report comprehensively on questions affecting the press.

The committee submitted its report in 1954. the committee recommended the setting up to a Press Council to uphold freedom of the press. The committee also favoured reasonable restrictions to be imposed by amending Article 19(2). The Amendment should include reasonable restrictions relating to: (1) Public order; (2) friendly relations with foreign states, and (3) incitement of an offence.

Freedom of the Press and Emergency

The years between 1971 and 1977 were turbulent in the history of the freedom of the press in India. But, the study of the press could not be viewed independently but was intertwined with political developments in the country. Significantly, the ascent of Mrs Indira Gandhi to the pinnacle of political power was very important. It was observed that Mrs Gandhi's ambition to retain power led to many undemocratic ways of holding to it. Obviously, important and historical facts compelled Mrs Gandhi to take an extreme step of imposing emergency on June 25, 1975.

The darkest chapter in the freedom of the press in India occurred during the 19 months period of emergency. Pre-censorship was imposed on newspapers. Justifying censorship, Prime Minister Mrs Indira Gandhi told the National Union of Journalists that "a section of the press was not concerned with the national interests and that it was helping build-up a vicious atmosphere in the country. It was necessary to prevent incitements to the people to defy laws". In Protest against the pre-censorship of newspapers, several leading dailies in the country left blank spaces and some other papers published extracts from famous poems of Rabindranath Tagore in the editorials.

A special session of Parliament was convened on July 12, 1975 to approve the proclamation of emergency. The Government of India ordered that the proceedings of this special session of Parliament be not reported to the press. This amounted to the denial of privilege given to the newspapers to report the proceedings of the Parliament under the Parliamentary Proceedings (Protection of Publication) Act, 1956. On July 26, Narayan Ganesh Gorey, the Socialist leader in Rajya Sabha on behalf of the opposition said that they would boycott the remainder session as a protest against the suspension of the regular

Parliamentary rules and the Government's decision to apply the press censorship to the reports of the Parliamentary proceedings. On December 8, the President in the exercise of powers under Article 123 promulgated three ordinances affecting the freedom of the press, namely, the Prevention of Publication (of Objectionable Matter) Ordinance; the Parliamentary Proceedings (Protection of Publication) Act (Repeal) Ordinance, and the Repeal of Press Council Act Ordinance. Within two months these ordinances were approved by Parliament. The Government also abolished the Press Council of India with effect from January1, 1976. The Council was established in 1966 to evolve a code of conduct for the press and to uphold the freedom of the press.

With the mounting pressure on Mrs Gandhi to hold elections, Mrs Gandhi declared elections on January 19, 1977. On March 20, 1977 censorship of media was lifted.

Many political parties pledged freedom of the press if they were voted to power in 1977 general elections. The Janata Party, which came to power, promised to uphold the freedom of the press.

In the two and a half years rule under the Janata Government, many significant things happened as regards the press. The Government reconstituted Press Council and also a Press Commission. The Second Press Commission which dealt with the freedom of the press argued that the newspapers had the fundamental right to freedom of expression under Article 19(i)(a), but that article does not confer on ordinary citizen any fundamental right to express their views through newspaper. The Commission, therefore, suggested that Article 19(i)(a) should be reviewed so as to permit an ordinary citizen to exercise his fundamental right to freedom of speech and expression through a newspaper. In this regard the argument of the Commission is as follows:

> A newspapers is published for the consumption of the public. The freedom of the consumer or the public to give expression to their views is also equally important. The public has also a right to information. Freedom of expression in its widest amplitude includes the right to information. The public has a right to know

the different trends of opinion and views operating in the country. But the newspapers generally refuse to publication of news and views which are not to their liking. Everybody cannot afford publication of newspapers under modern conditions for giving expression to his views which may be of vital interest to the community at large and he loses the opportunity to have his say, unless the Press agrees to publish his views. At present, the press has unfettered right to decide what to publish and what not to publish. Self-censorship by the press is as great a menace to the freedom of expression as Government censorship. Our constitutional law has been solicitous in protesting an idea when it comes to the market but has been singularly indifferent in creating opportunities for is expression. A newspaper should give publicity to view which are even hostile to it.

Freedom of the Press and Defamation Bill, 1988

As discussed in the preceding pages, the governments in power tried to stifle the freedom of expression (freedom of the press) when newspapers exposed the misdeeds of the governments. It is very significant to note that the freedom of the press was affected much during the period when the Congress Party headed by Pandit Jawaharlal Nehru (1947–64), Indira Gandhi (1969–77, 1980–84) and Rajiv Gandhi (1984–89). During the time of Rajiv Gandhi, a section of the newspapers in the name of investigative journalism brought out many corruption charges against individuals or ministers in Rajiv Gandhi's Cabinet. It was in this context that the Government decided to curb the freedom of the press by introducing the Defamation Bill, 1988, in the Lok Sabha on August 29, 1988.

The Government's attempt to bring in amendments to the Defamation Law in India was opposed by newspapers.

Journalists, politicians, lawyers all over the country opposed the Bill. Following the pressure an opposition from the press, Prime Minister Rajiv Gandhi made an announcement of the withdrawal of the Bill on September 22, 1989. He said:

> "A free press is an integral part of the inner strength and dynamism of our democracy. Without a free press, there can be no

democracy. The imperishable values of our freedom struggle have gone into making of the press in India. We uphold this legacy. We shall continue to do so. Our commitment to the freedom of the press is total. We have no intention of curbing, in any way, the freedom of the press".

Article 19(i)(a) and Court Cases

The importance of the freedom of the press has been stressed by many people in India on various occasions. In 1950, Pandit Jawaharlal Nehru said: "I would rather have a completely free press with all the dangers involved in the wrong use of that freedom than a suppressed or regulated press". The Second Press Commission commenting on the role of the press observed:

> While the primary function of the press is to provide comprehensive and objective information on all aspects of the country's social, economic, political and cultural life, it has also an educative and mobilising role.

In many cases, the Supreme Court emphasised the great value of the freedom of the press in a democratic society. But at the same time, the Court also endorsed reasonable restrictions imposed by the Constitution in Article 19(2) since freedom of expression or freedom of the press cannot be misused. As observed by the Second Press Commission that the press had a 'mobilising role', the press cannot take it granted that it should wrongly misguide or misuse its freedom in disturbing public safety.

The Supreme Court in various cases elaborated and interpreted Article 19(i)(a). Since Article 19(i)(a) does not specifically deal with freedom of the press, the intervention of the courts is necessitated for better understanding of its nature. The cases that came up before the court dealt with: (1) freedom of publication; and (2) freedom of circulation.

The Supreme Court elaborated the concept of the freedom of the press in the following cases: Romesh Thappar Vs. State of Madras (1950); Brij Bhushan Vs. State of Delhi (1950); Virendra Vs. State of Punjab (1957); Ramjilal Modi Vs. State of Uttar Pradesh (1957);

Express Newspapers Pvt. Ltd., Vs. of India (1958); Sakal Newspapers Vs. Union of India (1962); Benett Coleman and Co. Ltd., Vs. Union of India (1973); Indian Express Newspapers (Bombay) Pvt. Ltd., Vs. Union of India (1986).

The two cases *Romesh Thapar Vs. State of Madras* (1950) and *Indian Express Newspapers (Bombay) Vs. Union of India* (1986) have summarised the concept of freedom of the press as observed by the Supreme Court of India in its judgments from 1950 to 1986.

Press Council of India

The press in India in the early 50's was indulging in sensationalism, malicious, irresponsible and objectionable writings. In order to curb the activities, the Government passed an Act known as the Press (Objectionable Matters) Act, 1951. The Purpose of the Act was to contain the press from encouraging violence, and crime and scurrilous writings. The newspapers opposed the enactment of law in this regard, and alleged that the Government was impinging on this freedom of the press. The Government in order to appease the press, set up a Press Council to monitor the professions of journalism and uphold the freedom of the press. Following the recommendation, the government introduced the Press Council Bill in the Rajya Sabha which was in session and got it passed. With the dissolution of the Lok Sabha in April, 1957, the bill lapsed and the Press Council could not be set up immediately. However, on the recommendation of the National Integration 1965. The first Press Council Bill was introduced in Parliament in with Justice Mudholkar as its Chairman. But the Council was again dissolved in 1975 during the internal emergency on the ground that Council was not able to function effectively. Subsequently, when the Janata Party came to power, it again reintroduced the Press Council Act. On Account of the news Act called as Press Council Act, 1978, the Council came into existence on March 1, 1979.

The Press Council of India is empowered to performs the following to uphold the freedom of the press in the country:

(a) to held newspapers and news agencies to maintain their independence;

(b) to build up a Code of conduct for newspapers, news agencies and journalist in accordance with high professional standards;

(c) to ensue on the part of newspapers, news agencies and journalist the maintenance of high standards of public taste and foster a due sense of both the rights and responsibilities of citizenship;

(d) to encourage the growth of a sense of responsibility and public service among all those engaged in the profession of journalism;

(e) to keep under review any development likely to restrict the supply and dissemination of news of public interest and importance;

(f) to keep under review cases of assistance received by any newspaper or news agency in India from any foreign source including such cases as are referred to it by the Central Government or are brought to its notice by any individual, association of persons or any other organisation; and

(g) to undertake studies on foreign newspapers, including those brought out by any embassy of other representative in India of a foreign state, their circulation and impact.

The present study found that the press in India played different roles-radical and conformist in turn-at different points of history; moving from revolutionary zeal during the nationalist movement to uncritical, complacency in the years after Independence, from renewed commitment to democracy and social justice in the wake of the Emergency to largely unadulterated excitement over various issues in recent times.

It is obvious that the governments in power tend to impose restriction on newspapers to curtail dissemination of information. The possible reasons can be: (1) the government's view that they enjoy power by virtue of the mandate of the people and hence newspapers cannot question their authority, and (2) newspapers by enjoying grater freedom than a citizen would disturb public safety and sovereignty of the country.

But, in the modern world, freedom of the press is the heart of social and political intercourse. The press has assumed the role of the public educator making formal and non-formal education possible on a large scale particularly in the developing world, where television and other kinds if modern communication are not still available for all sections of society. The purpose of the press is to advance the public interest by publishing facts and opinions without which a democratic electorate cannot make responsible judgements.

Newspapers being purveyours of news and views having a bearing on public administration very often carry material which would not be palatable to governments and authorities. The authors of the articles which are published in newspapers have to be critical of the actions of the Government in order to expose its weaknesses. Such articles tend to become an irritant to the Government in power. Therefore, in order to titles on editors and proprietors of newspapers, inclusion press barons in cabinet and inner political councils, etc. the other kind of pressure is one of using force against the press. Enactment of laws providing for pre-censorship, seizures, interference with the transit of newspapers and demanding security deposits, imposition of restriction on the price of newspapers, on the number of pages of newspapers and the area that can be devoted for advertisements, with holding of Government advertisements, increase of postal rated, imposition of taxes on newsprint, canalisation of import of newsprint with the object of making it unjustly costlier, etc., are some of the ways in which Governments have tied to interfere with the free flow of information.

Democratic countries all over the world have mad provisions guaranteeing the freedom of the speech and expression *inter alia* freedom of the press while laying down the limits of interference with it. However, the entire concept of the freedom of the press is undergoing a change in the emerging new technology such as Internet and Satellite Television channels. It is no more relevant to argue that the freedom of the press is part of freedom of expression and speech. During the last 50 years in India the press has emerged as a big business. The study discussed earlier that the Constitution freedom of expression under Article 19(i)(a). In view of the growth of press as a big industry, freedom of the press should be specifically defined in the Constitution.

Although, Article 19(i)(a) is restricted by Article 19(2) in the Indian Constitution, the restrictions are necessary on the freedom of the press as observed in the case of *Romesh Thapar* Vs. *Union of India (1950)*. Notwithstanding the fact that the press knows its limits it has an obligation to society to inform the people with right information.

The law relating to Official Secrets which impinges on the freedom of the press also needs a fresh look. It may be appropriate to do away with the Act which is a legacy of the colonial rule. The right to gather news and have a free access to information have added a new dimension to the demand of free press. If the press is to discharge its function of informing people effectively right to free access to sources will have that the press has no right which does not belong to other citizens. But at the same time they seldom fail to emphasise, that, in a democracy, press has a special role to play. The obvious dichotomy in a judicial thinking has not perhaps been emphasised. Sahay (1979) rightly said, "The press freedom without access to information, is a meaningless jargon and implies merely the freedom to publish Government handouts, and leaders' speeches in Parliament and other public forums".

The present work traced the evolution of the Press Council of India and its function and found that the Council lacked judicial powers to penalise the errant newspapers. But, in the 1909s, the television channels have grown beaming various programmes. Therefore, the Press Council of India can be renamed as Media Council of India by bringing the newspapers, radio and television channels under the ambit of the renamed Council to uphold the ethics of journalism as well as the freedom of the media, instead of freedom of the press.

It is also found that he Government appointed only two Press Commissions to study the state of the press in the country. But, during the last 17 years after the submission of the Second Press Commission Report, many changes have taken place in newspapers as well as in the country. In the 90s, the legislatures in various parts of the country have imposed various restrictions on the coverage of their proceedings. And sometimes, the legislatures have passed strictures on the press as seen in the case Dinakaran* (1993). Therefore, it may be suggested that there is a need to appoint a Third Press Commission to study the newspapers role in particular and other media to recommend and review all the laws relating to newspapers.

As the country is entering the news millennium, it is advisable to bring an appropriate policy concerning newspapers on the issue of access to information, privacy of individuals and the freedom of the press.

Reference

1. The Government of India purchased Rs 1700 Crore Bofors Guns from a Sweden factory in which the Bofors Company allegedly paid Rs 64 crores as commission to middlemen, who were very close to Rajiv Gandhi.
2. In the Rs 420 Crore purchase order of sub-marines from West Germany, the Company allegedly paid commission to the middleman close to Indian Politicians.

---

* The Tamilnadu Assembly sentenced Muthu Pandian, news editor of Dinakaran, a Tamil daily, to simple imprisonment for a week for breach of privilege. Dinakaran was held guilty of having published certain remarks expunged from the House Proceedings in February, 1993. The House said that not only that he editor failed to apologies or appeal before the privileges Committee but also cast aspersions on the speaker.

Nonetheless, a detailed examination into the issues like the editorial freedom, the role of editor in the Indian press, nexus between politicians and journalists, Government allurements to the press which have an indirect impact on the freedom of the press must be undertaken to further debate on the press freedom in the Indian context.

Unit II

Chapter 7

Gandhian Journalism

The history of the free India is written with the unceasing pen of Gandhian journalism which emerged from the values and philosophy being practiced and propagated by Mahatma Gandhiji in his life and through his publications viz., *Indian Opinion, Harijan* and *Young India.* With courage of conviction, Gandhiji applied his principles in his life in journalism and could bravely write his quest for truth or experiments with truth in the modern era narrating his experiences while boldly facing the poignant situations to achieve his goals. Essentially, he believed that newspapers should have values when they were launched with a view to serving the people. Gandhian journalism began in India nearly after 140 years after the first newspaper was started by a European, James Augustus Hickey in 1780. Since then, very few publications came into existence, which were launched both by the Britishers and Indians. Prominent among them were Rajarammohan Roy's *Sambad-kaumadi* which was launched in 1822 while Fardoonji Murzban started the vernacular newspaper in Gujarati, *Bombay Samachar* in the same year. It was interesting to note that all the English dailies had 4000 subscribers, out which 125 were Indian subscribers in 1823.

> Mahatma Gandhiji was instrumental in launching, *Indian Opinion*, in 1903 a weekly which started publication in four languages – English, Hindi, Tamil and Gujarati with an intention to serve all Indians in South Africa. His work in journalism began

when he used the weekly to educate and mobilise Indians through the weekly columns on various aspects of life. Also he supported the publication financially. In his autobiography, he noted that lack of funding to the weekly forced them to discontinue the publication in Tamil and Hindi. Gandhiji, in fact, wrote only two books, '*My experiments with truth*' in Gujarati and '*Hind Swaraj or Home Rule*' which was written in Gujarati was translated by him into English. In the preface to the book *Hind Swaraj*, he said:

> It (*Hind Swaraj)* was written in 1908 during my return voyage from London to South Africa in answer to the Indian school of violence and its prototype in South Africa. I came in contact with every known Indian anarchist in London. Their bravery impressed me, but I felt that their zeal was misguided. I felt that violence was no remedy for India's ills, and that her civilisation required the use of a different and higher weapon for self protection. The Satyagraha of South Africa was still an infant hardly two years old. But it had developed sufficiently to permit me to write of it with some degree of confidence. What I wrote was so much appreciated that it was published as a booklet...In my opinion it is a book which can be put into the hands of a child. It teaches the gospel of love in place of that of hate. It places violence with self sacrifice. It pits soul force against brute force. It has gone through several editions and I commend it to those who would care to read it.

Hind swaraj used the technique of dialogue between the reader and the editor. The purpose of adopting of such dialogue seemed to be that Mahatma did intend to clarify the doubts that would linger in the mind of the reader. He answered many queries posed by the reader such as education, civilisation, culture and so on. Answering a query of the reader in *Hind Swaraj*, Gandhiji explained the objectives of newspaper. He said 'one of the objectives of the newspaper was to understand popular feeling and to give expression to it; another was to arouse among the people certain desirable sentiments, and the third was fearlessly to expose popular defects'.

Gandhian Journalism: Not a profession

As for giving ideas, I have originality. But writing is a bi-product; I write to propagate my ideas. Journalism is not my profession.

—Gandhiji in Harijan, August 18, 1946

Gandhiji outlined the basic purpose of newspapers was public service. In serving the people, the newspapers were expected to transmit news that would transform the individual from wrong doing to righteous behaviors. Almost Gandhiji's writings had aimed at moral transformation of the individual while reinforcing moral conduct in him. Writing in *Hind Swaraj*, he opined that 'the tendency of the Indian civilisation is to elevate the moral being, and that of the Western civilisation is to propagate immorality'. With this view, Gandhiji equated civilisation with good conduct in his answer to the reader in *Hind Swaraj*. Through his writings in *Young India* and *Harijan*, he emphasised on prayer as one of the means to purge himself/ her from the wrong doing and advised all readers to Chant Ram. For instance, he advocated nature cure to keep up sound health in an article through his journal *Harijan* on May 25, 1946. He wrote:

> Nature cure consists of two parts: Firstly, to cure diseases by taking the name of the god or Ramayana, and secondly, to prevent illness by the inculcation of right and hygienic living. The report from the village says that the inhabitants are cooperating with them in keeping the village, clean- I, hold that where the rules of personal, domestic and public, sanitation are strictly observed and due care is taken in the matter of diet–and exercise, there should be no occasion for illness or disease. Nature cure implies an ideal mode of life and that, in its turn presupposes ideal living conditions in towns and villages.

Stephen Hay (2005: 149) observed: 'His way of transmuting or perfecting his own conduct, and ultimately finding god, was through tightly interweaving the three strands of soul purifying prayer, self rule and selfless service of others. In 1927 he explained, I am endeavoring to see God through service of humanity, for I know that God in neither in heaven, nor down below, but in every one…'

On number of occasions, Gandhiji wrote on moral conduct of the individual and 'he believed a spiritually integrated person is no longer a slave of the passions, but is able to go about him or her daily affairs in the light of true self knowledge' (Parel, 2000:16).

In the present day context, dishonesty coupled with corruption is the root-cause of myriad problems, and the politician and the bureaucrat equally share the responsibility. Kothari (1993) noted with concern that 'a significant portion of citizens did not get enough to eat; did not have a secure roof over their heads or enough clothes to cover bodies. Men, women, and children toil from morning to night ...India's poverty is, therefore, not a poverty of resources. It is a ***poverty of Justice'.*** Viewed from Kothari's frame of issues, poverty of Justice was the root-cause of many problems. Stories in the Indian press abound on dishonesty of politicians and bureaucrats. For instance, Sainath's stories (1996) on poverty adequately reflect the dishonesty of politicians and bureaucrats in siphoning off the money meant for development.

> In August 1995, Prime Minister P.V. Narasimha Rao inaugurated an anti-drought project in Orissa. This one will involve spending Rs 4,557 crores in six years (over Rs 750 crores a year) on just a few districts including Kalahandi, Bolangir, and Koraput. Every paisa of that huge sum would be worth spending if it actually fought scarcity and built better infrastructure...In theory, drought-prone blocks come under a central scheme known as Drought-Prone Areas Programme (DPAP). But bringing blocks into DPAP is now a purely political decision. The central allocation for DPAP, a phalanx of other schemes then get money coming in under the employment assurance scheme (EAS), anti-desertification projects, drinking water missions and a host of other schemes. Well, *some* people do benefit (p. 317-318).

The malady in society is corruption which is rampant in every issue, and although newspapers in India focus on the corrupt issues, the adequacy of stories need to be more when compared with the other news values such as conflict, prominence and so on. For instance, judiciary too is no exception to this prevailing scenario.

Indian Opinion: the voice of Gandhian Journalism

Gandhi started the publication of 'Indian Opinion' in1903 and the first issue of Indian opinion was published on June, 04, 1903 although Gandhi, in his autobiography mention the year of publication as 1904. The prime objective of Indian Opinion was to protect the Indian interest and it was such a challenging task considering that there was no other medium of communication. Apart from this the other challenge was the control of press. Gandhi wrote about this situation,

"I believe that a struggle which chiefly relies upon internal strength cannot be wholly carried on without a newspaper, it is also my experience that we could not perhaps have educated the local Indian community, nor kept Indians all over the world in touch with the course of events in South Africa in any other way, with the same case and success as through the Indian Opinion, which therefore was certainly a most useful and potent weapon in our struggle". (Gandhi, 1950: p.142)

The objectives of the Indian Opinion were:

(a) to provide news to all the sections of society in their own language

(b) to advocate their cause

(c) to provide the information of the events happening in India

(d) to contain contributions from competent writers, Indians as well as Europeans

(e) to cover all the aspects on social, moral, intellectual issues

If one goes through the content and language of the Indian Opinion, one can see the art of conveying the message in the simple language which had the direct appeal to the audience. This can be easily verified in the first editorial of the Indian Opinion entitled 'ourselves' where Gandhi writes:

> "We need offer no apology for making an appearance. The Indian community in South Africa is a recognised factor in the body politic, and a newspaper, voicing its feelings, and specially

devoted to its cause, would hardly be considered out of place: indeed, we think, it would supply a long felt want. The Indians, resident in British South Africa, loyal subjects though they are of the King-Emperor, labor under a number of legal disabilities which, it is contended on their behalf, are undeserved and unjust. The reason of this state of affairs is to be found in the prejudice in the minds of the Colonists, arising out of misunderstanding the actual status of the

Indian as a British subject, the close relations that render him kin to Colonists, as the dual title of the Crowned Head so significantly pronounces, and the unhappy forgetfulness of the great services India has always rendered to the Mother Country ever since Providence brought loyal Hind under the flag of Britannia. It will be our endeavor, therefore, to remove the misunderstanding by placing facts in their true light before the public. We are far from assuming that the Indians here are free from all the faults that are ascribed to them. Wherever we find them to be at fault, we will unhesitatingly point it out and suggest means for its removal. Our countrymen in South Africa are without the guiding influence of the institutions that exist in India and that impart the necessary moral tone when it is wanting. Those that have immigrated as children, or are born in the Colony, have no opportunity of studying the past history of the nation to which they belong, or of knowing its greatness". (First issue of Indian Opinion, 4th June, 1903).

Most of the articles written by Gandhi in Indian Opinion were unsigned. Indian

Opinion was published in four languages namely English, Gujarati, Tamil and Hindi in the interest of the British Indians living in South Africa. Indian Opinion was foolscap sized three column journals and filled with discriminatory regulations involving Indians. The journal also provided space for the letters to editors of the local newspapers. Gandhi comprehensively wrote on intellectual and aesthetic subjects and here is an example of an article on 'Indian Art' published in the issue of the journal of September 17, 1903,:

"The Hindu palace-architecture of Gwalior, the Indian-Muhammadan mosques and mausoleums of Agra and Delhi, with several of the older Hindu temples of Southern India, stand unrivalled for grace of outline and elaborate wealth of ornament. The Taj Mahal at Agra justifies Heber's exclamation that its builders had designed like Titans, and finished like jewelers. The open-carved marble windows and screens at Ahmadabad furnish examples of the skilful ornamentation which beautifies every Indian building, from the cave monasteries of the Buddhist period downward. They also show with what plasticity the Hindu architects adapted their Indian ornamentation to the structural requirements of the Muhammadan mosque. English decorative art in our day has borrowed largely from Indian forms and patterns. The exquisite scrolls on the rock-temples at Karla and Ajanta, the delicate marble tracery and flat wood-carving of Western India, the harmonious blending of forms and colors in the fabrics of Kashmir, have contributed to the restoration of taste in England. Indian art-work, when faithful to native designs, still obtains the highest honors at the international exhibition of Europe".

Gandhi consistently wrote articles on other subjects as well. It is also important to notice that along with his scholarly contribution to the journal. He also contributed financially and during the first year of the journal, Gandhi spent 3000$. Gandhi wrote about it in his autobiography, "I had to bear the brunt of the work, having for most of the time to be practically in charge of the journal". (Gandhi, 1956: P-285).

Gradually, Gandhi became solely responsible for journal's management and policy but he didn't mention his name as editor. Although Gandhi faced financial burden but he had no regret for this. In his letter of January 13, 1905, to his political guru and mentor, Sri Gopal Krishna Gokhale, Poona, he wrote,

"When I saw that Mr Madanji could not carry on the paper without pecuniary assistance and as I know that he was guided by thoroughly patriotic motives, I placed at his service the bulk of my savings. I have already become responsible to the extent of nearly $3,500".

In December, 1904, the Indian Opinion entered into a new phase when Gandhi made it clear that the workers were to look not to the present but to the future; not to their pockets but to paper first. Gandhi rather declared that the policy of the journal was service.

It was Gandhi's noble effort that inspired many people along with Englishmen associated with the Indian Opinion. In the issue of December 31, 1904, the Gujarati edition of the Indian Opinion, published notes on the three Englishmen who left their job and join Indian Opinion and started assisting in printing and publication of the paper. Mr West, Mr Kitchin and Mr Polak joined Indian Opinion as they felt that the objective of Indian Opinion were worthy.

In 1905, there was the outbreak of plague in Johannesburg and Gandhi was consistently writing on the problems faced by the people. Gandhi was continuously fighting against the disabilities suffered by the Indians in South Africa. The major disabilities were:-

(a) Restrictions on immigration and trading

(b) Traveling in trains and cabs

(c) Walking on footpaths

(d) Racial arrogance and trade policy.

The columns of Indian Opinion were full of such cases. Gandhi tried to get news from other countries also and for this he needed reliable correspondents in other countries especially in England and, the letter of January 13, 1905 to Gopal Krishna Gokhale is an example of the Gandhi's intent in which he had written, "I am also anxious to secure either honorary or paid correspondents who would contribute weekly notes in English, Gujarati, Hindi and Tamil".

The objective of Indian Opinion was also to inspire the people and Gandhi used to write the biographies of great man and women like Tolstoy, Lincoln, Mazzini, Elizabeth Fry, Florence Nightingale, Ishwar Chandra Vidya Sagar, and Raja Ram Mohan Roy. Another example of such inspiring story is here from the Indian Opinion of March 2, 1907 under a sub-heading 'An Indian Poetess'.

"The Ladies Conference at Calcutta brought to prominence a lady orator, Mrs Sarojini Naidu, already known as a poet of considerable distinction. Mrs Naidu is a Bengali lady by birth and has married a Madrasi gentleman. She spoke without notes and made an impressive and most eloquent speech.

It is further stated that she is not accustomed to speak in public. It is a very hopeful sign of the times that our ladies are coming to the front and are taking active part in the great work of national reform. A gifted lady like Mrs Sarojini Naidu, with her persuasive and attractive eloquence, should be able to render important service to the women of India".

Gradually the Indian Opinion became the mouthpiece of South African Indian on the issue of Registration policy by South African Government where Indians and other Asians had to mention important physical identity masks and thumb impression on the certificates, failing which they were to forfeit their right of residence and liable to be fined or imprisoned. Struggle against registration started all over and Indian Opinion played a key role in the struggle. The Indian Opinion translated the ordinance in Gujarati for the large number of Indians. The Indian Opinion of May 3, 1913, wrote,

"In spite of the bill being rushed forward a stage further; we imagine that it will never reach the third reading stage. But it is well for passive resisters to keep themselves in readiness. It is to be hoped that, if the struggle revived the impending third campaign will be the purest, the last and the most brilliant of all. We share the belief with the theory, that one true passive resister is enough to win victory for right. Right is on our side".

Further on the issue on 20 September, 1913, of the Indian Opinion Gandhi wrote about the passive resisters that who has crossed the border that will return to their homes after the struggle gets over, as, "Hitherto passive resisters have challenged arrests by crossing the Transvaal border. That is how; the present struggle too, has been commenced. We may, on this question of crossing of the border, at once say this method of resistance does not mean that we are asking for breaking of the provincial boundaries. On the contrary as soon as the struggle ceases, those who will have crossed the borders from different provinces will return to the province of their domicile".

The resistance against the injustice act continued and because of Gandhi's effort and contact the movement gradually spread in the large part of India and England. Gandhi's consistent touch with the editors of other countries especially England also helped to widespread the movement. The number of subscribers of the Indian Opinion rose from 1,200 to 3,500 but there was financial problem. The paper was restructured to meet the challenge. The size was reduced from 16 to 8 pages. Gandhi was consistently indicating about the shape of things to come. Gandhi wrote a letter to Mr A.H. West, on or before December 29, 1909, when he was about to change the size of the Indian Opinion,

"The size (of the Indian Opinion) should be changed as suggested. No apology need be offered in the paper for it. The English columns should be reduced. No leading matter of opinion (be) given for the present except explanatory- notes. A. H, matter should be severely condensed. Energy should be devoted to the art of condensing. It may be divided into Passive Resistance, Natal notes, Cape notes, etc. Reports of Bombay and other meetings may be considerably shortened. The English columns then should simply give news on the disabilities throughout South Africa and about matters we are interested in 'The Gujarati' columns ought not to be reduced; but if the Gujarati subscribers fall off, even that may be reduced almost to any extent, you there, in Mr Polak's and my absence, being the sole judge".

Though Gandhi had mentioned that no apology would be offered, the Indian Opinion of January 1, 1910 published the reasons for the change in the size of the newspaper also explaining the condensation of the content so that the same amount of the information can be given even after reducing the pages as he explained, "With the present issue, this journal appears under a somewhat changed dress. The size, too, has been reduced. The Transvaal struggle has put a very severe strain on our resources. It has now become too great for us to continue the old form and size. It is within the knowledge of most of our readers that our publication is not a commercial concern, but our capacity for the service of the community to whose interests Indian Opinion is devoted is limited, and our limitation has necessitated the change the readers will notice in its appearance. Though the size has been reduced, we hope that we shall be able by means of condensation to give the same amount of information. Our readers who are interested in the ideals we endeavor to promote can render useful service by finding subscribers for the journal which they may call their own. It is our desire to give more varied matter as our resources increase. It is, then, for the readers to say when they shall have a better service of news".

Although Gandhi had reduced the size of the paper, but he couldn't sort out of financial problems and shared his views with Maganlal in the letter dated January 20, 1910, "It is desirable not to give more than a month's credit for Indian Opinion. You should only take a limited risk. Let the amount be debited to your account. It will not be deducted from your current allowance. You should never take liability for more than ten subscribers. However, whatever liability you have taken upon yourself in the Cape Colony is binding on all as you did not know the new rule. The new rule is, I believe, very good at least for the present. We will have to carry many (fresh) burdens; it is, therefore, better to cut down these. This (not allowing too much credit) seems to be the prevalent practice of newspapers. As people gradually get used to it, they will follow it of their own accord. We pay the license fee in advance because of compulsion, i.e., physical force. That we shall take the subscriptions in advance will be on the strength of soul-force. The subscriptions will then come in automatically. I have no time now to dilate upon this".

The Language of Gandhian Journalism:

Language is a tool of communication for journalists, and use of language in news reports plays a significant role in informing the public about an event. Though a journalist does not witness an event, he or she tries to construct it with the help of information given to him/her by a second party. Sometimes, a journalist may be present at the event; he or she constructs it by understanding it. In such a situation, is the journalist presenting fact to the public? News is a representation of reality that happens in the environment and the language facilitates the projection of reality. In the profession of journalism, use of value-free words is to be practised to be very objective in reporting an event without any bias. Since the use of language is not mere accidental, they carry the intentions of the writer. Often, the ideology of the writer can be understood through his/her writings. Fowler (1991:5) said 'the contents of newspapers are not facts about the world, but in very general sense ideas'. Thus, the analyses of media discourses can assess the ideological practice of journalists and their representation through language.

On another occasion, he advised the newspapers to give importance to the language being used in the newspapers. In order to avoid the law, language cannot be changed to suit the needs of the time. The following passage is illustrative of his mind—

> The last, though not the least, question is: What is the duty of a newspaper in a country where there are laws like the "Seditious Writing Act" and the "Defence of Indian Act" to "restrict its freedom?" In order to get over this limitation our newspapers have evolved a style of writing which makes it possible to interpret what they say on a particular matter, which may seem to fall within the purviews of these Acts, in two different ways. Some have perfected this art to a science. But, in my opinion, this causes harm to our country. People develop a tendency to equivocate and fail to cultivate the courage to speak the truth. It changes the form of the language which, instead of being an instrument for expressing one's thoughts, becomes a mask for concealing them. I am convinced that this is not the way to educate our people. Both people and individuals must cultivate the habit of speaking their minds. Newspapers are in a position to impart such training to them. The right course, and the one which will ultimately be found to be of the greatest advantage to us, would be that those who are afraid of the above laws and who do not want to get entangled in them should stop publishing newspapers, or that

they should frankly state their true views and bear the consequences. Justice Steven has said some where that there can be no hatred in the language of a man who has no hatred in his heart. And if there is any hatred one should frankly express it. In case one hasn't the courage to act thus, one should stop publishing a newspaper. In this lies the good of our people and our country. From Selected Works of Mahatma Gandhiji, Vol VI, p. 312)

Profits Vs. Public Service:

Journalism has become an industry in the modern days, and commercialisation of the press has been increasingly found in every aspect. Kuldip Nayar (1994) aptly commented as 'the press became more and more commercialised. The old concept of a newspaper representing ideas and nation's ethos had worn out and the profession became an industry'. The contents are aimed at attracting the public and thereby to increase the circulation of the paper. In the process of increasing the circulation, newspapers solicit advertisements from the potential businessmen. Gandhiji's view was that newspapers were meant for public service, they should not compromise on their role in society, and the concept of profits should be relegated to the background. When newspapers solicit advertisements from the businessmen, the newspapers tend to be influenced and they yield to the pressure of those advertisers. Often, adverse news against advertisers is suppressed in support of the advertisers. Being in the service of the people, the newspapers cannot "soil" their pages with such advertisements. For instance, Gandhiji appealed to the readers of *Young India* to support the weekly with their subscriptions, in order to avoid advertisements. Thus, Gandhiji observed succinctly:

> 'It is now and established practice with newspapers to derive their main income from advertisements rather that from subscribers. The result is deplorable. The very newspaper which in its editorial columns strongly denounces the drink evil publishes advertisements in praise of drink. We read about the ill effects of tobacco a well as where to buy good tobacco or which brand of cigarette to smoke in the same newspapers. Or, it may on the one hand, publish a severe denunciation of a certain play

and, on the other, else where in its columns, a long advertisement of it. The largest source of revenue is derived from medical advertisement, which is the cause of mush ham to our people. They, almost wholly, nullify the other services rendered by newspapers. I have seen the harm caused by the advertisements, for many people are lured into buying the medicines – supposed to increase virility, overcome debility, etc. Many of these medicines are those which encourage immortality. It is strange that such advertisements find a place even in religious papers. This custom has been adopted from the West. Whatever the effort, we must either put an end to this undesirable practice or, at least, reform it. It is the duty of every newspaper to exercise care in accepting advertisements for publications in its pages'. From Selected Works of Mahatma Gandhiji, (Vol. VI, p. 311-312).

Further, on another occasion, he expressed his displeasure at the modern newspapers. He pointed out: 'It is generally seen that newspapers publish any matter they have without regard to its need or importance just to fill in vacant space. This practice is almost universal. It is so in the West also. The reason is that most newspapers have an eye on profits. There is no doubt that newspapers have done great service to the people and these defects are therefore overlooked. But to my mind, they have done equally great harm. There are newspapers in the West which are so full of trash that it would be as into read people with their prejudices. At times they produce bitterness and strife even between different families and communities. Thus, newspapers cannot escape criticism merely because they also serve the interests of the people. On the whole, it would seem that the gain and loss from newspapers are almost equal'.

Interpretative Journalism:

Interpretative journalism is increasingly becoming feature of the modern day newspapers. Newspapers because of their inherent weakness of slow disseminators of information as compared to television indulge in interpreting news with their comment. Earlier views which were confined to editorial page interpolate with news, and newspapers pass value judgments on the events. One of the ethics in journalism often underlines non-involvement in the events, and the journalist is an objective spectator of the events. Specifically, the emergence of television has posed a problem to viewers in the context of live coverage of issues. The journalist in order to analyse the situation is identifying himself with the situation as in the case of embedded journalism where journalists' trips are sponsored by the source. Objectivity is losing its' relevance as said earlier. Long back Gandhiji observed:

> The reporting of speeches in Indian newspapers is generally defective. There are very few who can write down a speech verbatim while it is being delivered or afterwards from memory. This results in much distortion and interpolation. The best rule would be to send the proof of the reported speech to the speaker for correction and publish its own report of the speech only if the speaker doesn't revise the proof sent to him. From Selected Works of Mahatma Gandhiji, (Vol. VI, p. 310).

Although Gandhiji was insisting that the information should be cross-checked by journalist before publication, it is not practiced by modern day journalists. One alibi for journalists is that they are rushing to cover many news events, and find less time to verify the facts. In a survey conducted by Murthy (2005), it was found that all the respondents reported that they would not cross-check information in the press notes. Added to it, more than 50 per cent of the respondents informed that they would face a problem with language to express the situation that they had witnessed. Thus, Jacquette (2007: 246) explained the reasons: (1) news reporters have a complexly interested set of perceptual, personal, and cultural perspectives from which standpoint they collect information, (2) which they must then try to communicate to a readership or audience in a particular choice of texts and images, and (3) for persons whose background and pre-suppositions they may likely have some grasp of, but which will also include persons of very diverse perceptual, personal, and cultural perspectives.

Developmental Journalism

I have taken up journalism not for its sake but merely as aid to what I have conceived to be my mission in life. My mission is to teach by example and precept under severe restraint the use of the matchless weapon of satyagraha which is a direct corollary of non-violence and truth...To be true to my faith, therefore, I may not write idly, I may not write merely to excite passion. The reader can have no idea of the restraint I have to exercise from week to week in the choice of topics and my vocabulary. It is training for me. It enables me to peep into myself and to make discoveries of my weaknesses. Often my vanity dictates a smart expression or my anger a harsh adjective. It is a terrible or deal but fine exercise to remove these words.

Gandhiji, *Young India*, July 2, 1925

Developmental journalism covers the entire gamut of socio-economic and cultural events, and it does not differ drastically from regular news coverage. Rather, its emphasis is more on developmental aspects keeping in view the context of development; and it examines critically and reports the relevance, enactment and impact of developmental programmes. Thus, Mahatma Gandhiji in India practiced development reporting even before the term, development journalism[1] came into existence. Mahatma Gandhiji, who was a development journalist, felt that the newspaper's role was to educate the masses, he profusely wrote on contemporary topics such as Hindu-Muslim unity, removal of untouchability, prohibition, promotion of *khadi* and other village industries, and the popularisation of spinning wheel as a means of supplementing the income of the semi-starved and unemployed village peasants in India (Krishna Murthy, 1966:79-80). During Independence, the Press was an effective medium in the hands of nationalists as well as social reform groups. They exposed social evils like casteism, child marriages, ban on remarriage of widows, social, legal, and other inequalities for which women were subjected. It also helped them in carrying out a massive campaign to educate the people on the eradication of untouchability (Krishna Murthy, 1966; Desai, 1993:237; Yadava, 1985). Because, journalism in those days functioned as a mission to awaken the masses socially and politically (Yadava, 1985; Parthasarathy, 1991).

Thus, Gandhiji set an example to the journalists in practicing development journalism with an intention to reform the society. He believed that the role of newspapers was only public service, and hence he wrote a series of stories on various issues such as health, birth control, and women upliftment and so on. For instance, he wrote a series of articles on birth control in *Young India* and *Harijan* beginning in 1925 as he was against the use of contraceptives to control the population. On April 4, 1925, he wrote: "If it is contended that birth-control is necessary for the nation because of over-population, I dispute the proposition. It has never been proved. In my opinion, by a proper land system, better agriculture and a supplementary industry, this country is capable of supporting twice as many people as they are in it today". On another occasion, he was can did in saying about women's problems of forcible use of contraceptives. He wrote in *Harijan* on May 2, 1936: "To ask India's women to take to contraceptives is to say the least, putting the cart before the horse. The first thing is to free her from mental slavery, to teach her the sacredness of her body, and to teach her the dignity of national service and the service of humanity". At the same time, he was a visionary though he denied it, and he foresaw the things that would happen in the coming decades. One trait of a development journalist is that he should signal the coming events before the people would understand the consequences of any action. Gandhiji as a development journalist continued to write about the birth control methods in *Harijan* on March 28, 1936. He said: "I know what havoc secret vice has played among school boys and school girls. The introduction contraceptives under the name of science and the *imprimature* of known leaders of society has intensified the complication and made the task of reformers who work for purity of social well-nigh impossible..."

About educating rural masses, Gandhiji wrote articles in *Harijan*, forgiving the farming population rudimentary instructions about food. 'Milk and banana make a perfect meal,' he wrote in *Harijan* of February 15, 1935 in an article entitled 'Green Leaves and their Food Value'. 'For nearly five months I have been living on uncooked foods. The addition of green leaves to their meals will enable villagers to avoid many diseases from which they are now suffering,' He devoted another article to the debate on 'Cow's Milk versus Buffalo's, and still a third to the supreme Indian problem: rice. In his booklet, *Key to Health,* and elsewhere, Gandhi gave warning against machine – polished rice. Polishing removes an over coat rich in vitamins, especially B_1, he explained: lacking those vitamins, Indians, for most of whom rice is the chief staple food, are subject to numerous debilitating diseases, notably beri-beri which means 'I cannot'. Hand–pounded rice, Gandhi explained, retains the vitamin – rich coating (Fischer, 1994:407).

At other times, Gandhi explained about the nutritional value of the mango kernel and the groundnut or peanut. Gandhi knew that the improvement of seed, the proper use of fertiliser and the proper care of cattle could solve some of the basic problems of life. Gandhi also paid attention to non – agrarian aspects of village life. He wrote in *Harijan* on August 29, 1936 that 'we have to concentrate on the village being self contained, manufactured mainly for use'. 'Provided this character of village industry is maintained, there would be no objection to villagers using even the modern machines and tools that they can make and afford to use. Only they should not be used as a means of exploiting others.'

In *Harijan* of July 26, 1942 Gandhi described the ideal Indian village: "It is a complete republic, independent of its neighbors for its vital wants, and yet interdependent for many other wants in which dependence is necessity. Thus every village's first concern will be to grow its own food crops and cotton for its cloth. It should have a reserve for its cattle, recreation and playground for adults and children. Then, if there is more land available, it will grow useful money crops, thus excluding... tobacco, opium, and the like. The village will maintain a village theatre, school and public hall. It will have its own water works ensuring clean supply. This can be done through controlled wells and tanks (reservoirs). Education will be compulsory up to the final basic course. As far as possible, every activity will be conducted on a cooperative basis." To this modest blueprint, which, however, seemed like a sketch of heaven to India's permanently underfed farmers, Gandhi added another wild dream: electricity in every village home (Fischer, 1992). Gandhiji as a development journalist showed an example to the present day newspapers how to practice development journalism.

Further, after Independence, that mission was partly carried by researchers as well as newspapers in conducting a few experiments in development journalism to accelerate rural development. Selden Menefee and Audrey Menefee conducted an interesting study of mimeographed newspaper in Mysore containing some developmental information. Known as *Menefee experiment*, a small newspaper called *Gram Samachar* (village news) was published in Kannada, the local knowledge, for 13 weeks to test the effects of communication on the villagers. For the purpose, four villages were chosen near Mysore in Karnataka. The researchers found an increase in the information level of the regular readers because of the newspaper (Menefee and Menefee, 1967). In another experiment, a researcher started a rural newspaper, *Gramyavani*, in 1993 in Deulpudi, a village in Ganjam district of Orissa to give information to the rural people. The fortnightly newspaper reaching eight villages of the *panchayat* continued for 16 months. A major objective of the newspaper was to provide development-linked information to the people. The contents of the newspaper included agriculture, health, forestry, and animal husbandry. The newspaper brought awareness among the villagers exposed to the newspaper (Jena, 1995). The two studies proved that the newspapers could raise the information level of the people and thereby contribute to accelerating developmental processes at the individual and societal level.

Does Gandhian journalism which emerged nearly a century back have relevance today? During this century, Gandhiji showed to the world that his practice of non-violence, and strong determination to achieve his goals in the face of stiff resistance proved to be successful. Culture as a news value can be relevant even today in the wake of proliferation of newspapers and news channels. In the arena of international communication, a serious issue is often discussed i.e cultural imperialism[1]. With the continuous of supply of news or events by alien channels in the form of entertainment, it is argued that the channels have a hidden agenda to promote their culture in the form of consumerism which is an anathema to the Indians. Gandhiji aptly described these consumer goods as bodily comforts which provide the well being of the Individual physically while distancing her/him from culture of the country. An observation of newspaper content reveals that civilisation as described by Gandhiji is taking deep roots which are perpetuated by the modern mass media contents. Gandhiji said in *Young India* on June 1, 1921.

> I do not want my house to be walled in all sides and my windows to be stuffed. I want the cultures of all lands to be blown about my house as freely as possible. But I refuse to be blown off my feet by any. I refuse in other people's houses as an interloper, a beggar or a slave. I refuse to put the necessary strain of learning English upon my sisters for the sake of false pride or questionable social advantage.

Enough steps must be taken by all citizens concerned to curb the prevailing environment of decultarisation of India. In fact, the argument to halt cultural imperialism of the West which started in the early 1970s when the UNESCO set up a commission to study the mass media content at the instance of the Third World countries. Diplomats like Mustapha Masmoudi[2] (1979) Tunisian Ambassador and permanent delegate to UNESCO and journalists like D. R. Mankekar (1981) in India raised their voice through mass media programmes to make the native culture insular from the external influences.

The second aspect of the Gandhian news values is peace. Peace as a news value is increasingly relevant in the beginning of the twenty-first century. As defined by Gandhiji, non-violence is a conscious attempt to detach oneself from violence in spite of having strength and prowess. Thus, the emergence of peace journalism as suggested by Johan Galtung has greater relevance today. The mightiest personality in the twentieth century, Gandhiji showed to the world the need to practice non-violence. It was observed that 'over times peace journalism could help society at large think and speak about non-violence and creativity when dealing with conflicts' (McGoldrick, and Lynch, (2000). The need for peace journalism can be understood that the dishonesty and valueless environment that prevailed in the society also reflects in the media. For instance, a study of headlines in *The Hindu* (page 12) on February 2, 2009 showcased the low level of societal norms.

- Congress: report constitutionally erroneous
- How Chief Election Commissioner pursued BJP allegations
- Minister slams bribery in judiciary
- Nobody has power to get case registered against a sitting judge, he says
- Centre must accept CEC's advice: BJP
- Apex court to hear SEBI plea today
- CEC does not have *suo motu* power: Nariman
- "Ensure safe passage for civilians in Sri Lanka"
- Kalyan factor won't erode Muslim vote bank: Mulayam
- ED moves court on Satyam

A careful study of these headlines reveals the use of the words: 'erroneous', 'allegations', 'bribery in judiciary' 'SEBI plea in court' 'Muslim vote bank' and others. In another newspaper, even harsh and violent words have been used in the editorial. For instance, *Indian Express* editorial (Monday, February 2, 2009) contains the following:

> It's about Tamils, not the Tigers
>
> The latest bout of **breast- beating and fist shaking** that is going on over the fate of Sri Lanka's Tamils, now that the Liberation Tigers of Tamil Eelam are penned into a tiny enclave in the north of the Island, is a case of too little, too late. It may seem unfeeling not to join the state of shocked mourning that seems to have

broken out suddenly all over Tamil Nadu, but the Sri Lankan army's steady, inexorable progress in the war against the LTTE was never a secret.

The use of negative words bribery, allegations, and plea in the court reflects the state of the society as media is said to be a mirror of society. In contrast to the Gandhian Journalism, the words depict the negative meaning in the minds of newspaper readers, and the Gandhian journalism abhors the use of such words.

Although, the third news value, development is always relevant in the country, developmental reporting has not gained much currency among Indian newspapers. Obviously, the Indian press is known for its wide coverage of political news (Murthy, 2000), gossip (Sainath, 1996: 436) and sensationalism (Goswami, 1994). Hence, vital issues such as primary education, population control, the state of urban decay, power crises, etc. get a backseat (Rai, 1992; Singh, 1994; Shourie, 1995). Further, reporting on rural development does not receive much importance in the Press although 70 per cent of the population in India lives in rural areas. Rural stories rarely get front-page coverage unless they are disastrous events such as starvation deaths, flood, famine or a policy pronouncement (Gupta, 1994). Because development is a very wide subject and it is a long-drawn process, and therefore two types of reporting emerge in relation to the treatment of development news. In two types of reporting–process and events–the trend in newspapers is to focus on events instead of process. Since, development is a process, it requires a constant study and comprehension of the subjects. In journalism, journalists are keen on reporting events. The Second Press Commission (1982) observed: "The reporting of non-official initiatives in rural development, educational reforms, leprosy eradication and so on is less extensive than the in-depth reporting of the implementation of official development programmes. It is unfortunate that our newspapers become aware of such non-official activities only after they have been honoured by Jamanalal Bajaj foundation or Magsasay award".

The role of the Press underwent a sea change during the post-Independence period. In terms of contents, the Indian newspapers fall into two categories: elite and sensational papers as contents or rather news in newspapers play a key role in judging the character of the paper. Elite newspapers focus on serious issues while sensational papers are keen on trivial issues. Rather, the difference in the Indian Press is slowly fading between the two categories. Circulation is oxygen for the survival of the newspaper, and the papers adopt new strategies. Principally, news is made to attract the large sections of the readers. On this count, the elite papers of late adopt the same strategies being adopted by the sensational papers. The chief reason for this trend is commercialisation of the Press on account of the entry of businessmen into the profession of journalism. Veteran journalist Chalapati Rao (1982) observed: the broad feature of the Indian Press is that it is an industry, which is owned and managed by other industries. Further, he commented, "The working class, the poor peasant, the lawless labour, does not exist for mass media. We are hopelessly witnessing the rapid growth of the big business press and the government".

As commercialisation has set in, the newspapers focus on contents that attract the attention of the readers. Political news is given a prominent place in all the newspapers, irrespective of language. In a study conducted by Murthy (2000), it was found that political news ranked the highest in the selected English and regional newspapers. On the front page, two themes politics, and crime, moral problems occupy three-fourths of the space. Because the front page is the most significant page, newspapers focus on political and sensational events to grab the readers' attention.

Newspapers devote a substantial part of their resources for the coverage of political news. Obviously, the vicissitudes of the political parties, mudslinging and allegations against each other form the grist to the reporters' mill. A senior journalist and freelance writer Tavleen Singh (1994) comments, "There are other things seriously wrong with Indian journalism like, for instance, our obsession with politics and politicking to the exclusion of real issues. We will, for instance, give you reams and reams on Kanshi Ram's problems with Mulayam Singh Yadav but tell you nothing about the state of governance in Uttar Pradesh".

News stories on crime and moral problems also get considerable attention on the front page. Stories on theft, burglary, cheating, and law and order problems appear more frequently on the front page. Such issues contain news values that enable papers to boost circulation. Pritish Nandy (1994a) aptly observed: Issues like poverty, homelessness, and unemployment are no longer on the front page. What you have, instead, is the odd sex and violence story to keep the flag of investigative journalism flying.

Public controversies surrounding politicians or celebrities get much space. News is also sensationalised. Chalapati Rao (1982) observed that the present day newspapers, which seek to be popular by trying to be sensational, are practicing the cult of personality in the crudest possible form. Of late, the private issues of public personalities get front-page treatment.

Slowly, the definition of news that is taught in the journalism classrooms is radically changing. The newspapers have their own definitions of news. The popular dailies define news differently from the traditional definitions of news. The old definition of news concentrates on public interest, which is modified in the present day context as news with a public personality in the focus (Murthy, 2004: 29).

Therefore, the priorities of news are changing. Pritish Nandy (1994b), the former editor of the *Illustrated Weekly of India*, writes:

> What about quality journalism? Changing the world for the better? Frankly, who cares about it? Entertainment is the opiate of the masses today and journalists are busy competing with their own advertising departments to bring you leisure-led marketing vehicles that celebrate designer trash. Be it magazines or TV shows or even newspapers and colour offerings, they are all falling over each other to showcase the talent less and trivial. The packaging is skilful and the content is zilch.

Flimsy and non-relevant issues get more space in the newspapers. Ninan (2003) observed that the trend in 1970s was news editors frowned if a company name was mentioned in the copy. Because, public was more worthy than private, politics more worthy than business and governance more worthy than entertainment. Contrary to the earlier trend, in the present day journalism, news about personalities is salient, and it's personal journalism instead of public journalism. Newspapers compete with television channels in covering the glamour. Executive editor of *India Today*, Kaveree Bamzai (2009), made a cryptic comment: Unfortunately the accent is so much on glamour and on who is a celebrity and who's not. I think the whole notion of achievement has become diluted. There is a celebrity culture obsession where a Rakhi Sawant or a Mika are more popular than say someone who has brought electricity to a village or brought IT to a village...I suppose if you are a woman, you are expected to be glamorous and success is measured that way, so that gets accentuate".

Conclusion:

Gandhian journalism needs to be looked closely and it has great relevance even today. The Gandhian trait of positive journalism has radically undergone a change. For instance, Gandhiji observed that the British judges' consideration of contempt of court was praised by him. He admitted the "reprimand" given by judges was acceptable. He truthfully published it in the newspaper, and yet he defended himself. But, the modern newspapers don't even publish the Press Council of India reprimand or censure to the newspapers for violation of journalistic ethics. Courage of conviction and truth telling are the bedrock of the journalism profession. The foundations of Indian press as laid by Mahatma Gandhiji are receding to the background in the present day owing to media's slow adoption of the western model of journalism, tabloidisation which emphasises on sensationalism, sex, and surprises. News reports are biased and personal involvement of journalists is quite discernible in the newspapers. Vilanilam (2009: 89) observed:

> "...The old Journalism of the Gandhian era, of journalists with noble goals, motivated by the need for social change in India, has disappeared, yielding to the journalism of the pocket book, of the purse in short – of pure greed. Journalism as service to

society has been replaced by journalism aimed at profit and affluence for media promoters and media workers".

Therefore, Gandhian journalism has relevance even today, and journalists working in the media establishments must bear them in mind when they are working. In view of the prevailing environment, the media in India must retrospect its' role in society in light of Gandhian journalism. When the newspapers fail to live up to their expectations, Gandhiji advised:

> Unfortunately, the newspapers have become more important to the average man than the scriptures. I would fain advise them to give up reading newspapers. They would lose nothing by so doing whereas real food for their minds and spirits lies in the scriptures and other good literature (Harijan, April 27, 1947).

Chapter 8

Gandhi's Free Speech

When the atrocious adversities of the detestable dynamic rule of the British Empire flooded the land of gods with the tears of blood, a man strong by thoughts, wealthy with love put forth his determined steps, his indispensable words of *satya* and *ahimsa* after winning over the ruthless racism in South Africa. A leader who rewrote the history of the diversity with his discreet, distinguished pen which he gained in the war of colours that pinned a writer, a speaker onto the shyest man ever, a journalist whose worthy words turned into articles, leaflets, letters, messages, quotes, speeches etc, for every word that dripped from his thoughts was like a dilating diamond reflecting the shine of his vision, a lawyer whose statement went unquestioned for its purity and divinity shined over even the flawless argument arresting the flow of words, a Mahatma whose verbal output astonished the communicators, the Gandhi who left back a free pen, a free country celebrating his literary treasure.

Gandhi was a true orator, a genuine speaker and an honest writer whose striking simplicity, scenic sincerity, streaking serenity elevated the verbal communication to the heights of his vision. Gandhi had always taken the first steps, may it be through his journalistic writings or through his message oriented speeches; he let his words lead his people towards the constitution of independence. Collected Works of Mahatma Gandhi, a hundred volume project, is one of the largest entreats of Gandhi's writing and speeches, that seeped in his innumerable articles, telegrams, speeches, discussions, interviews, petitions, persuasions, quotes, books, messages etc. It was a literary hunt that was initialised by one of the first government holders, Jawaharlal Nehru who actively incorporated the process of collecting and complimenting Gandhi's writings and the oral writings of his speeches in a single series, for he adorned this process as "a duty we owe to ourselves and to future generations", by restoring such a statement, Nehru complimented Gandhi's verbal communication as the tribute of the Leader of Satyagraha to his people. The first President of India, Dr Rajendra Prasad portrayed his words as adulation to the Mahatma in the introduction of the mammoth work titled "Collected works of Mahatma Gandhi", as follows:

> "Here are the words of the Master covering some six decades of a superbly human and intensely active public life-words that shaped and nurtured a unique movement and led it to success; words that inspired countless individuals and showed them the light; words that explored and showed a new way of life; words that emphasised cultural values which are spiritual and eternal, transcending time and space and belonging to all humanity and all ages."('Homage', *CWMG*, Vol. 1, v).

In a quest to lead his people who were ahead in different paths of non-violence, Gandhi proved that his non-violent pen was mightier than the violent sword that stabbed not just people but the struggle of independence. His words were the ball bearers of his vision, for they inflicted the urge towards ahimsa, the upheaval of mankind. He wanted to upraise the cry of the unreachable, and his instinct of leadership led him to the boundaries uncrossed through the effective communication that he established through not just his writings of satyagraha but by spreading the outrage of swaraj marked by non-violence by word of mouth that he dwindled through his followers. Gandhi defended his writings against the petition of violence by boldly stating that: "My life is a standing testimony against the libel". Gandhi stormed his thoughts over the blended bind of pages through his Bona fide books such as Sarvodaya, Hind Swaraj, Satyagraha in South Africa, Ethical religion etc. By mourning violence in his mother tongue, Guajarati through his leading articles in Navajivan and Harijan Bandhu, that also witnessed the message of the Mahatma to his followers in the form of his Atmakatha (Autobiography). Gandhi also turned his pen in Gujarati over the readership of Indian opinion with his powerful literature that assimilated his thoughts to a vast audience all over Gujarat. But his own question that has shaken his thoughts in a literary conference admiring the boundaries of Gujarat is as follows:

> "For whose sake are we going to have our literature? Not certainly for the great gentry of Ahmedabad. They can afford to engage literary men and have great libraries in their homes. But what about the poor man at the well who with unspeakable abuse is goading his bullocks to pull the big leather bucket?" (CWMG, Vol.63, 413).

Gandhi was a leader not of a single culture, a single tradition, a single language for he captured the hearts of millions introverting their differences but extroverting the love and unity that he spread on them with the single culture of *ahimsa*, the single language of *satya*, and the single desire for 'Swaraj'. Swarming his mission through the road of words that were dictated by his truth, Gandhi let his senses speak their agony through the inner voice that kept him intact. He wanted his people to be free at their thoughts, because he wanted them to 'think audibly' and to 'speak the strength of the truth', for he knew that once said, the words cannot be taken back, so if it is truth it will never ever be questioned under the bars of justice. He floated as the lotus preserving the odour of the pond, preserving the truth in the world, thereby his tone led not because it was audibly authoritative but since it was amatively authentic, which can be felt in his expression ornamented as follows:

"To be true to my faith [in Satyagraha], therefore, I may not write in anger or malice. I may not write idly. I may not write merely to excite passion. The reader can have no idea of the restraint I have to exercise from week to week in the choice of topics and my vocabulary...My aim is not to be consistent with my previous statements on a given question, but to be consistent with truth as it may present itself to me at a given moment. The result has been that I have grown from truth to truth [...]. My words and deeds are dictated by prevailing conditions. There has been a gradual evolution in my environment and I react to it as Satyagrahi."('Foreword', in *CWMG*, Vol. 90, v, Vol. 53, 485).

Gandhi was a leader who stimulated his followers towards the path of patenting freedom but with adhering adherence to truth which he crowned as the greatest leader of all times, of all decades, of all epics, of all cultures, traditions, languages, of all struggles and even of the statured struggle of the satyagrahi. As a leader, Gandhi embraced the conflict resolution whether in Kheda, Champaran, Delhi, Calcutta, Noakhali, Dandi or Johannesburg with the inflicting non-violence that spread even onto his whirling writings and soothing speeches that didn't hurt anyone except the enraging violence that burnt the hearts of the people. Besides the newspapers, open letters and articles with which he mediated the inconsolable sufferings and grievances of the people, Gandhi blew the conch shell of the war for independence through cable and telegraph communication. Gandhi was a leader who groove into the insights of the struggle by not just injecting an internal rejection of the British force but also by gathering an international support for India in its battle for freedom, in its struggle to communicate the resistance of the people. Therefore, even in his well acclaimed Dandi March, Gandhi propagated his classic message out to the international audience with the help of a combined cable-radio company that connected British colonies out to the world which was set up during the yester year of the Salt march. Gandhi advocated the verbal communication to succeed over his ambition 'to wipe every tear from every eye', and thereby lifted his verbal instinct to the world, to strengthen the power of the freedom movement by gathering an international opinion against the British imperialism which was evident in his words that favoured the fervour for freedom:

"I know I have countless friends in America who are in deep sympathy with this struggle but mere sympathy will avail me nothing. What is wanted is concrete expression of public opinion in favour of India's inherent right to independence and complete approval of the absolutely non-violent means adopted by the Indian National congress. In all humility but in perfect truth, I claim that if we attain our end through non-violent means India will have delivered a message for the world."(CWMG, Vol. 43, p. 180)

Gandhi sprouted as a true leader by this message that is though complete in sense, but incomplete in action. The blurred vision of the Mahatma is visible within his lines so statured. It is that Gandhi wanted India to concrete as a leader of the lands extending its waters. The Mahatma anguished not just for the independence of his motherland, but wanted its struggle for freedom to be written not just in the country's history but to be acclaimed in the golden words of *satya* and *ahimsa* in the world history.

Fight for free speech in South Africa:

Gandhi might never have accustomed with the ramping racism suffered by the Indian settlers in South Africa, if he had not suffered humiliation on the grounds of racial discrimination during his arrival in South Africa. Today, we wouldn't have had a free India breathing the sacrifice of its freedom fighters, if the timid, coward lawyer wrapped in the shyness of silence wasn't subject to war of the whites. It was during these South African years when the mahatma was born, when the leader was made in the agonising anguish against the humiliation of the coloured and due to the heartless hindrance of their rights which the whites still enjoyed. In 1893 A twenty three years old Gandhi assisted an Indian merchant to South Africa in a black civil suit but never ever presumed that the colour of his suit shadowing his skin could ever be a problem. The Natal, the Cape, the Transvaal, and Orange Free State colonised the South Africa, which was under the resistance of the British Empire after the Boer War (1899-1902) against the Dutch colonisers. The British and Dutch living in the South Africa were termed as the white people who in agreement with the British rulers of India exported Indian labour under contract. Trade jealousies and racial prejudice that presumed the whites as the superior race condemned the rights of the coloured people who initially enjoyed the law of the land. Gandhi who always resisted standing up to speeches and struggles which is unambiguous through his following statement:

> "This shyness I retained throughout my stay in England. Even when I paid a social call the presence of half a dozen or more people would strike me dumb [...]. It was impossible for me to speak impromptu. I hesitated whenever I had to face strange audience and avoided making a speech whenever I could. Even today I do not think I could or would even be inclined to keep a meeting of friends engaged in idle talk." (M.K Gandhi, *An Autobiography,* 57)

Dumbstruck the world with his incredible fight that he started off with the colonisers in South Africa Gandhi confronted his struggle in the colonies of Natal and Transvaal that were weighted with Indian settlers, and his campaign addressed the issues regarding franchise, immigration etc. Gandhi revealed the problems of the people through intensive use of white press such as that of the Natal mercury which added words to his symbolic actions. Gandhi penned his struggle through the Green pamphlet, Hind Swaraj, and also through many articles adorning the columns of the white press. Gandhi rolled his struggle against racism with the words that retorted him back to the coloured country in his book, Satyagraha in South Africa', where he writes:

> "During my stay in England I had occasion to talk to many Indian anarchists. My booklet, Indian Home rule...had its birth from the necessity of having to meet their arguments as well as to solve the difficulties of Indians in South Africa who held similar views."(MK Gandhi, *Satyagraha in South Africa, op.cit.* p. 211).

Criticism was nothing new for the leader who took it as a compliment because he believed that people criticise because they know the best of him. In an answer to the criticism of his Hind Swaraj, Gandhi completed his book in the true sense by saying:

> "...having had the position of a publicist practically forced upon me by circumstances; I felt bound to write for those for whom Indian Opinion caters. The choice lay between allowing the

readers of the Indian Opinion, anxious though they were for guidance, to drift away in matter if the insane violence that is now going on in India, or giving them, no matter how humble, a lead that they are asking for. The only way I saw of mitigating violence was the one sketched in the pamphlet." (CWMG, X, p. 296).

The phase of revolution of leadership outcast its colours with the leader of time and space, the leader who rescued his people from the clutches of ethical embarrassment, and social suffering under the rule of colonisation which added to their already existing hierarchical differences that distinguished human from a human. Gandhi sprinkled his words that structured as phrases, messages and quotes over the aristocracy of caste system, and over the bureaucracy of British system. Gandhi was a literary economist for he counted every word that he uttered for he was a leader who knew the value of his literal audibility that even if toned differently could deviate from his vision of non-violence. He never regretted any of his dialogue, conversations, writings and interviews, which can be advocated in his following flow of words:

> "My hesitancy in speech, which was once an annoyance, is now a pleasure. Its greatest benefit has been that it taught me the economy of words. I have naturally formed the habit of restraining my thoughts. And I can now give myself the certificate that a thoughtless word hardly ever escapes my tongue or pen. I do not recollect ever having had to regret anything in my speech or writing. I have thus been spared many a mishap and waste of time." (*Ibid.* 58).

His journey to South Africa couldn't isolate him from the India's struggle for independence. He ventilated open letters to the India's readership with the native pen which plunged through the newspapers such as The Hindu, The times of India, The Statesman, The English which competed to publish the mahatma in their columns quenching for his writings. Even during his South African years, Gandhi emerged as a Leader of the Hind Swaraj that he had not only written but also screwed in action for the same. Gandhi was emerging his leadership that he wrenched over his conscience through his struggle from the distant lands for his motherland. Gandhi switched on his plan over the government in South Africa where he waged a 'war without violence', a war that was armed with the journals that reciprocated the bullets of words. He percolated his thoughts into his action and advocated not for people but for truth and justice that existed from when the life landed on this land of order. Questioning the legitimacy of the appeal for equal rights in South Africa, Gandhi condemned the practice of untouchability in their home land. He protested against caste hierarchy that his country concreted and as a true leader urged his followers to erase such differences before asking the government for their rights. Entrenching the varnishing value of rights of his people through the space of journalism inculcating thought, Gandhi admits that—

> "I believe that a struggle which chiefly relies upon internal strength cannot be carried on without a newspaper, but it is also my experience that we could not perhaps have educated the local Indian, nor kept Indians all over the world in touch with the course of events in South Africa in any other way, with the same ease and success as through Indian Opinion, which therefore was certainly a most potent weapon in our struggle."(MK Gandhi, *Satyagraha in South Africa, op.cit.* p. 131).

Enhancing his power to assimilate his consciousness with his doings, the blunt blushing lawyer was sharpened with the attributes of Satyagraha that he evolved with qualities enduring the whiteness of actions which the white people lacked. Analysing the exemplary evolution of Gandhi as a leader, Khushwant Singh of the Hindustan times wrote, 'It was a metamorphosis from a crawling caterpillar, turning into a chrysalis and emerging as a butterfly- a monarch butterfly with wings made of Khadi'.

Conflict Satyagraha: the struggle for free speech

When Gandhi returned to India, he was obscure of its situation and thereby restrained from any political activity for about three years. With the advice of his political guru and leader, Gopal Krishna Gokhale, Gandhi intensively travelled to impound words to his blurredness of the conditions of his people. But he didn't stop to tune his readers and listeners with the down pour of his unshakable statements that held on the hopes of the people miserably suffering the demeaning deeds of the unwelcomed imperialism destroying their livelihoods. Gandhi publicised the local movements and conflicts through his national columns that were more in keen to report Gandhi. The mahatma restored this instinct of journalism to widen the struggle for the local movements that were earlier confined to boundaries that could never be identified. May it be the peasant movement of the indigo planters in Champaran, or the Ahmedabad and Kheda Satyagrahas, Gandhi abstained violence from knocking the doors of the conflicts. In Champaran, Gandhi issued a series of leaflets to communicate with the mill workers who were facing famine conditions due to the sudden inflation in rents and levies that were illegally imposed on them by the European planters. Introducing a sequence of seventeen leaflets, Gandhi verbalised the significance and principles of the Satyagraha that he wanted them to instigate in their activities. Gandhi reconsidered his Champaran struggle, for by now he understood that the peasants had to be provided with not just with wages that evaporate but with the assurance of a better quality of life that sustains which could be sanctioned only when country will attain Purna Swaraj, which is engrossed in his Leaflet No. 10 where he reconciles, 'Even if wages were to be doubled, in all likelihood abject poverty would remain unless other measures were also adopted.'(CWMG, XIV, pp. 242-43) While in the leaflet 13, Gandhi urged the workers to restrain on their pledge if they believe his Satyagraha. And the success of his Champaran Satyagraha went in way with the fast that he had undertaken to ratify the false criticism by proving that he can stand on his oath of fast to an extent that he can allow it to kill him and thus restoring the not just the belief of the workers but also their pledge that led to ultimate victory. So why did the mahatma choose written statements over spoken verbosity. This was because Gandhi wanted the message of civil resistance through Satyagraha to be well understood by the peasants. Thereby if Gandhi gears up with speeches, there will be no scope for correction as words said remain imprinted in the minds of the people. Also there is a chance of misinterpreting the modulation of the verbal tone.

Henceforth, Gandhi prefixed his wider non-cooperation movement with the leaflets that leathered his local Champaran Satyagraha. Moving to the Kheda Satyagraha that gained momentum in pace with the Ahmedabad workers strike, Gandhi declared the launch of the Satyagraha following the failure of settlement with the officials of the Kheda district who refused to come in lines by leasing the collection of revenues from the peasants who suffered not just crop failure but also inflation in prices of basic commodities. Gandhi ignited his peaceful civil resistance to a gathering of 5000 people and appealed them not to pay the land revenue that year but also assured them not to be afraid of the penalties that the government may issue. Gandhi stormed a written pledge addressing the same which the peasants signed without any second thought. It was later published in many leading newspapers that thronged even their commercial space with the words of the mahatma. The pledge reads as follows:

> Our village has had crops under four annas. We therefore, requested the government to postpone collection the next year, but they did not do so. We the undersigned therefore solemnly declare that we shall not pay the assessment for the year whether it is whole or in part; we shall leave it to the government to take any legal steps they choose to enforce recovery of the same and we shall undergo all the suffering that this may involve. We should also allow our lands to be confiscated should they do so. But we shall not by voluntary payment allow ourselves be regarded as liars and thus lose our self-respect. If the government shall graciously postpone for all the remaining villages collection of the revenue, we who can afford it, would be prepared to pay the revenue, whether full or in part. The reason why well-to do among us would not pay is that, if they do, the needy ones would, out of fright, sell their chattels or incur debts and pay the revenue and thus suffer. We believe that it is the duty of the well-to-do to protect the needy against such a plight. (CWMG, XIV, p. 279)

Gandhi ejected the arrow of a magnificent verbal communication by drafting the pledge against the sufferings of the peasants. Also Gandhi allowed the media to intervene into the struggle by publicising it to the country but weirdly in the case of Ahmedabad strike Gandhi didn't encourage the space for media and locked his speeches and communication to the sufferers because it was an internal dispute that didn't require to be dramatised to the public through the exorbitant vehicle of communication. In a letter to a friend, Gandhi writes, 'Never mind if the voice does not reach the thousands, nay millions. They come not to hear but to see. And they see far more than what we can imagine.'(*Collected Works of Mahatma Gandhi,* page 332) Gandhi was a discriminative leader, for he longed not to satisfy the people but wished to sustain the respect of his people whose identity he wanted to build through the Satyagraha for Swaraj. The conflict resolution of Gandhi can be well described in the words of B.R. Nanda, an exuberant Gandhian scholar who described the Satyagrahi as follows:

> "The truth is that in Gandhi's philosophy of Satyagraha, the enemy was not regarded as an eternal enemy, but a potential friend. It is the duty of the Satyagrahis to reason with the adversary, to try to dispel his prejudices, to disarm his suspicions, to appeal to his dormant sense of humanity and justice, and, eventually to try to prick his conscience by inviting suffering at his hands. As Gandhi told a correspondent in April 1939, the Satyagrahi's object was 'not avoidance of all relationship with the opposing power', but 'the transformation of the relationship'. In South Africa, Gandhi negotiated, fought, and finally reached an agreement with general Smuts. His parting gift to the chief antagonist was a pair of sandals which he had himself stitched. [...] In India, through a quarter of century, Gandhi corresponded with all the Viceroys-Chelmsford, Reading, Irwin, Willingdon and Linlithgow-keeping his lines of communication open even while he engaged them in non-violent battle." (Nanda, *In Search of Gandhi*, 141)

Gandhi substantiated the words of the scholar through his statement that goes as follows:

> "India cannot tolerate such punishments nor will the British statesmen even uphold it. The British public would be horrified at it…I have far greater faith in British statesmanship than the commissioner has."(CWMG, XIV, p. 349)

Drifting to the more public movements of Gandhi who imparted his political petition of Satyagraha in his people, and revolutionary petition of Swaraj over the European government, the mahatma launched the Non-cooperation movement in 1920 against the Rowlatt Bills that halted the rights of the people. Prior to his launch of a national wide movement, Gandhi used letters to negotiate and persude the government. In one of his letters, Gandhi wrote: 'I read all the speeches on the Rowlatt bills today. I was much distressed...Under the circumstances, I hope, at any rate, that all the members will leave the select committee, or if necessary, even the council, and launch a countrywide agitation.' Thereby Gandhi through his effective verbal communication stroked off his communication with the government by introducing non-cooperation with the law of the colonisers by boycotting councils, law courts, and educational institutions financing the government. Identifying the Rowlatt bills as to stab the liberty and freedom of Indians, Gandhi screwed in a series of writings and speeches against the bill. Standing against his falling health Gandhi drafted and signed a pledge which reads as follows:

> Being conscientiously of the opinion that the bills known as the Indian Criminal Law (Amendment) Bill No.1 of 1919 and the Criminal Law (Emergency Powers) Bill No. 2 of 1919 are unjust, subversive of the principles of liberty and justice, and destructive of the elementary rights of individuals on which the safety of the community and the State itself is based, we solemnly affirm that in the event of these Bills becoming law and until they are withdrawn, we shall refuse civilly to obey these laws and such other laws as a Committee to be hereafter appointed may think fit and we further affirm that in this struggle we will faithfully follow truth and refrain from violence to life, person and property. (*CWMG*, XV, p.102)

As a pledging leader, Gandhi thereafter launched the civil disobedience movement in reaction to the non-cooperation from the government. Gandhi caught in the holds of violence of his people under his innumerable verbal petitions, and uprooted the war of violence with his verbal Satyagraha that he flamed with his conscious words. With his drizzling downpour of literary calibre, Gandhi created ordinance in the growing chaos of conflicts. Pleading his people to withstand the hard knocks of going against imperialism, Gandhi argued that a definite ruthless imperialism is better than an indefinite dynastic rule. More than a conflict leader, Gandhi evolved as a conflicting leader for his mode of struggle coined the era of Satyagraha.

Journalist Gandhi:

Gandhi aroused the shaded journalist in himself as a student of law wherein he bolded his words as a freelance journalist who flowed his literary rhyme over cultural issues that touched the mind of the young Gandhi. Even as a leader of great movements, Gandhi kept alive the inherent journalist in himself by striking the columns of newspapers with his simple but affective words that changed the opinion of more than a country. Indian Opinion, a well acclaimed newspaper of the mahatma stranded as the reflection of his vision during his preliminary struggle that eroded in South Africa. Gandhi widened the space of his agitation by incorporating various linguistic columns in his newspaper which influenced a greater part of the national audience. Indian Opinion had four sections namely, Hindi, English, Gujarati and Tamil, which have dawned the rays of Satyagraha over the in-phase patriotism of the people. As an editor of 'Young India' Gandhi compiled not news but his message to his people as a well versed editorial leader of the readership. His Gujarati monthly Navajivan also thundered its impact not just to that particular readership but also to the entire audience who were stretching their thoughts over the translation of the language in which Gandhi adorned the future he anticipated, the language that was blessed to guide the mahatma. Both Young India and Navajivan stormed in reporting the history of a constitution by steering the Satyagraha of the Satyagrahi in his words, in his actions, in his non-cooperation movement, in his civil disobedience movement that was climaxed with the Salt march. The pen of the journalistic leader never stopped; even today it is flowing unperturbed, though its style changed over time, its path towards *satya* and *ahimsa* never deviated. It is true that Gandhi portrayed the role of both a leader as well as a journalist but at the end of the saga of Satyagraha, a leader won over a journalist, which is unquestionable through the following anguish of Gandhi:

> "In the very first month of Indian Opinion, I realised that the sole aim of journalism should be service. The newspaper press is a great power, but just as an unchained torrent of water submerges whole countryside and devastates crops, even so an uncontrollable pen serves but to destroy. If the control is from without, it proves more poisonous than the want to control. It can be profitable only when exercised from within. If this line of reasoning is correct, how many of the journals in the world would stand the test? But who would stop those that are useless? And who should be the judge? The useful and the useless must, like the good and evil generally, go on together, and the man must make his choice." (M.K. Gandhi, *Autobiography*, 263-64)

Gandhi upheld the necessity for ethical journalism than the freedom of press. He wanted a free pen but not a powerful pen that he claimed as to be an uncontrollable hurricane. He knew that the country needed a leader more than a journalist. But at the same time he could connect to the nerves of the people only through journalism that celebrated verbal communication beyond the boundaries of the barred country. Thereby Gandhi refrained himself as a journalistic leader who informed the country nothing new, for '*satya* and *ahimsa* are as old as the hills', as the mahatma quotes. Gandhi is the inspiration to every leader, every journalist, every lawyer and every communicator, for he is an ambidextrous clinched with every quality which felicitates his Satyagraha. Rajkumari Amrit Kaur is one such admirers of Gandhi as a journalist, who relished the privilege of witnessing his journalistic attitude. In her words:

> "To those of us who had the privilege of working with Gandhiji every week when the Harijan was being edited by him, it seems strange to be writing for its columns without submitting the same to the searching gaze of that prince of journalists. The care and thought he bestowed on whatever he himself wrote, the eagle eye with which he vetted every word of what even a man like Mahadev Desai (his secretary) wrote, his insistence on right

> expression, on the adherence to truth where facts were concerned, on the necessity of not using one word more than necessary, his appreciation of good literary style, his ruthless weeding out of much or wholesale discarding of what one thought was good, all these are never to be forgotten lessons. But the remembrance of them makes one pause and wonder whether any one of our poor efforts can ever come up to the high standard of journalism which was Gandhiji's incomparable contribution to public life."(*Gandhi the writer*, 202-03)

Commercial Freedom to Free speech:

Gandhi established an unwithered gigantic communication within his countrymen by storming his volunteers who were the soldiers of his Satyagraha, to bind his people with the truth of ahimsa, with the peace of patriotism and with the acoustic belief in his Satyagraha. Gandhi lead the different streams of struggles merge into the ocean of independence by uprising 'the common cause'. Gandhi in the following pledge of his followers:

> "We the volunteers are called upon to enlist ourselves in order to do village construction work, and this village reconstruction work is nothing but the organisation of peasantry and workers upon economic basis. We want to enter into the hearts of the peasants. We want to identify ourselves completely with the masses. We want to make their woes our own. We want to feel with them in everything in order to better the lot of those on whose toil we the people of the city are really living. We must therefore make common cause with the workers."(CWMG, Vol. 38, 311-12)

Gandhi identified himself as a volunteer of his Satyagraha by spraying the innocence of his words through his speeches. He fluttered the wings of freedom through his intense pecking of words to chirp the truth of Satyagraha with the verbs that confront it. His speeches were misted with the colour of Khadi. Though his language lacked the efficacy and bountifulness of a stupendous orator, his tone had the deep insight of morality that couldn't either be comprehended by the greatest of speakers or could be conceived by the incredible truth seekers. Gandhi didn't want to hide the treasure of truth under the rhetoric, reconcilable similes and metaphors that can paint the truth with the adversities of understanding. His crystal clear clarity of words is expressively expounded by John Hanes as he writes:

> Gandhi's literary achievement is more remarkable in view of the fact that he was never, in any sense of the phrase, a literary man [...] he had no special grace of style. Seldom, if ever, in his writings, did he rise to the heights of eloquence and beauty. Gandhiji's interests were never aesthetic, but rather pragmatic. He had no desire or ambition, no time, to be an artist. His one thought was of his own people, and his struggle to make them free. So he wrote with disciplined simplicity, seeking only to make himself clearly understood. The result was the one most important quality of literary act, namely, clarity [...] [He] mastered his medium. He wrought a style which was perfect for his purpose of communication. To read his writings is to think of content and not of style which means a triumph on the adaption of means to ends. (*Journalist Gandhi-Selected Writings of Gandhi, 11-12)*

So, what differentiated a leader from a communicator? It is the language with which he communicated that disclosed the chapter of a leader in Gandhi. As a pacesetter, Gandhi not only boycotted the European councils, courts, institutions and amenities but also the European language that erased freedom from its dictionary. Because, Gandhi wanted 'Swaraj' out not 'independence' as he says, 'even if I speak a little of English, I have the feeling that I am committing a sin'. Gandhi wanted to radiate Hindi as the Official language of the country for it was the communication means for people in majority of the provinces. As a leader, Gandhi not only stressed on the importance of communication but also italicised the Satyagraha of communication that needed the truth of the majority but not the untruth of the European minority. Gandhi emphasised on the articulation of dialogue as he says, 'I know [it] will be the lingua franca when swaraj is granted to the whole of India'. It is not that, Gandhi wanted to eliminate the western language as he himself quoted his Satyagraha in English many at times and even edited newspapers in English-Indian Opinion, Young India etc, it is that Gandhi didn't wanted the coloniser's language to rule the country. Gandhi had an enforced efficacy in his English which even the Englishmen couldn't concrete. In the words of Edward Thompson, a professor in Oxford University:

> "Perhaps, his unsurpassed command of English idiom comes partly from this perfect control over his mind. The hardest thing in our language for a foreigner is our prepositions. I never met an Indian who mastered them as Gandhi has. I learnt this during the Round Table conference, when two or three times he asked me to draft some statement for him. If you are a professional writer, you try to be careful about your prepositions, and I admit that I took a deal of trouble over this drafting. Mr Gandhi would glance over my work, and would make just one subtle prepositional change-you might think that the change was a trifle. But it did its work. Perhaps it left a loophole (and politicians are suspected of linking loopholes). Anyway, it changed my meaning into Mr Gandhi's meaning. And our eyes, as they met and each of us smiled at the other, showed that we both knew that this had happened."(*Mahatma Gandhi-Essays and Reflections*, 290-91).

From a simple communicator Gandhi turned into a complex leader whose words though could be rowed over, but when it comes to his doings, even the dictating detective cannot conclude his verbal leadership to a point. Reaching the shore of understanding his verbal communication, let us constitute into his immortal leadership qualities complimenting his auxiliary verbal elucidation.

The Learner:

"Live as if you were to die tomorrow. Learn as if you were to live forever."- Mahatma Gandhi ("The Greatest Quotations of All-Time", page-393).

Gandhi always urged that if two of his statements crossed swords, then to accept his second statement for he was always up the slope of learning. He was always ahead in the war of improvement for his train never stopped at the discrimination of age. No matter how small or big the person is either by age or other social constraints, Gandhi always tried to learn something or other from everyone. Even from the imperial ruthless rulers of ancient India, Gandhi learnt how one shouldn't be in this exotic society. Gandhi was a man who cannot be reciprocated in any way, in the words of Shashi Tharoor:

> Mahatma Gandhi was the kind of person it is more convenient to forget. The principles he stood for and the way in which he asserted them are easier to admire than to follow. While he was alive he was impossible to ignore. Once he had gone he was impossible to imitate. *(From Midnight to the Millennium*, 22)

The Listener:

"It is unwise to be too sure of one's own wisdom. It is healthy to be reminded that the strongest might weaken and the wisest might err" (*Everyday Useful Quotes*, page 429).

A listener of his conscience, a listener of the morals, a listener of his followers, Gandhi was that prism that brightened more than a diamond. His path was not unaffordable for even the poorest of poor can take shelter in its shade of truth and non-violence. But his path is inaccessible even to the wealthy if they fall down to the wretchedness of ruthlessness. Gandhi was a constant listener, but the martyr was brutally criticised as of being dauntlessly dominant under the realm of politics. As an answer to talkers, Nehru stressed on the moral impact of Gandhi as follows:

> "Politics cease to be just expediency and opportunism, as they have usually been everywhere and there is a continuous moral tussle preceding thought and action. Expediency...can never be ignored, but it is toned down by other considerations and a longer view of more distant consequences...Bernard Shaw has said that though he (Gandhi) may commit any number of tactical errors, his essential strategy continues to be right. Most people, however, are not much concerned with the long run; they are far more interested in the tactical advantage of the moment".(Nehru on Gandhi, views on Political Culture- by Prem Misir, Posted on October 26, 2010)

Gandhi at the dimensions of free speech

The morals of mahatma had a fluency in influencing the

monitoring minds of his people. He was voted as a monitoring mentor, an addressing advisor, a panoptic pacifier and a nerving negotiator. The mahatma became the democracy by being of the people, for the people and by the people, contradicting to the present perverting politicians who have pirated democracy as far the people, off the people and buy the people.

During his struggle for freedom in South Africa, an incident narrated by Sen (1945) shows how a Pathan (soldier) named Saiyad Ibrahim did not seek for revenge but:

> ...bared his back and said to Gandhiji: "Look here, how severely they have thrashed me. I have let the rascals go for your sake, as such are your orders. I am a Pathan, and Pathans don't take but give a beating." To him Gandhiji said: "Well done, brother, I look upon such forbearance as real bravery. We will win through people of your type," and he was right, for, years later hundreds of Pathans took the pledge of non-violence, and many came to the Congress fold sheathing their swords rather than brandishing them to fight the battle of freedom. (*Gandhi, a biographical study*, page 63)

Gandhi was a man of propelling prayers, which created a sense of peace in his followers whenever they approached his circle of morality. He was a transforming pacifier who sublimed the sufferings of his people directly into their mission. His toothless truthful smile had the infinite patience of hope which he showered in his vicinity. It was during the time when light of hope was shattered in the agony of violence, when the Mahatma ceased the destroying flames of himsa with his restoring flames of ahimsa. Describing the Satyagrahi as a pacifier, Nehru continues as follows:

> "Freedom came to us, our long sought freedom, with a minimum of violence. But immediately afterwards we had to wade through oceans of blood and tears...Horror pile on horror and a sudden emptiness seized us... The light seemed to go out. But one bright flame continued to burn and shed its light on the surrounding gloom. And looking at that bright, pure flame, strength and hope returned to us...there was the Spirit of India, strong and unsullied,

> rising above the turmoil of the present...during the past four months, in a dissolving world, he has been like a rock of purpose and lighthouse of truth." (*CWMG*, XC, p. I)

More than an advisor, Gandhi was a persuader who warned the wings of freedom to be cautious of the coagulating clouds of violence that still vaporised over the nucleus of differences. In his lamenting words, Gandhi put forth his plea as a father of a nation as he writes:

> It is worse than anarchy to partition a poor country like India whose every corner is populated by Hindus and Muslims living side by side. It is like cutting up a living body into pieces. No one will able to tolerate this plain murder. I do not say this as a Hindu. I say this as a representative of Hindus, Muslims, Paris and all. I would like to say to my Muslim Brethren, 'Cut me to pieces first and then divide India. You are trying to do something which was not attempted even during the Muslim rule of Two hundred years. (*CWMG*, LXXIII, p.25)

Free Speech: The Vision

The vision of the Mahatma was never accomplished. Though the world had congratulated the land of diversity for the freedom that it was presumed to have acquired, but in the reality of reign, India had rented freedom from the world on the lines of development that it had never gained. Therefore, the plight of the country is diced in its ability to stay intact with the principles of the great soul that could never rest over the land that couldn't taste freedom from the hypocrisy of political intricacies. One would really wonder how a man of such ornamenting morality was born in a country blinded with violence, even the prime leaders of the Indian independence stressed on issue. In the havocking tone of words, Nehru addressed the convocation of freedom as follows:

> "...He did not descend from the top; he seemed to emerge from the millions of India, speaking their language and incessantly drawing attention to them and their appalling condition. Get off the backs of these peasants and workers...all you who live by

their exploitation; get rid of the system that produces this poverty and misery."(*The Story of Gandhi*, page 3)

Conclusion:

A man blinded with *satya* and *ahimsa* led a nation blinded with violence. He could never see the path before him but at the same time never led his followers to a pit as he always walked with a stick before taking every step. He wrote with the purity of words; spoke the serenity of morals for he could never see anything bad in anyone. He used his spectacles not to see the world but to reflect his blindness over his people. And as he writes not to be written:

> If anything that I write in these pages should strike the reader as being touched with pride, then he must take it that there is something wrong with my quest, and that glimpses are not more than mirage. Let hundreds like me perish, but let truth prevail [...]. I am not going either to conceal or understate any ugly things that must be told. I hope to acquaint the reader fully with all my faults and errors. My purpose is to describe experiments in the science of Satyagraha, not to say how could I am. In judging myself I shall try to be as harsh as truth, as I want others also to be. (The Essential Writings-by Mahatma Gandhi, p. 3)

Gandhi, the scientist of Satyagraha earns an unwithered pen that still expounds his experiments with truth.

The man who was too noble for a Nobel prize has been leading the lands, the waters, the hills and all other embodiments of truth with the simplicity with which he coloured the crookedness of India's Independence.

Chapter 9

Gandhi's Free Attire

A leader is not the one who never fails but is the one who never quits and doesn't allow his followers to quit. Engraving confidence in every breadth that breathes his vision, a leader creates leaders. Once when the rare star brightened, a leader was born, he who turned the plight of India through his whistling vision, he who is still alive through his dreams that have turned into an inspiration to the young India. His statues speak, his thoughts still murmur in the distant blow of air. He is the man with the stick, he is the father of a fuming nation, he is the mahatma; he is none other than Mohandas Karamchand Gandhi, the legend who has enthralled the world as a whole. Being crowned with immense popularity and perseverance, Gandhi is still alive in the minds of the people as the folk hero, as the lightening leader, as the soldering soldier. One would really wonder, how could Gandhi imprint his presence among the people of various languages, and various dialects of each of these languages? How did Gandhi spark his non-violent movement among the masses? Definitely it's all possible not just through verbal communication, there has to be something abstract that connected to the rhythm and rhythm of their patriotism and that is non-verbal communication. He spoke a lot without uttering even a single word, for his non-verbal symbolism lifted him to the heights of serenity and belief.

Spinning yarn, wearing Khadi, marching against the salt law, Gandhi stunned the world by screwing his vision into his simplicity.

It is said that one has to practice before he preaches, but Gandhi didn't have to preach his doings for his actions echoed to the people and to their sufferings. He bestowed the blanket of his non-violent movement over his followers, who have raised him from a leader to a mahatma. His journey as a leader of the struggle for independence had neither the multi-tone speeches nor the mesmerising words to elite his followers to his vision, what he had was the engraving silence, unruffled fasts, charioting charisma that turned his struggle into a victory, that turned him from being a truth seeker to the truth itself. He adorned the light of patriotism in every individual movement and at the same time controlled that light from turning into fire. Truth and non-violence as his weapons silence and serenity as his words, kindness and humbleness as his chariot, Gandhi eroded the war field from getting stained with violence and bloodshed. When asked, what would be his message to his followers, Gandhi had a simple answer, "My life is my message", may be this answer seems less of words but has more of meaning indeed has more of message that doesn't need to be put into words. Contradicting to the present armchair politicians who portray themselves as leaders through their unwilling speeches on the starving without even meeting them, Gandhi not only connected to the people, but also connected to their situation. For instance, he always chose to travel in third class, for he wanted to surmount his life as an Indian from the view of the India's poorest, rather he wanted to start his mission shouldering the sufferings of the real sufferers, so that he can atleast seed the hope for a developed India.

Gandhi carved a large part of his life travelling to the untouched parts of India and even beyond its boundaries to be accustomed with the different social and political issues that were not discussed in the igniting sessions of the congress. And where ever he went he showered a definite flow of words and an indefinite flow of his thoughts through his physical presence. Adjoining his life with shunning symbols shining his vision, Gandhi whirled the whirlpool of the world by standing as a symbol by himself. Not only plugging into the grievances of the people that had turned into distant struggles, but also by erasing the boundaries of their struggles by raising the flag of freedom movement, Gandhi engraved himself not only in the history to be learnt, but also into the future to be made. His non-verbal communication is like the spectrum of light that though has many colours stating its presence, at the end all merge into the white light, into the vision of a mahatma who always tried to inflict his leadership qualities in every person by staying as common as a common man but thinking as different as one really can. There are different phases of his non-verbal leadership where people were lead by his actions, his doings, and his thoughts, towards an independent India that had taken birth in his scavenging protection. Considering the legendary march against the salt law where each of his steps led to thousands of steps, where his thirst dwindled across all his followers, Gandhi broke the salt law not with the handful of salt he made but with the country full of followers he gained. Quoting his unfathomable fasts which created more a depth influence than the speeches of the ornamenting orators, Gandhi by introducing such indefinite hunger strikes stated that he has nothing more valuable than his life to give for the release of his mourning motherland which according to him was not under the clutches of the imperial British empire but was brutally crushed under the social differences that allowed such a rule to ruin our rare history. Each of his non-verbal persuasion has its own inherent meaning to be dug to the coherence of leadership. So, let us understand his mighty symbolism through the perspective of leadership.

Khadi as the symbol of free attire:

Generally, a leader is visualised to be tied and tucked in the uniform that reflects his duty and armed with weapons honouring his attire. One might feel that Gandhi who portrayed himself in Khadi is not complimenting to the visualisation of a leader, but by observing the insights of the mahatma, one can clearly witness the greatness of his simplicity because Gandhi was always tied and tucked in his vision and was also armed with the weapons of truth and non-violence, in addition his white garments reflected the colours of his thoughts that touched the horizon for a developed India. Gandhi believed in firmness of thoughts over outer appearance, rather it is to the contrary in the sense he waged a war through this clothing, a war that had no bloodshed but was surely stained with his rooted thoughts which were winding the wind for waving the flag of an independent India. He rose as the sheltering sun, the blanketing rain, and thereby ridged over as the true leader by colouring the country with Khadi, and by turning his notion into a civil-disobedience movement. By wearing hand spun Khadi garments, Gandhi also wanted to uplift the power of man over machines for he never wished to see machines undermining the capacity and will power of humans. He was not against machines for he himself used wheel to spin yarn, it is that he wanted machines to run in parallel with man, but not faster to an extent that he cannot catch up with them. As a leader, Gandhi always wanted to see an employed India and for that he believed that if machines grab the work of man, it would be synonymous to that they are grabbing his employment and thereby his daily bread. Gandhi was a man of sapience of not just the present but also of the future for he knew that the population of his country would take a steeping rise to an extent that it cannot make every citizen work for his living and thereby injected his intuition in his freedom struggle and thereby fought for an independent India in the reality of its meaning. He wanted the country to be free not just from the imperialism of colonisers but also from the imperialism of poverty. In the words of an American researcher:

> Engaged in the simple labour of spinning, dressed as one of the poor in loin cloth and chadar, this important and powerful man communicated the dignity of poverty, the dignity of labour, the equality of Indians, the greatness of Indian civilisation, as well as his own saintliness. The communicative power of costume transcended the limitations of language in multilingual and illiterate India. His impact on the West was enhanced by his resemblance, in his simplicity of dress and saintly manner, to Christ on the Cross...When Gandhi tried to convince all Indians to wear plain white Khadi, he threatened not only regional industry and caste hierarchy but also the roles of separation of the roles of daughter, wife and widow which are central to perception of female identity. (*Clothes Matter, Dress and Identity in India* p. 73)

He drove the vehicle of the freedom movement with the wheel over which he spun yarn, over which he spun his vision of a self sufficient country, which also reflects in the soaring flag of India wherein the chakra is nothing but the symbol of India's man power. Gandhi dug the depths of being a leader by sustaining his vision even after his demise, rather his vision will sustain till the country won't stand up to it. Who in this world of diversity thought that there can be a light that merges their varsity? Except that thin old man, weak of being, fragile of strength who brought together innumerable cultures and ethnicities into the single struggle with the single culture of patriotism. Who thought that a piece of cloth could be so powerful? Other than the mahatma who made his clothing speak, rather represent the agony of his people. He made his clothes mourn the violence and at the same time brighten the purity of truth and non-violence. He wanted people to stand for independence not by word of mouth, but by doings of action. Therefore, simply by choosing their clothing, people were asked to let their notion for independence win over British imperialism. Henceforth, by creating a sartorial revolution through Khadi, Gandhi evolved as a Leader in Khadi.

Silence, the Speech Fast:

Silence values every uttered word, for it knows that the resonance of each word never ends just by completing it. Gandhi always fought for truth through his well acclaimed Satyagraha and silence is the biggest truth that one can say without even saying a word. Always trying to groove himself through the echo of his consciousness, Gandhi sailed through the ocean of silence with great thrive and thirst. He believed that one must master over himself before trying to lead others towards the path of one's perseverance and silence allows us to lead ourselves. So Gandhi not only led his people but also their hearts for he touched their souls through his mammoth silence. He used to observe silence for a day, a month and sometimes for an indefinite time over which he allowed his silence to speak his thoughts. His vow of silence is sometimes referred to as 'speech fasts' because Gandhi believed that if food is a necessity so is speech, rather the freedom of speech. And under the British colonisation, people were devoid of such freedom that instigates and illuminates all other rights that were starving to be sanctioned, therefore Gandhi upheld the shying silence to take on the flame of speech so that one day it will be free. By staying in the meditation of silence, Gandhi allowed the clamour of the nature to resonate vibrantly, which was lost in the blare and glare of the worldly noise and through his silence he lightened peace not just in his vicinity but in every person who lit him as his leader. Silence was the ultimatum of his non-violent movement wherein he gave up his worthy words, rather shielded them from being stabbed with the crown of violence. As a leader, Gandhi had to take many destined decisions, for that he had to talk, counter and debate within himself before presenting it to the public, and silence him gave him the space to build his thoughts over the foundation of the freedom struggle that he had to lead with the leaders of varied conscience. It is just this horizon of speech that differentiated him as a saint leader accustomed with the mantra that mourns death and celebrates life. He didn't want to limit his struggle with words that cannot confront to the people of a diversified country like India, and henceforth expanded his communication through silence that has immense meaning in its voidances that even the words of meaning may never ever fill up.

Gandhi stood up as a lending leader by sprinkling the treasure of abstract words through the holy silence that he embraced with contenting commitment. Swearing on to the pledge to wake up his country to the dawn of independence, Gandhi allowed his silence to swallow his sufferings with the will power to let his land taste freedom at the edge of this struggle. Sometimes, he even breathed his silence to creep into all his senses to instigate, rather let his consciousness take the right decision. Clinging to silence wherever, whenever possible, Gandhi reflected peace to every word he uttered. According to the mahatma, silence is a form of prayer that tunes with the mind, sings with the heart and connects every person to the plea of persuasion. Thereby he led his people through the baritone of silence that peeped into his struggle to keep up its non-violent nature. Rather he simmered the fire for independence but at the same time preserved its agony through the fight for freedom with silence, the master weapon that was sharper than the weapons that slewed in violence. He never wanted to lead people, but he always wanted his thoughts to show them the way, the path of peace and prosperity with the tinge of unity in diversity. Gandhi has left back his vision that is the answer to all the problems that the country faces, he is and will be remembered in the taste of salt, in the silence of thoughts, in the speech that touches our hearts filled with the peace and patriotism that he imbibed through his aesthetic silence. So, even now we can hear the enthralling speech of the mahatma if we observe silence with the deepening devotion towards his vision.

Gandhi's non-verbal persuasion:

Gandhi pledged on strong stances not just through his precious words which were the justifying jewels still shinning as bright as they were uttered, but also by adding life to his words because every vein of his carried his vision, every breathe inhaled the thought of his pledge, and every fast of his filled his hunger with the thirst for independence to his motherland that was brutally bereft of freedom. May it be for the improvement of labour conditions for workers or to stabilize the communal riots, Gandhi undertook fasts to persuade the people and government towards truth and justice by being stubborn to his senses. When situations went out of his control, he kept his life at stake by going into indefinite hunger strikes to bring the circumstances into the track of peace and non-violence, rather stated that violence kills him when it really did kill his people. He held on his followers as a leader of heights for he went through the same pain as that of a worker when snatched of his rights, as that of the deprived when termed as 'untouchables', as that of a Hindu or a Muslim stabbed by the harassing violence, as that of a women burnt due to the customs that she was never born with. His fasting was a symbol of his love for his countrymen, and he wanted to bind his country with the same love into the common culture, the common religion, the common language of freedom that already flagged in his thoughts even before the country was declared free for he knew when the people come together as a unified wall, they can bounce back any kind of imperialism, and when that happens our country will never ever allow any administration to disturb its boundaries. Also, according to Gandhi fasting is a means of self-purification because it is never determined as it happens when one's vision wins over his senses, and it purifies one's flickering senses with the notion that is already being pumped by his heart. To increase the waves of revolution and socio-political change, Gandhi used his weapon of fasting wherein he self-suffered to decrease the suffering of his people who were crushed in the clutches of injustice. By fasting, rather by bringing all his senses into the unified struggle, Gandhi pierced the flavour of unity in his movement for he believed that what is the use of such a diversity that doesn't allow diversity in thoughts and actions. Fasting is a form of prayer and meditation for the mahatma who laid down many guidelines for performing fasts with the truth that one resonates by not lying to himself. Gandhi concreted the idea that fasting should be a struggle for social change but should never be intended for personal gain.

As a reforming politician, Gandhi allowed media intervention in his struggle purified with his sacrifice through the gushing gesture of fasting, thus giving various forms to his non-verbal symbolism through the innumerable verbal communications that addressed the same. Fasting is a tradition inherent in many Indian cultures, so Gandhi didn't invent something new but surely discovered fasting as a means of social persuasion and rather as a fight for sloping independence. Also by introducing such tradition in his freedom movement, Gandhi connected his notion to many cultures that observed fasting as a custom.

Though numerically Gandhi undertook fifteen fasts during life time, but each of his fasts is equivalent to infinite patriotism that he showered over his country that is blessed to give birth to such a miracle who so easily converted the rooted ruptures of traditions into the amendments of his struggle, such that we can even presume that he invented such means of satyagraha and thereby turning from the chapter of cultures that differentiate us towards the chapter of freedom struggle that unites, rather binds us with the tears of blood that were shed for us. It was never hard for the mahatma to digest emptiness for his hunger for food was exotic before his hunger for the upliftment of his people suffering from the starvation for freedom. He poured his life over the freedom sapling that was to take birth and surely had taken but retarded in its growth since the time he left his life, his vision to be unclaimed. Let us see what the mahatma had to say about fasting:

> "A complete fast is a complete and literal denial of self. It is the truest prayer. 'Take my life and let it be always, only, all for Thee' is not, should not be, a mere lip or figurative expression. It has to be a reckless and joyous giving without the least reservation. Abstention from food and even water is but the mere beginning the least part of the surrender." (Harijan 15-4-1933, p. 4)

Spreading the essence of Satyagraha:

When the country was in the stillness of that of a graveyard, Gandhi returned from South Africa as a hurricane uprooting the tranquillity of violence with the storm of Satyagraha, the war for truth and justice. There was an agitation, rather restlessness in his silence that made him to blow his agony in the smoke of the steam engine to get in tune with the problems of the people. He travelled to every nook and corner of the country with the hope that his decisions won't shadow the grief and suffering of anyone for he knew that his countrymen who were adorned with the boiling blood, sparked with ignition will never accept non-violence to overcome their problems. Henceforth, he had to travel to prove his point by pondering non-violent strike against their grievances by torturing the government with their peaceful agitation. Gandhi believed that violence was nothing new for the British rulers as was horrifyingly havocked with their unpardonable cruelties like lathi charge, divide and rule policies, bonded labour etc, so if the Indians go on the same track of violence they can never succeed over the colonisers as they acclaimed violence as their birth right. But peace and non-violence was never in their dictionary and if Gandhi's countrymen master in this chapter which was unperturbed by the imperialism, surely they can replace the impounding imperialism with indexing independence.

This leader saw more than a breathing death, more than the tears of thirst, more than any other leader, for his steps never stopped at the door of impossibility for he knew his love and peace can sustain his people and their freedom. Wherever his steps halted, Gandhi vibrated the thoughts of his vision with a verbal resonance that echoed more than its meaning but his presence itself made the difference that he wanted to create for he was structured as an avatar by the people who thronged indefinitely to have his *darshan* atleast from the rare of view, far of hearing, but surely closest by heart. Gandhi many at times went on long walks that he crowned as *padyatras* that purified the land that could touch the feet of the mahatma but repented over its inability to smoothen the path for him. He always chose to reach even far of places with his ability but whenever time challenged him, he had to bow before it by contracting the distance with the speeding locomotives. A country, whose land ended indefinitely for many leaders, appeared as definite path for the Mahatma who not just glimpsed the diverse sufferings of the diverse country, but also addressed their problems with his mantra of civil-disobedience wherein he united the people acclaiming their rights within the statured boundaries. His age never limited his ability, for he believed that old are those ruptured in the thought of impossibility. Till your breadth affects the air, till your heart doesn't stop, why should you stop? Gandhi had a simple logic that restored his title of being an active leader till the end of his life. His thoughts travelled to the people faster than time that ticked his very existence. His adorned his *padyatras* to villages as the tour to the temples of India, as he believed that India was born through her villages though time deteriorated their value, they remain as pure as were. Also Gandhi was accustomed with his weapons such as peace and non-violence through the calmness and serenity which he found in villages that affected not only his attire but him as a whole. There is always a rhetoric fight in his tours and voyages because his presence itself challenged the colonisers dwelling the rare of lands far from the freedom struggle that represented the lands of the leaders. Gandhi was the leader of land that extended over the blanket of sky as he is global leader whose vision travelled to various anthems, various flags and various leaders. The people of the infinite land will always be lead by this leader who still wishes to travel to the anguish of his people through his vision imprinted over the land that didn't create any boundaries, over the sky that cannot reflect violence, over the water that raises the sun of hope and happiness, over the wings of a bird celebrating freedom.

Simplicity: The charisma of Gandhi:

Fading in his white robes, Gandhi had nothing spectacular in his appearance, but still created an authentic aura that attracted the conscience of the people who viewed him as the God in the temple of non-violence. His words were not weighted with vocabulary but the words that ornamented him were dipped in the ocean of poetry yet couldn't equalize to his abstractness. His voice wasn't so splendid, yet his prayers created goosebumps, his speech had neither melancholy nor melody, yet people bunched in numbers for the slightest of chance to vibrate their feelings in it. So, what is that which created magic in his simplicity? It is the truth and commitment with which Gandhi astonished his simplicity. He was a true satyagrahi who changed the dimensions of violence to such diminishing levels that it was not visible before the upheaval of non-violence. Many of his contemporary leaders explained his chanting charisma in their exotic words. Let us rejoice one of such description of the mahatma by the person who wrote one of the important chapters of independence, Jawaharlal Nehru, the first Prime Minister who inaugurated the throne of Indian government:

> "The little man of poor physic had something of steel in him, something rock like which did not yield to physical powers, however great they might be. And in spite of his unimpressive features, his loin cloth and bare body, there was a loyalty, a kingliness in him which compelled a willing obeisance from others. Consciously and deliberately meek and humble, yet he was full of power and authority, and he knew it, and at times he was imperious enough, issuing commands which had to be obeyed. His calm, deep eyes would hold on one and gently probe into the depths; his voice clear and limpid, would purr its way into the heart and evoke an emotional response.

Whether his audience consisted of one person or a thousand, the charm and magnetism of the man passed on to it, and each one had a feeling of communication with the speaker. This feeling had little to do with the mind, though the appeal to the mind was not wholly ignored. But the mind and reason definitely had second place. The process of 'spell-binding' was not brought by oratory or the hypnotism of silken phrases. The language was always simple and to the point and seldom was an unnecessary word used. It was the utter sincerity of the man and his personality that gripped; he gave the impression of tremendous inner reserves of power [...].Every gesture had meaning and grace without a false touch. There were no rough edges or sharp corners about him, no trace of vulgarity or commonness, in which unhappily our middles classes excel. Having found an inner peace, he radiated it to others and marched through life's torturous ways with firm and undaunted step." (Nehru, *An Autobiography*, 137-38)

Wherever he went, he was welcomed and received with great thrall and enthusiasm because his deeds created the path to their hearts in such a way that the people never had a second thought or a back step in accepting him as their leader. He extended his charisma through his independent nature wherein every person from a leader to a worker was at the same level of being his countrymen. He believed that no work is small till it builds the country towards the path of perpetual prosperity that is complimented with peace and truth. His critics who commented over his deeds as of being pedalling politics, couldn't sustain the truth of the satyagrahi, and at times nailed his greatness over of the wall of criticism, even today Gandhi has many critics but it is the way people want to keep alive the charisma of Gandhi by reprimanding and countering his thoughts and vision so as to understand them in the best of ways possible. His death couldn't erase his charisma which is preserved in every decision of the country, in every right that people have, in every breadth of the free India that keeps him alive.

Gandhi versus Gandhi

Many people scorched under the brightness of British imperialism and dumped under the literacy of illiteracy, never could understand Gandhi's Satyagraha, non-cooperation and civil disobedience movements what they knew was that in the path of the mahatma they will attain their rights, they will regain their life. Therefore, Gandhi turned as a symbol of independence, as the anthem of freedom. Gandhi became the iconic satyagrahi with the titles of 'Mahatma', 'Bapu' but ironically his name was used to propagate selfish motives to the heights of publicity. Gandhi condemned such false practices and persuaded his followers to discriminate the good from not just the deemed writings but from his actual writings as well. In the words of Bapu:

> My writings cannot be poisonous, they must be free from anger, for it is my special religious conviction that we cannot truly attain our goal by promoting ill-will [...]. There can be no room for untruth in my writings, because it is my unshakable belief that there is no religion other than truth [...]. My writings cannot be free from hatred towards any individual because it is my firm belief that it is love that sustains the earth." (*MMG*, 40)

The fact that Gandhi detached violence even in his writings wrenches the readers with exclaiming astonishment and infighting intendment to know about the mahatma with more of his words. As Nehru quoted in his speech, Gandhi was really a 'mad' man who sacrificed his life for the people who are celebrating not freedom but corruption printing him as the symbol. Gandhi has become a 'brand' with commercial buildings cashing his name, cashing his sacrifice. A man who underwent the adversities of the British Raj is now undergoing the demoralisation of Licence Raj.

Gandhi always stood for truth and his words still reverberate in the rhyming anthem of the country but the weak man couldn't stand before his people who are singing his struggle but not his vision. The flag of independence is still as glorious as was hoisted before the mahatma, the anthem is still as bright as was heard by the Bapu, but the people aren't going in the way shown by the mad satyagrahi who is still hoping for a change through such verbal writings.

Gandhi is an inevitable symbol of India's independence, and rolling back to years that witnessed his presence, he was independence. Enriching this statement with the words of Nehru:

"Congress was dominated by Gandhi and yet it was a peculiar domination, for the congress was an active, rebellious many sided organisation, full of variety of opinion, and not easily led this way or that. Often Gandhi toned down his position to meet the wishes of others; sometimes he accepted even an adverse decision. On some vital matters for him, he was adamant, and or more than one occasion there can be a break between him and the congress. But always he was the symbol of independence and militant nationalism, the unyielding opponent of all those who sought to enslave her, and it was as such a symbol that people gathered to him and accepted his lead, even though they disagreed with him on other matters. They did not always accept that lead when there was no active struggle going on, but when the struggle was inevitable that symbol became all important, and everything else was secondary." (*The Discovery of India*, 399-400)

Also Gandhi is an inevitable brand of commercialisation. Let Gandhi retort to this contradicting statement.

"I claim for the Charkha [spinning wheel], the honour of being able to solve the problem of economic distress in a most natural, simple, inexpensive and business like manner. The Charkha, therefore, is not only not useless...but is a useful and indispensable article for every home. It is the symbol of the nation's prosperity and, therefore, freedom. It is a symbol not of commercial war but of commercial peace." Mohan Mala, 1921 (YI, 8th December, 1921)

From free speech to free attire

Gandhi's deeds never went unnoticed, for his followers and the multitude media penned his doings to verbal conclusions. Gandhi didn't have to speak his actions, for the media evolved varied verbal conscience to his non-verbal symbolism. He was a leader who never aspired for the glare of media, but surely used the freedom of press to instigate his campaign of independence with the publicity enough to ignite the spark of freedom struggle in the people. His non-verbal communication was touched by the verbal writers who portrayed the symbolism through their articles, poetry, prose, statements, quotes and even today the saga continues but there is still an infinite forest of his symbols to be addressed. Even his verbal communication had the flavour of symbolism and inherent meaning.

Many research hunts were carried out to read between the lines of the mahatma. Gandhi was always in the lime light of freedom struggle with every writing, every speech, inspired by the mahatma whose life can be written with only with the white ink, never to complete. Gandhi was a symbolic journalist whose writings were so ideal that they blossomed as the symbols of his Satyagraha. Gandhi believed that when the people will become self-dependent, then itself India will attain independence. And when that happens, the colonisers will presume that they are ruling but actually they are making a fun out of themselves by trying to rule the rulers. So in a mission to make his countrymen independent and self sufficient, Gandhi turned his people to Khadi, initiated the civil-disobedience movement, marched over the non-cooperation agenda, and penned the 'swadeshi' journalism. Gandhi believed that the craze to modernise is equivalent to the craze to be ruled, so people would rise to independence when they will give up the pursuit to westernise, which is evident in his words:

"Don't be dazzled by the splendour that comes to you from the west. Do not be thrown off your feet by this passing show. The Enlightened One has told you in never to be forgotten words that this little span of life is but a passing shadow, a fleeting thing, and if you realise the nothingness of all that appears before your eyes, the nothingness of this material case that we see before us ever changing, then indeed there are treasures for you up above and there is peace for you down here, peace which pass the all understanding, and happiness to which we are utter strangers. It requires an amazing faith, a divine faith and surrender of all that we see before us." (YI, 8th December, 1927)

The fight within

A leader must have a blend of qualities that erect his supreme quality of leadership. As a leader, Gandhi radiated his vibrant qualities to his followers for he was the embodiment of idealisation, for he was the mahatma. A leader should be a role model; he should not just show the path but should sublime his steps into his followers'. But the deeds of the Mahatma were so absolute, were so ideal that they couldn't be realised by his people. He was thereby embellished as an avatar that would fulfil their wishes by blessing them with independence. More than a leader, Gandhi evoked as a Mahatma pondering to the abstractness of his people. In the words of a heavenly poet to the mahatma:

"I know your teaching is to fight against evil by the help of good. But such a fight is for heroes and not for men led by impulses of the moment. Evil on one side naturally begets evil on the other, injustice leading to violence and insult to vengefulness. Unfortunately such a force has already been started, and either through panic or through wrath our authorities have shown us the claws whose sure effect is to drive some of us into the secret path of resentment and others into utter demoralisation. In this crisis you, as a great leader of men, have stood among us to proclaim your faith in the ideal which you know to be that of India, the ideal which is both against the cowardliness of hidden revenge and the cowed submissiveness of the terror-stricken. You have said, as Lord Buddha, has done in his time and for all the time to come,- *Akkodhena jine kodham, asadhum sadhuna jine*,- "Conquer anger by the power of non-anger and evil by power of good".

You have come to your motherland in the time of her need to remind her of her mission, to lead her into the true path of conquest, to purge her present day politics of its feebleness which imagines that it has gained its purpose when it struts in the borrowed feathers of diplomatic dishonesty. This is why I pray most fervently that nothing tends to weaken our spiritual freedom may intrude into your marching line, that martyrdom for the cause of truth may never degenerate into fanaticism for mere verbal forms, descending into the self-deception that hides itself behind sacred names." (CWMG, Vol. XV pp. 495-96)

Knitting the wool of freedom over the country that dripped the drops of violence over a century, Gandhi mesmerised the world by flashing the potent ability of non-aggression in aggravating the Western rule with its esthetical ease. Gandhi drilled as a magnificent magician who with his whispering wand of non-violence turned the colonies of the British administration into a connecting country coordinating its rules. Henceforth, Gandhi spaded as a charismatic leader propelling the people with his spell-bound semblance. Thereby, Gandhi became the rhythm of the national anthem, the ripple of the repelling waves, the fume of the fluttering flag, the leader of a legendary land, and the mahatma of his manifesting motherland. Let the title of mahatma freeze on this poet of Satyagraha, because there can be many leaders, but there is only one mahatma. The journey of freedom, where Gandhi started on truth and ended on truth, is the inerasable part of the history. And the flowing flag, the resting rights, and processing patriotism are the proofs of his daunting impact in the struggle that he signed to be victorious over the viceroys of imperialism.

Gandhi is ornamented with efficacies that are not just confined to leadership. His qualities are like the rays sweeping though the fog of exoticness, and as one wipes the mist of disbelief, he can feel the exploding rays of the mahatma reflecting from his aura. Even the dictating dictionary has less of adjectives and adverbs to describe the mahatma with his stupendous qualities. It is even difficult to summarise the satyagrahi in less of words. But an attempt is made to lighten the spectrum of his leadership qualities through the sail through his non-verbal symbolism.

Discipline and Self enlightening: the wings of the Satyagrahi:

"The best way to find yourself is to lose yourself in the service of others"- Gandhi (*Virtuous Living*, page 115)

A man who pronounced discipline not just in his silence but also in his verbal anguish, Gandhi restrained his consciousness with his destined self discipline that he concealed over his vision. No one knew Gandhi, as much the mahatma apperceived himself through his frequent non-verbal monologue with his instinct. The realisation that he painted on himself escorted his Satyagraha with the tone of discipline. The mahatma declared that as one grows in his consciousness, he would understand the happening of events encircling him as to why he feels as he feels, why he behaves as he behaves, why he condemns as he thinks. Gandhi quotes self awareness as one's ultimate leader and as one trains to communicate with it through his aesthetical discipline, he will rise to the realisation of life and its mission. By encoding his intuitive discipline in the silence that he thrives for, Gandhi polished the obscurity of his vision, thus disclosing the mission of his life to himself.

Reading from the mind of the mahatma, let us see what the mahatma himself had to say about self-discipline:

Brahamchraya means control of all the organs of sense. He who attempts to control only one organ, and allows all the others free play is bound to find his effort futile. (*Bapu's Letters to Mira.* p. 257)

To hear suggestive stories with the ears, to see suggestive sights with the eyes, to taste stimulating food with the tongue, to touch exciting things with the hands, and at the same time to expect to control the only remaining organ, is like putting one's hands in the fire and expecting to escape being hurt. (*Bapu's letters to Mira* p. 257)

Humility: The soul of the mahatma

The ever multiplying followers of the mahatma reveal his dripping honey of humility that sustained the ahimsa in the freedom struggle that is written in the history of a father's country. He didn't restrict his humbleness to words but allowed it to sink in his life. The 'half naked fakir' illuminated his simplicity in his clothing as he didn't want to be well dressed when two thirds of his countrymen were bereft of adequate food, shelter and clothing. The heights of his humility reflect in his following statement:

"Britishers must leave as friends" (*Gandhi's Passion,* page 41)

Gandhi proved that the greatness of a man is not in the power that he dictates to control the life of the people, but in the power that he assimilates to the people with humility. The following narration of Thomas Weber, researcher on the Salt March, serves as testimony of his humility:

On the fourth day, at the lunch halt at the tobacco growing village of Dabhan, Gandhi was received with great enthusiasm. Perhaps the enthusiasm of the welcoming committee was ebbed a little as Gandhi walked straight through the village, past the temple and the village square, to the untouchable quarters where he drew water from the well and bathed. The high-caste Hindus who accompanied him were faced with a dilemma-whether to mingle with the casteless or be rude to their honoured guest. And for someone like Gandhi to draw his own water, rather than have a servant do it for him was a small practical sermon on the kind of free India he envisaged. The salt march was the means, all the small examples set by him and his marchers along the way were to be glimpses of the end. [*Gandhi Marg*, 22(4): 423]

"The seeker after truth should be humbler than the dust, only then, and not till then, will we have a glimpse of truth"-M. K. Gandhi (The Essential Writings-by Mahatma Gandhi, p. 3)

Satyagraha-The war without weapons

Inspired by the astounding epics of the land, Gandhi envisioned his vision of Satyagraha. He interpreted the 'Dharma Yudh' through the lens of the struggle for independence and formulated 'Satyagraha'. His unshaken faith in truth has shaken the plight of his country. Gandhi objected his struggle to be called as 'passive resistance', as his actions were not passive, thereby sought for hunt to title his struggle, wherein he penned a competition in the local newspaper, Indian Opinion, and 'Sadagraha' was selected as the best entry. Gandhi reformed the term as 'Satyagraha' to highlight the importance of truth in his agitation. Starring the mahatma's vision from the diary of Mahadevbhai and from Yeravda Mandir:

"Truth has no form. Therefore everyone one will form such an idea or image of Truth as appeals to him, and there will be as many images of Truth as there are men. These will be true as long as they last. For they enable a man to obtain everything he wants.

"Truth should be Truth in thought, Truth in speech, and Truth in action. To the man who has realised this Truth in its fullness, nothing else remains to be known, because all knowledge is necessarily included in it. What is not included in it is not truth and so not true knowledge." (The Encyclopaedia of Gandhian Thoughts, page 350)

"The fight of Satyagraha is for the strong in spirit, not the doubter or the timid. Satyagraha teaches us the art of living as well as dying"-Mahatma Gandhi. (*T-7-76)*

Sacrifice: The value of humanity

"All humanity is one undivided and indivisible family, and each one of us is responsible for the misdeeds of all the others. I cannot detach myself from the wickedest soul."-Gandhi ("The Greatest Quotations of All-Time", page-315)

However, small the personal meetings were, Gandhi made every person feel that he is the only one in the world with whom Gandhi relished to talk. Gandhi moved his naturalness of love for all to the doors of justice as rights for all. He assured that belief can change even a cold blooded man as did it change many violent seekers to a Satyagrahis. His love for humanity has endorsed in him the far going forgivingness, triggering trust, approachable open mindedness, and unfathomable freedom to his motherland. And as the mahatma quotes,

"You must not lose faith in humanity. Humanity is an ocean; if a few drops of the ocean are dirty, the ocean does not become dirty" (Facilitator's Manual for the Class of Non-violence p. 31)

He concretes his faith and love for humanity for he knows that he is a part of it.

The man in one:

Gandhi identifies himself nowhere superior to his followers. He never wished to be plunged with power rather always wanted to empower his people. Even after the attainment of independence, Gandhi didn't hold any position. When the country was spirited with the celebration of independence, Gandhi was in East Pakistan (now

Bangladesh) trying to resolve the disputes over the partition. Till the time for his permanent tapasya didn't blow, Gandhi went on tirelessly, growing strong by age for the freedom he wanted. He never aspired to be protected by his followers, instead shielded them with Swaraj that he gained with his weapons of Satya and Ahimsa. Gandhi never liked the titles he was adorned with for he didn't regard himself to ever live up to the title he is adorned with. He even regretted the title of 'Mahatma' that he was crowned with by the 'Gurudev', Rabindranath Tagore as he says:

"My experiments in the political field are now known, not only to India, but to a certain extent to the civilised world. For me, they have not much value; and the title of 'Mahatma' that they have won for me has, therefore even less. Often the title has deeply pained me; and there is not a moment I can recall when it may be said to have tickled me." (*CWMG*, volume 68, p.386)

Ahimsa

Gandhi didn't confine his moral values to the abode of hearing but also spread those with the adhering adore of action. He transformed his morals into weapons against the injustice. Ahimsa, the pen with which Gandhi signed the struggle of independence has affected his life to the divinity of living as he writes:

Ahimsa is not merely a negative state of harmlessness, but it is positive state of love, of doing good even to the evil-doer. - (*Young India,* August 25, 1920)

Ahimsa is a weapon of matchless potency. It is the summum bonum of life. It is an attribute of the brave, in fact, it is their all. It does not come within the reach of coward. It is no wooden or lifeless dogma, but a living and life giving force. – (*Young India,* Sept 6, 1926)

Ahimsa is not the way of the timid or cowardly. It is the way of the brave ready to face death. He who perishes sword in hand is no doubt brave; but he who faces death without raising his little finger and without flinching, is braver. (*Young India,* Oct. 11, 1928)

Conclusion:

Gandhi was the rainbow of qualities where the colour of each of his characteristic merged into the other. The greatest of saints, the tallest of scholars, Gandhi was a man beyond the words of any greatest writer. His qualities can never be unleashed with the words of any writer other than the mahatma himself: "I look only to the good qualities of men. Not being faultless myself, I won't presume to probe into the faults of others." (*Be the change!* p. 55)

The greatest quality of this leader is that he finds no characteristic in him that he can acclaim. Though the mahatma's non-verbal attributes can never be summed up in the elasticity of words, but nevertheless it is difficult to not quote the classic words of Bhikhu Parekh as he condenses the Satyagrahi's non verbal communication as follows:

After a long reflection and experimentation he [Gandhi] evolved a distinct mode of discourse that was also a form of praxis. Convinced that human actions derived their emotional energy from 'heart' which could only be addressed and activated by judiciously selected language of symbols, and recognising that Hindu culture was deeply symbolic, he evolved a powerful cluster of culturally evocative symbols including such things as the spinning wheel, the Khadi, the cow, and the 'Gandhian cap'...Partly by conscious design and partly as spontaneous expressions of his own way of life, his dress, language, mode of speaking, food, bodily gestures, ways of sitting, walking and talking, humour and staff, became a symbol of a specific way of life. Each evoked deep cultural memories, spoke volumes and conveyed highly complex messages. (*Gandhi*, pp. 8-9)

Limiting Gandhi's majestic non-verbal leadership to such a verbal writing is a hectic and herculean task and is rather impossible, therefore there are and will be many such verbal communications but even an infinite of them can't be equated to the mahatma's non-verbal symbolism.

Gandhi is that ray which can take birth only once for the freedom of morality against mortality.

Chapter 10

Gandhi's Free Communication Versus Ethics

Ethics in the profession are only guidelines, which are necessary in the process of information dissemination. These ethics relate to language use, and the means adopted in securing information for ensuring objectivity and fairness in presenting facts to the public. Collection and dissemination of information is the duty of the press. Because, the press as a mass communication channel operates in a public sphere for the benefit of the readers, the actions of the press are expected to be above ground. The public scrutinises the actions of the press on all occasions and expects the press to reflect values and ethics of the profession. In the process of collection and dissemination of information, the press adopts different means to obtain information and occasionally suppresses news from the public because of extraneous reasons. The press is, therefore, expected to have certain norms and ethics in the collection and dissemination. Former press council of India chairman P.B. Sawant (2001) noted that the code of ethics all over the world emphasises the following: (a) honesty and fairness, (b) reply to critical opinions, (c) objectivity in reporting, (d) prohibition to receive gifts, (e) respect for privacy, (f) distinction between fact and opinion, (g) not to inflame hatred, (h) not to use dishonest means to obtain information, and (i) general standards of decency and taste.

Nevertheless, Sonnenberg (2004) reported a study done in 31 countries on the ethical code, and it was found that journalists adhered to 57 principles and 10 principles were found to be common in all these countries. These 10 principles are: truthfulness, honesty, accuracy of information, correction of errors, prohibition of discrimination on the basis of race/ethnicity/ religion etc., respect for privacy, prohibition to accept bribes or any other benefits, fair means in information collection, prohibition to allow any outsider to have influence on the journalistic work, prohibition of discrimination on the basis of sex/class etc., freedom of speech, expression, comment, criticism, professional secrecy.

Though these codes specifically mention that public accountability and privacy of the individual seem to be important, the media violate them while asking for absolute freedom to discharge its duties. Thus, in many countries, certain elements of free press are regulated such as press freedom, freedom of expression, privacy, libel/ defamation/slander, right to reply, access to public information, discrimination, pre-condemnation and court proceedings, responsibility of the publication, censorship, source protection and minors. Thus, Gandhiji, while favouring press freedom, advised the press to observe self-restraint. He wrote in *Young India* on May 12, 1920:

> Freedom of the press is a precious privilege that no country can forgo. But if there is, as there should be, no check save that of the mild character, an internal check should not be impossible and ought not to be resisted.

Ethical journalism: The overview

The word 'ethics' is closely linked to questions of appropriate conduct within society. Etymological meaning of 'ethics' goes back to the Greek 'ethos' meaning reliable character, virtuous people, proper conduct etc. Ethics is a branch of philosophy concerned with actions that are morally permissible and actions that are not. Ethics in media constitutes a normative science of conduct applied voluntarily. World over efforts have been made to set ethical guidelines, rules, norms, codes and principles to help journalists to make right choices when they are in a dilemma. This research paper is an effort to carve out Gandhian concept of ethical journalism. *(Blackburn, 8 May 2003)*

Media profession is changing and it can be said that at present scenario most of the media organisations are becoming "social entertainers". It is no accident that no television channel in India today has any place for mass oriented content. Newspapers lack in-depth study or research on subjects relating to the nation. Events are more important than issues. It is true that media has become a product that trapped in the hands of free market capital forces and neglecting developmental issues related to mass. Hence, it would be relevant to go through Mahatma Gandhi's canon of journalism that is considered as one of the greatest journalism of all time and started the various aspects of development journalism.

Mahatma Gandhi consistently wrote for a common man. Gandhi himself applied his basic perspective to several fields, not only to politics, including governance, and economics, which were his focus of interest, but also to others such as treatment of nature, including animal life, education, social relations, religion, science, technology, and culture. In education, he stressed character building as its main aim; in social relations, love, empathy, and respect for the other; in religion, tolerance, openness, and freedom from dogma; in science and technology, humaneness; and, in culture openness combined with refusal to be blown off the feet. Gandhi believed that Great men are always above their time. If time passes, the relevance of their thought becomes more important. Gandhi continuously emphasised the necessity for identification with the villagers, who represented the masses of India and their needs be met. For Gandhi, the sole purpose of journalism was the service to the entire sections of the society. As Gandhi wrote in Young India "I have taken up journalism not for its sake but merely as aid to what I have conceived to be my mission in life....I may not write merely to excite passion. The reader can have no idea of the restraint I have to exercise from week to week in the choice of topics and my vocabulary. It is training for me. It enables me to peep into myself and to make discoveries of my weaknesses."

(Attenborough, 10 Dec 2007)

Gandhi and Media Ethics:

Media ethics are applied ethics which deal with the ethical standards of media which includes print, broadcast, film, theatre, art forms, internet and traditional media. Media ethics set guidelines, rules, norms, codes and principles for media. With changing forms and expanding reach of mass media, the issues pertaining with the media ethics have come to the fore once again. Ethics of entertainment and infotainment media, ethics of business media, media and democracy and changing ethical standards in global media network are being debated fiercely. Commercialisation of media and communication content, privacy, right to reply, communal writing, sensational, freebies and sting operations have raised new ethical concerns. Freedom of mass media is premise of the liberal democracy where media plays a role of facilitator and express people's voice. New trends, especially the media convergence and technological changes have brought new dimensions to the ethical debate. Efforts are being made worldwide to create norms and standards for media coverage. Though media has freedom to publish and broadcast information in form of news or entertainment it has to oblige to certain norms, rules and regulations. The governments of nation states world over have made some provisions to protect rights of citizens but also independent bodies comprising of media professionals have eventually drafted norms and regulations. These are voluntary norms expected to be followed by journalists and media. In the age of media credibility crisis, these ethical norms are devised to help to restore the faith and confidence in media. (Kieran, *26 Mar 1998)*

Mahatma Gandhi was the most effective mass medium of the twentieth century. His journalism belonged to an era when there was neither radio nor television. Such was the power of his 'soul communication' that whatever he said and wrote reached the farthest corners of this country within days and to the entire world thereon. Mahatma Gandhi, in a journalistic career spanning nearly four decades, edited six journals. None, including *Harijan* and *Navajivan*, could boast a circulation of more than a few thousand copies. But such was Gandhi's grasp of the basics of mass communication that he ensured that his daily "outpourings of heart and soul" reached all. If one were to ask the question as to who came first-Gandhi-the-freedom-fighter or Gandhi-the-media-crusader-the truth would be that Gandhi-the-journalist pre-dated Gandhi the freedom fighter by at least 20 years. In less than a few months' stay in South Africa, Gandhi realised the need to become a journalist to fight for the rights of the Indian community. And he brought the highest qualities the profession could boast of-courage in the face of adversity, unswerving adherence to truth, pursuit of public causes, and objectivity in presentation. His letters to the editors of South African dailies are a lesson to all journalists on how to fight injustice in a country where the laws are loaded against one section of the people, without giving offence to the rulers themselves. After 10 years of relentless crusade, Gandhi realised that the twin tasks of mobilising public opinion and influencing official decisions required a regular newspaper. Thus, was born *Indian Opinion* in June 1903. He was clear about the nature and content of his newspaper. It would not carry any advertisements nor try to make money.

In *My Experiments with Truth*, he wrote: "Week after week I poured out my soul in its columns and expounded the principles and practice of satyagraha as I understood it. I cannot recall a word in these articles set down without thought or deliberation or a word of conscious exaggeration, or anything merely to please. Indeed, the journal became for me training in self-restraint and for friends a medium through which to keep in touch with my thoughts." *(Sharma, August 1994)*

Free communication vs. Ethical communication: the perspective of Gandhi

Given the flexibility and freedom in courageously pursuing the path of truth, what is the essence of Gandhian perspective? Primacy of ethics dominated his entire life.

He sought nothing short of moral development for all, and through it their spiritual development, while first following himself what he preached. Rather, his precepts followed from his practice and experience. This gave him great credibility all over the world, and allowed him to reform his society and polity. His ethics were as much relevant to society and its institutions as to individuals. He subjected these institutions and even whole civilisations to stern evaluation, applying his principles of ethics. We do not have to labor hard to know what Gandhi's essential principles of ethics were, for he declared them often truth and nonviolence. He would reduce them again to one basic word, truth. Relentless pursuit of truth is the one principle in which were integrated all his strands of thought and applications to life's problem as Gandhi mentioned "the press is called the fourth estate. It is definitely a power but to misuse that power is criminal. I am a journalist myself and would appeal to fellow journalists to realise their responsibility and to carry work with no idea other than that of upholding the truth" (Gandhi, The Harijan: 1947).

Besides using various communication modes and mediums like intra-personal, interpersonal, group communication and also verbal and non-verbal symbolic communication, Gandhi successfully used the newspaper medium for communication. Gandhi was associated with Indian Opinion, Young India, Navjivan and in later part of his life with Harijan, Harijanbandhu, and Harijansevak in English, Gujarati and Hindi, respectively.

Gandhi was an effective communicator-journalist as receivers of his message believed in his words as Gandhi was the embodiment of what he preached. His strongest weapon of Satyagraha, he applied as a parameter to his own life as mass leader and journalist communicator. Gandhi's concept of Satyagraha is an integrated concept and includes truth, non-violence, non-stealing, chastity or brahmacharya, poverty or non-possession, bread labour, fearlessness, control of the palate (asvada), tolerance, swadeshi and removal of un touch ability — basically a self restrained life style model for an individual Satyagrahi. (Mishra, 2010)

Though he has not categorised the concept of journalist, Gandhi has dropped clear hints of what he expected from journalism and journalists. His rules for Satyagrahis are applicable to journalists. The Gandhian Satyagrahi journalist will not harbour anger against anyone and in pursuance of truth he will suffer anger of opponents and put up with assaults but never retaliate with anger or lose his/ her balance and insult opponents. Here opponents are those who want to quell the truth. Journalist must not submit out of fear, of punishment. He/she should merely follow the truth and take it to the logical conclusion. Satyagrahi journalists never intend to embarrass the wrongdoers and his objective must be to convert and not coerce. Journalist should have inward conviction and must believe in truth and non-violence as his/ her creed and have faith in the goodness of human nature which he/she expects to evoke by truth and love. 'The press is called the Forth Estate. It is definitely a power but to misuse that power is criminal. I am a journalist myself and would appeal to fellow journalists to realise their responsibility and to carry on their work with no idea other than that of upholding the truth' he said in Harijan. *(Attenborough, 10 Dec 2007)*

The controlled free communication: Ethics not the barricades of freedom

The spirit of Gandhian viewpoint is shaped by his firm faith in and commitment to truth and non-violence. For him, the substance of truth is morality, and non-violence is its essential part. Ahimsa or non-violence is a positive principle, which includes compassion and care. Truth finds expression through ahimsa; both are meant to be practiced. He said, 'it is not enough for thought to be based on truth, the life must express it'. And that is what he did. After Jesus Christ, there are scarcely those like him who lived what they preached, and lived to such rightness, in spite of being engrossed so much in politics. This is what lends reliability and respect for Gandhi and his beliefs. Though he saw in non-violence a powerful weapon for the empowerment of the weak and destitute, he refused to call it as a weapon of the weak. On the contrary, non-violence was the weapon of the ethically strong and brave, according to him. He strove to get justice to the underprivileged and make them stand on their own feet with solemnity. He believed that journalism can be the effective tool to bring about the change that is needed for the upliftment of the society but on the other hand, it can act negatively when we don't understand its importance and value.

The media, collectively, gets a bad name when journalists lose the trust of those whom they set out to serve. Gandhi, the father of nation, warned: '.......just as an unchained torrent of water submerges the whole countryside and devastates crops; even so an uncontrolled pen serves but to destroy......' (Thakurta, 2012: p. 9). He did not believe in a centralised state and power. Power both political and economic had to be decentralised and distributed, to be meaningful to the people. His principle of selfrestraint on wants is a key to environmental; sustainability, and also integrated with his fight against inequality. The legacy of Gandhi is still alive. He has been a motivation for numerous mass movements for social justice and environment protection.

Gandhi's contribution to religious thought is not less important. Gandhi's contribution lies in providing a resolution to a difficult modern dilemma. On the one hand, in spite of a long history, religion has failed to make human beings civilised enough. On the other hand, science and technological progress also failed in making human beings rational enough to raise all human beings to a position of dignity, happiness, and moral responsibility. Though, he discarded neither, but put conditions on both. He accepted religion in so for as it left us with an ordinary legacy of ethical values, which needs to be followed. He accepted science and technology only to the extent that they did not deprive human beings of their dignity and livelihood. For him, spirit of religion is principles. His religiosity was unique, for he was a rationalist among believers and a believer amid rationalists. He emphasised both reasoning and faith in one self and moral value in a creating unity. He eschewed all sectarianism in religion. 'Tolerance' is not what really captures Gandhi's approach to other religions. He not only advanced from patience to equal respect for all religions, but even beyond that by insisting on sharing the best from all religions.

He sincerely put this faith early in life to practice. He believed that no religion was perfect, and that one had to learn from all of them. His religion was merely one of truth and non-violence, devoid of any need of rituals and priests.

Spirit is a harmony which covers all its diversity. From this point of view, there is something important about Gandhian thought which can be said to make up a Gandhian perspective. We can use this perspective or approach to understand many facets of our individual as well as social or collective life, such as politics, economics, environmental issues, and education, and derive lessons or guidance for action. This is what Gandhi himself did. His thought was essentially a guide for action on a variety of fronts, in advancing the cause of justice, peace, and freedom.

To say that there is spirit in Gandhian thought which characterises all his thinking and action in different situations and contexts does not mean, in any way, that he was dogmatic, inflexible, or rigid sectarian. Far from it, it was an essential character of his approach to slum dogma and rigidity in thought. Gandhi denied that there is anything called Gandhism.

Ethical Standards over the flow of journalism:

Gandhi could achieve high moral and ethical standards due to his managerial skills. We all know Gandhi as a man of principles, discipline, and dedication to his work and a brilliant strategist and all these qualities Gandhi achieved due to his managerial skills that he had Gandhi achieved high ethical standards by setting up examples and in the early days of the Indian Opinion, he was doing almost everything single handed. Gandhi personally trained some workers when he was running the Young India and the *Harijan*. He always kept a watchful eye on each detail. Gandhi had realised success of a newspaper did not depend only on qualitative content but also on efficient management. Gandhi was well aware of the fact that in spite of excellent editorial and rich content circulation was also important to run a newspaper and for this it needed great management skills at each strategic point. Gandhi implemented new things for the success of his newspapers. He introduced a new tone in his correspondence unlike the official firm and extremely synthetic in an average newspaper office, he used simple and direct language. It was short and very to the point. Gandhi's newspapers suggest that his purpose of journalism was to serve the society in all respect and inspire the mass for a greater cause. He talked to the people in their own language to communicate the message. His over reaching concern for addressing the communication needs of the general public became evident when he expressed that English alone could not be a medium of the newspaper. Hence, it is clear that Gandhi's practice of journalism set high ethical and moral standard by practicing mass oriented and value based journalism.

(Nair, 1 Oct 1994)

In spite of some inspiring examples of practices of development journalism by today's media the questions that arise at this point is Can Gandhian model of development journalism be practiced consistently under the prevalent economic system of capitalism, which functions on the basis of selfishness and unlimited multiplication of wants? It is true that some media outlets have taken initiatives on developmental issues and consistently working on the education, health, environment and other issues. But in a huge country like India where more than 70 per cent people still live in rural areas and they are not covered in this regard. It is a matter of serious concern that no private media talks about the issues related to rural India. Poverty continues to pose a threat to millions of people, journalists have no choice but to continue reporting development issues and what is there impact on public. Gandhi developed a model for journalists to practice development journalism with a purpose to improve the society. He believed that the role of newspapers was only public service, hence, he wrote a series of stories on various issues such as health, birth control, and women empowerment and so on. He consistently wrote on the importance of educating rural masses and this approach is still relevant in India with a major population of illiterate section. In a country like India, which is plagued with problems like illiteracy, lack of health care facilities, pollution, corruption, and the apathy of government officials etc, the role of the Press in development is desirable.

Chapter 11

Gandhi's Free Religion

In a forward Gandhiji wrote for 'The Sayings of Mohammad', on 24th March 1938 in Calcutta, he expressed his feelings about spirituality thus:

"*I am a believer in the truth of all the great religions of the world. There will not be no lasting peace on earth unless we learn not merely to tolerate but even to respect the other faiths as our own. A reverent study of the sayings of different teachers of mankind is a step in the direction of such mutual respect*". (Abdulla, 1997)

Such an esteem feeling could only come from a person whose soul has become one with the Universal soul. For such a person, there is no difference between religions, cultures, nationality, caste, gender or in my form of creation; the created and the creator are one and the same. Overall, Gandhiji spread the supreme messages of Unity and equality, the dignity of labour and the supremacy of spirit over matter, and exhorted everybody to shed Gandhiji claimed himself to be a 'Sanatana Hindu'. He says:

(i) I believe in the Vedas, the Upanishads, and all that goes by the name of Hindu Scriptures, and therefore in Avatars and rebirth;

(ii) I believe in the Varna dharma in a sense, in my opinion, strictly Vedic but not in its popular and crude sense;

(iii) I believe in the protection of the cow in its much larger sense than the popular; and

(iv) I do not believe in idol –worship

In addition to the above, in an article Gandhiji wrote to an American friend, 'Why I am a Hindu'. He further writes:

"*On examination I have found it to be the most tolerant of all religions known to me. Its freedom from dogma makes a forcible appeal to me in as much as it gives the votary the largest scope for self-expression. Not being an exclusive religion, it enables the followers of that faith not merely to respect all the other religions, but it also enables them to admire and assimilate whatever may be good in other faiths.*" (Gandhi Smriti Darshan Samiti, 1994)

True to the Indian spirit and tradition, Gandhiji considered all religions to be different paths to the same goal God. Gandhiji had studied Christianity and Islam, and had many Christian and Muslim friends. He tells us in his autobiography how certain aspects of Christianity - the life and death of Jesus, the Sermon on the Mount, and the crystalline purity of some Christians, appealed to him. Similarly he read a translation of the Koran and the life of the prophet, and was struck by the courage with which he and his followers had faced the humiliations and hardships heaped upon them. Many years later, he advised his English disciple, Miss Slade (Mirabhen) to read Koran and to find out 'gems' in it. Gandhiji, though believed in the sacred scriptures of many religions, declined to be bound by any interpretation, however learned that might be, if it was repugnant to reason or moral sense as can be seen from his declaration that 'untouchability' is an ineffaceable blot which Hinduism carries with it. He strongly questioned the latter day religious authority for sanctioning caste system in Hinduism as he believed that Vedic Hinduism had no such social stratification wherein a group of humans are classed as 'untouchables' and denied of basic human rights. He strongly believed that there cannot be any moral argument in support of such a social evil. Gandhiji rightly declared:

"It is irreligious, not religion, to give religious sanction to a brutal custom" (Sengupta, 2001).

Free Religion in words of the Mahatma:

Every attempt to define religion will be futile as it is something which is to be realised, lived and experienced. From the time immemorial religious thinkers have been trying to define religion, but there are few definitions on religion which throw light on all the important aspects of religion. To quote Dr Radhakrishnan:

"*Religion is a growth which is perennial and its evolution has gone on obeying the primary laws of human progress. As religion is still in the process of growing and until the growth is completed an adequate definition cannot be found*". (Radhakrishnan, 1966)

Thus, we can see that religion is a growing, dynamic and personal affair. Gandhiji says that:

"*For me every, the tiniest, activity is governed by what I consider to be my religion.*" (Kripalini, 1991)

Hence, religion is not what one gets after doing the scriptures of the world. It is not what is grasped by the brain, but what the heart grasps. It is worth mentioning here that the concept of religion as handled in popular English today is drastically different from how Hinduism, Buddhism, Jainism, Sikhism etc. handled in the past. The Sanskrit term is 'Dhma' for all these; which is a concept entirely different from the concept of religion. Today we call them religion just for want of another word; and the term religion is indeed unable to represent accurately what the word 'Dharma' stands for.

'The man who became one with the Universal Being' - this was the sub-title of Roman Rolland's book, 'Mahatma Gandhi', published in 1924. Rolland wrote:

"*One thing is certain, either Gandhi's spirit will triumph, or it will manifest itself again as were manifested centuries before, the Messiah and the Buddha*". (Nanda, 1985)

Twenty years later Albert Einstein could write of Gandhi:

"*Generations to come, it may be, will scarcely believe, that such a one as this ever in flesh and blood walked upon this earth.*" (Nanda, 1994)

Mohandas Karamchand Gandhi was born in the complex Vaishnavite tradition of Kathiawad in 1869 just twelve years after the suppression of 1857 revolution. The country was, at that time mentally suffering the humiliation of the defeat. It was a period of subdued resentment against the British Imperialism. The agony was still prevailing in the hearts of the people who find no way to fight against the Britishers to make India free. In the mean-time many public-spirited men started thinking that spiritual decline of their men was responsible for political subjugation. Several religious institutions like Brahma Samaj, Arya-Samaj and Theosophical societies came into being to reform the mind of the people with a view to making them aware of their rich ancestral religious traditions. This was a period of religious renaissance. The gem of religious sentiment spread all over India by the time Gandhiji was born.

Again, Kathiawad was the centre of Vaishnava sect founded by Vallabhacharya. Gandhiji's family followed this traditional theistic faith of Vaishnavism. Gandhi's father Karamachand Gandhi and mother Puthlibhai were stern believers in God and used to visit temples and saints. This might have imprinted religious impressions on the mind of Gandhi from his very childhood. His grand-father, Uttamchand Gandhi, apart from being a follower of Vallabhacharya, was also attracted to 'Ram Charit Manas' written by Tulsidas. This attraction passed on to Karamchand Gandhi and ultimately to Gandhi, Gandhi studied 'Ram Charit Manas' too deeply and this book created an indelible impression on him towards 'Ram' from his very childhoods.

Porbandar was also a meeting place of the people belonging to ail major religions of the world. Eclecticism has become a way of life and men worshipped as they pleased without any interference from others. Karamchand Gandhi had many friends among them are people belonging to various religious faiths held religious discussions in Gandhi's residence. Gandhi listened to them. Gandhi also studied some Gujarati religious books like 'Ramayan', 'Bhagavad Gita' and 'Manusmriti' from the library of his father. Gandhi learnt from his mother the Indian maxim - 'There is nothing higher than Truth'. He also learnt that non-violence is the highest value (Ahimsa parama dharmah). Though this latter was universally acknowledged among the Hindus in all parts of India, it is most rigidly practiced by the Vaishnava and particularly the Jains; the combined influence of all these turned his native place Gujarat into the land of strictest vegetarianism. Gandhi grew in that atmosphere. It was Puthlibai's spirit of devotion, saintliness and unorthodoxy in regard to religion that gave Gandhi's broad-minded religious spirit. (Jacob, 2013).

In London Gandhi studied Edwin Arnold's translation on the 'Bhagavad Gita' - 'The Song Celestial'. This book left immediate and life-long effect on Gandhi. He writes:

"*It opened to me a new view of life. It touched my spirit as perhaps it can only touch a child of the East*". (Vyas, 1985)

In another place Gandhiji writes about the deep attachment he had for 'Gita:

"*It is (the 'Gita') my mother. I lost my earthly mother who gave birth to me. But this eternal mother completely filled her place by my side ever since. She has never failed me. Whenever I am in difficulty or distress, I seek refuge in her bosom*". (Kumari, 1999)

From the 'Gita', Gandhi derived the eternal message of selfless action i.e. Nikshama Karma. His philosophy of life and religion were rooted in the 'Bhagavad Gita'. 'Gita taught him the idea that self-realisation is possible only through righteous action and non-violence. Service to God also accompanies service to humanity. Every devotee must devote himself to action in order to establish righteous and spiritual universe. Gandhi did not interpret the Kurukshetra War as historical event, but:

"*Under the guise of physical warfare, it described a duel perpetually going on in the hearts of mankind and the physical warfare was brought into make the description of the internal duel more thrilling. This preliminary intuition became more confirmed on close study of religion of Gita*". (Desai, 1956)

Gandhiji studied about all the major religions of the world. To him Buddha and Christ were never theorists, they were activists, they were for direct action in accordance with their ends. These two prophest never advocated force as a means of conquest. They were never afraid of using moral force to fight against evil. He took them as apostles of love and gentleness. Edwin Arnold's 'The Light of Asia' gave him touching impression regarding the life and teaching of Buddha. He followed the teachings of Buddha because Buddha was opposed to caste-distinctions, sacraments, rituals etc. the practice of which brings forth differences in individuals. Buddha was a source of inspiration to him because Buddha tried to evolve new social values and accepted cosmic view of salvation. Gandhiji fully accepted the eight-fold path of salvation of mankind enunciated by Buddha, particularly non-violence as most appealing.

Gmdhiji was aIso acquainted with Islamic Religion. He regarded it as a religion of peace. Islam means in its way denial of self/ annihilation of the self. This religion also preaches complete surrender to God. The ideals of Islamic religion such as universal brotherhood, self-sacrifice, social justice etc. influenced Gandhiji to a great extent. Islamic religion appealed to him because this religion preaches that a Muslim is one who performs righteous actions, puts his life into danger and is over-powered to dedicate his life for truth.

Gandhiji was influenced by Leo Tolstoy. The seed of thought and action, philosophy of non-violence and the importance of manual labour was implanted by Tolstoy to germinate in the mind of Gandhi. Gandhi says:

"*The law that to live man must work first came to me upon reading Tolstoy's writing on 'Bread Labour*". Madhavav and Saraja (1993)

According to Gandhi, it is not possible for a man to realise absolute Truth. Gandhiji holds this view because humanitarian attitude makes him to think so. To him individual salvation is not possible until the entire mankind does not attain it. As there are infinite numbers of selves it is not possible for all of them to attain salvation at a time. He holds the view:

"*I do not believe that individual may gain spiritually and those that surround him suffer. I do believe in the essential unity of man and for that matter of all lives. Therefore, I believe that if one gains spiritually, the whale world gains with him and if one falls, the whole world falls to that extent*". (Varma, 1982)

Gandhiji holds that whatever be the functioning of our mind or capacity, each of us has some limited ideas of Truth as he sees it. He has to act upon it regardless of consequences and with unselfish motive and not compromising with what he himself considers as opposition to truth. At first he must be satisfied with relative truth. And if he goes on working following this principle then this will serve him as beacon light and assist him in the realisation of the supreme Truth. Relative truths must be regarded as stepping stones towards the realisation of the Supreme Truth. Gandhiji advises everyone of us to strive for perfection though we may fall short of it. He says:

"*The goal ever recedes from us, the greater this progress, the greater the recognition of our unworthiness. Satisfaction lies in the effort, not in the attainment.*" (Mukherjee, 1957)

Gandhiji holds that man's ultimate aim is realisation of God, and all his activities, social, political and religious, have to be guided by this ultimate aim, for he accepts the metaphysical position of the identity of God and the self. The immediate service of all human beings becomes a necessary part of the endeavour simply because the only way to find God is to see Him in His creation and become one with it. This can be done only by service to all. Being part and parcel of the whole, one cannot find Him apart from Humanity. And Gandhiji's God is myriad-formed; he never fails to see God in any situation in which man places himself. Gandhiji saw Him in the people around, so all departments of life, all walks of life are filled with His presence. No part of life is devoid of relevance for redemption, no compartment purely profane. One's everyday life is never capable of being separated from one's spiritual being. Gandhiji felt that he could save ordinary man through his involvement in politics. As he says:

"*I felt compelled into political field because I found I could not do even social work without touching politics.*" (Chacko, 1986)

Freedom in his land of Multi-religion:

Though Gandhiji was not a very religious minded person in his younger days, he slowly developed respect and regard for religions, mainly through the influence and example of his father. Hindus, Jains, Parsis, Buddhists and Muslims used to visit his father both for religious as well as political discussion. Gandhiji says: " In Rajkot, however, I got an early grounding in toleration for all branches of Hinduism and sister religions." So his home was a kind of 'dialogue centre.'" Even though Gandhiji grew up in a devout Hindu household, steeped in Vaishnavism and was also exposed to strong Jain influences, his acquaintance even with his own religion was very meagre. It was in 1888,when he arrived in London to study law, that he read Bhagavad Gita, the most precious book of Hinduism. Here Gandhi also came into contact with the books on 'Key to Theosophy', The Bible, especially the New Testament and the 'The Light of Asia' by Sir Edwin Arnold. Even at that time he began to identify the unifying teachings of the Gita, the Light of Asia and the Sermon on the Mount in the Bible and thus he started to practise an interreligious spirituality. With this background Gandhiji continued his experiments with religion and God. (Gandhi, 1991)

a. Hinduism:

Among the Hindu Sacred books that have influenced Gandhiji, the Bhagavad Gita, which is the most valued part of the Mahabharata, comes first. Gandhiji appreciated the Gita deeply. "The Gita has been a Mother to me ever since I became acquainted with it…I turn to it for guidance in every difficulty, and the desired guidance has always been forthcoming." According to Gandhiji the central teaching of the Gita is 'anasakti' or selfless action, which is the most excellent way to attain self-realisation. For Gandhiji anasakti includes and transcends ahimsa. "He who would be anasakti (selfless) has to necessarily practise non-violence in order to attain the state of selflessness. Ahimsa, therefore, a necessary preliminary, is included in anasakti, it does not go beyond it." According to Gandhiji, Gita is not a historical work, but a philosophical and ethical work. Its subject matter is simply the realisation of Brahman and the means to it. Thus,

Hinduism, especially the Gita has played a vital role in moulding Gandhiji's religious philosophy. (Gandhi, 1998)

From whatever we have said above about Gandhi's understanding of and love for Hinduism, one may have the impression, that Gandhi was a traditionalist and he believed in the traditional Hinduism in the form it was depicted in the various ancient 'Shastras' or in the form in which it has been traditionally accepted and followed. But this is not literally true. Gandhi was in many respects very much radical in his approach and he did not hesitate to criticise those aspects of Hinduism, which did not appeal to his reason. Quite often he felt that Hinduism as commonly viewed was not the pure and real Hinduism: it was, as he said, a 'parody" of that. Gandhi, as a matter of fact, was more an interpreter and reformer of Hinduism than a traditional believer of it.

Gandhi not only brought about many social reforms in Hinduism, but he also tried to analyse some of the basic concepts of Hindu religion in his own way. For example, although he accepted the Hindu belief in the existence of God and the various 'Avataras', he analysed the Hindu concept of God in his own way. He took God as Truth. At any rate, what we have said above is enough to indicate that although Gandhi was a staunch Hindu, he did not always understand Hinduism and its various concepts in the way in which they were traditionally understood.

b. Islam:

Gandhiji was acquainted with Islam at an early age through the Muslim friends of his father. Later he read Irwin's version of Prophet Muhammad and was moved by it. Literally Gandhiji accepts Islam to be a religion of peace and considers peace to be its objective. Gandhiji had great appreciation of Prophet Muhammad and the spirit of Islamic fasting. He once said that he learned from Muhammad that only he could fast who had inexhaustible faith in God. Gandhi in his own way found the teaching of the Prophet of Islam fully compatible with the principle of Ahimsa or non-violence. Gandhi had a good appreciation of the Islamic fast. In Tolstoy farm he encouraged each one to fast according to his religion. Although there were only few Muslims, they were encouraged to fast according to the rules of the Quran. "He extols the distinctive contribution of Islam as its unadulterated belief in the oneness of God and a practical application of the truth of the Brotherhood of man for those who are nominally within its fold." Gandhiji appreciated the positive aspects of this religion and sacrificed his life for Hindu-Muslim unity. (Gandhi, 1991)

Gandhi was also impressed by the social and personal codes of behaviour that Islam prescribes. In the Koran there are progressive codes of social behaviour and there is hardly any aspect of social life on which the Koran does not reflect and prescribe rules and regulations. There are regulations for marriage, divorce, dowry, inheritance, funeral ceremonies, etc. The five pillars of Islam prescribe rules for person behaviour. Prayer, fasting, alms-giving and hospitality are duties that every Muslim has to perform. All these influenced Mahatma Gandhi's thought and it is on account of these that he liked Islam so much. Furthermore, the Islamic ethics of the brotherhood of man and service to humanity impressed Gandhi a good deal. We found in Islam a base for real love and kindness for all. Gandhi found many of the injunctions of the discipline of Brahmacharya in Islam in the form of its prohibition of perfumed oil, intoxicating drinks, illegal sexual intercourse, etc. Virtues like obedience to parents, avoidance of adultery, cheating and lying, refraining from theft, murder, etc. are also emphasised in Islam and all these influenced Gandhi in the formation of his code of ethical virtues.

c. Christianity:

Gandhiji came in contact with Christianity at an early age. He developed a dislike for it because of the wrong approach of the missionaries towards Hinduism. He got the impression that to be a Christian means to eat beef, drink liquor and change one's own clothes. Moreover, he heard that the new convert had already begun abusing the religion of his ancestors, their customs and their country. It was in London that he began to read the Bible, for the first time. The New Testament, particularly the Sermon on the Mount, went straight into his heart. It was in South Africa that he studied well the Christian literature, though it was mainly Protestant. As a result of this pursuit, the Bible became a part of his scriptures. But it does not mean that he accepted everything given in the Bible. He had serious difficulties with regard to the Bible and its accepted interpretation. Gandhiji did not believe that Jesus is the only incarnate Son of God and salvation can be secured only by becoming a Christian. (Gandhi, 1991)

Nevertheless, Jesus Christ influenced Gandhiji deeply. For Gandhiji the Sermon on the Mount and the Gita were imparting the same message to him, and he says: "Today supposing I was deprived of the Gita and forgot all its contents, but had a copy of the Sermon, I should derive the same joy from it as I do from the Gita. The ethical teachings of Jesus commanded the reverence of Gandhiji. The Sermon on the Mount considerably influenced his doctrine of 'Satyagraha' and non-violence he called Jesus the Prince among Satyagrahi's, because He showed the purest form of passive resistance or soul-force. According to Gandhiji, non-violence is the central teaching of the 'Bible and Jesus' non-violence is par excellence. The influence of Christianity on Gandhiji was profound and he lived up to the teachings of Jesus Christ. (Gandhi, 1991)

Gandhi called Jesus the prince of Satyagrahis. In this connection, we may very well refer to the following sermons of the Bible:

"You have heard that it hath been said: An eye for an eye and a tooth for a tooth. But I say to you not to resist evil but if one strikes thee on thy right cheek, turn to him also the other.

And if a man will contend with thee in judgment and take away thy coat, let go thy cloak also unto him. And whosoever will force thee one mile, go with him the other too.

You have heard that it hath been said Thou shall love thy neighbour and hate thy enemy. But I say to you: Love your enemies, do good to them that hate you and pray for them that persecute and calumniate you.

Blessed are the poor in spirit: for the theirs is the kingdom of heaven.

Blessed are the meek: for they shall possess the land.

Blessed are they that mourn: for they shall be comforted

Blessed are they that hunger and thirst after justice for they shall have their fill.

Blessed are the merciful: for they shall obtain mercy.

Blessed are the clean of heart for they shall see God.

Blessed are the peace-makers: for they shall be called the children of God.

'Blessed are they that suffer persecution for justice' sake: for theirs is the kingdom of heaven.

Blessed are the when they shall revile you and persecute you and speak all that is evil against you, untruly, for my sake: Be glad and rejoice, for your reward is very great in heaven. For so they persecuted the prophets that were before you."

Gandhi loved Christianity so much because of its absolute emphasis on love as the most important ethical virtue.

d. Buddhism and Jainism:

Gandhiji regarded Buddhism and Jainism as off-shoots of Hinduism. Gandhiji calls Buddha a Hindu of Hindus and holds that he broadened the base of Hinduism by giving it a new life and newinterpretation. According to him Buddha was "saturated with the best that was in Hinduism, and he gave life to some of the teachings that were buried in the Vedas and were overgrown with weeds. The Buddha's life of renunciation and his doctrine of compassion and toleration had influenced Gandhiji to a very great extent. Gandhiji says: "Many friends consider that I am expressing in my own life the teachings of Buddha. I accept their testimony and I am free to confess that I am trying my level best to follow these teachings." Gandhian life style of simplicity and voluntary poverty closely reflect the ethical principles of Buddhism.

Buddhism is regarded as atheistic in nature. It is said that Buddha did not believe in any God and preached a purely ethical religion. His religion is man-centred and humanistic instead of being God-centred. Apparently this view seems to be quite sound and correct, but Gandhi did not take Buddhism in this way. To be sure, he did not doubt that Buddhism was a very elevated kind of humanistic religion, but he did not subscribe to the view that Buddhism was atheistic. According to Gandhi, it is not true that the Buddha did not believe in God. What is true is that he did not believe in God as a person who needed sacrifices. According to him, the Law itself, i.e., the Dharma itself, was God. God was not separate from his own Law. The Law and the Law-maker are one-this, according to Gandhi, was the underlying faith of the Buddha. Therefore, he cannot be called an atheist. He believed in God; only, he believed in God as an impersonal Law, the Law of the moral Government of the universe.

Jainism, however, had a greater influence on Gandhiji. When the father of Mohandas died, mother Putlibai sought advice on family matters from Beeharji Swami, a Jain monk. Gandhiji took three vows upon the advice of this Jain monk and was allowed to go to England for studies. The ascetic tendency in Gandhiji, concepts of vegetarianism, non-violence and his recourse to vows and fasts are the best manifestation of the influence of Jainism. According to Jainism the five cardinal vows constitute the right conduct. They are Ahimsa (Non-violence), Satya (Truth), Asteyam (Non-stealing), Brahamacharya (Chastity) and Aparigraha (Non- attachment). Gandhiji accepted this code of conduct and prescribed it to the inmates of his ashram. Jainism also influenced him to take up his many fasts unto death. He absorbed the great ideals of Jainism and purified it. (CWMG, 1994)

We shall here attempt a brief analysis of the five ethical vows and virtues in the light of the Jaina view about them: ...

(1) Ahimsa (Non-violence) - It is the most fundamental rule of conduct in Jainism. It is understood and practised in Jainism

in its widest sense. Violence or injury or harm caused to any living being in any form is himsa. So ahimsa is to be practised not only in deed, but also in word and thought. Keeping ill-will against anybody in thought or speeking harsh words to anyone is as good as an act of himsa as inflicting any bodily injury to anybody. So ahimsa is more than mere avoidance of killing somebody. It is much more deep in meaning. Even forcing someone to do something against his will or curtailing somebody's freedom is deemed as himsa in Jainism. Causing injury to another from one's negligence is also himsa. Negligence (Pramada) implies the passions of attachment (raga) and aversion (dvesha) and any action done under their spell is violence. Non-violence understood in such wide sense is the rule of conduct according to Jainism. Practising ahimsa in the Jaina sense is not something very easy. It is a kind of tapas. On its positive side, ahimsa implies a Life of love for all.

(2) Satya (Truthfulness)–Generally speaking, this rule of conduct enjoins abstinence from giving false statements or telling lies. But the mere statement of fact is not truth. Truth, if it is harmful to others, should be avoided, It must be spoken with beneficent intentions. Otherwise, it will offend or harm somebody and that will be himsa. Exaggeration of fact, finding fault with others, using indecent speech, etc. are all examples of untruth according to Jainism and, therefore, they must be avoided: (a) Denial of the existence of a thing with reference to its position, time and nature; (b) Asserting the existence of a non-existent thing with reference to its position, time and nature; (c) Representing a thing as something else; (d) Reprehensible speech, (e) Sinful speech; and (f) Unpalatable (Apriya) speech.

(3) Asteya (Non-stealing)–Generally speaking, this means abstention from taking someone else's something which is not given. But as a Jaina rule of conduct, asteya is more comprehensive and includes within it the avoidance of all sorts of dishonesty and conceit. Buying a valuable article at

too low a price, appropriating something that has been forgotten about by its possessor, having greed for the property of others, taking in one's possession a thing whose ownership is doubtful, etc. are all examples of stealing and they must be avoided. Jainism regards stealing as a kind of violence (himsa), because wealth is the external vital force of a person and taking it away without his consent offends or hams him. Even abetment of theft or purchasing of stolen property or doing any kind of illegal business is a kind of stealing according to Jainism because each such behaviour dispossesses the rightful owner in some way.

(4) Brahmacharya (Celibacy)–This vow has been much emphasised in Hinduism and Buddhism also, but Jainism Lays far more emphasis on it. It extols the life of a celibate or a monk much more than any other religion. This vow or rule of conduct stands for abstinence from sexual intercourse, particularly from all sorts of illegal sexual intercourse. Samantabhadra has included within this vow, renunciation of contacts with any woman other than one's wife. Not only the actual commitment but even the thought of adultery is a violation of this vow. In general, brahmacharya means abstinence from excessive desire for any sort of sense enjoyment. Thinking about such enjoyment is also a violation of the vow.

(5) Aparigraha (Non-possession or non- attachment)–It stands for not only abstinence from excessive material possession but also for the avoidance of desire for such possession. So, its exact meaning is...non-attachment rather than non-possession. Excessive desire for material possession is parigraha or even Steya, because in a way it is depriving others of their legitimate rights. Attachment is generated by 'rnoh' or attraction towards Worldly possession and it results in himsa. So it must be avoided. For, otherwise, one cannot pursue right conduct. Desire for worldly objects is the root of all evil and, therefore, it must be shunned.

The days preceding the British rule in India are characterised generally as a period of peaceful co-existence of various religions. Instances of occasional feuds did not affect the harmonious relationship among them, as those conflicts were caused more by the political ambitions of the rulers rather than matters relating to religion. Diverse beliefs, faiths and customs did not come in the way of development of harmonious relationship, since acceptance of each other's religion was a significant trend among members of different communities in those days. The deterioration in communal harmony was a development that occurred much later. It appears that the idea of communalism gained its strength with the coming of the British through their 'divide and rule' policy.

In South Africa, Gandhiji had a very good relationship with the Muslims. He fought for the various issues of Indian Muslims. It gave Gandhiji the realisation that communal unity was imperative for achieving Indian freedom. The main communal tensions in India were between Hindus and Muslims. Gandhiji himself admitted that the "Hindu-Muslim problem is the problem of problems." Therefore, when Gandhiji returned from South Africa, he devoted himself fully and wholeheartedly to solve communal conflicts whenever it arose. Gandhiji felt that if Hindu-Muslim unity was established, unity with other communities could easily be strengthened. (Chakravartty, 1991)

Hindu-Muslim conflict has remained a focal point of Indian politics since the days of India's freedom movement. Conflict and coexistence between Indian nationalists and communalists, both Hindus and Muslims, greatly influenced the course of Indian national movement; a relationship which, in later years of the freedom movement turned sharply antagonistic resulting into a vertical split in the movement and the partition of the country. The interplay of religion and politics has always appeared to be detrimental to the growth of secular nationalism. But the history of Indian freedom movement is full of such interplays and compromises and Gandhiji's role in solving these conflicts was indeed historic. Far from being communal, Gandhiji was a true secular leader, although deeply religious as an individual. The question of Hindu-Muslim unity always remained at the centre of his thoughts and dedicated his whole life for the cause of communal harmony.

The free religion of the mahatma:

Gandhiji is considered as a man of religion. But this concept about religion is entirely different from the conventional religions. The following explain his ideas about religion, faith and God. Gandhiji says :

1. I want every one of you cultivate faith in God and religion. Mine is not a religion of the prison-houses. It has room for the least among God's creation.
2. I do not regard any of the great religions of the world as false.
3. My religion is a matter solely between my Maker and myself.
4. The soul of religion is one, but it is encased in a multitude of forms.
5. I want lasting peace that springs from toleration of each other's religion.
6. My personal religion peremptorily forbids me to hate anybody.
7. In matters of religion, beliefs differ and each is supreme for himself. If all had the same belief about all matters of religion, there would be only one religion in the world.
8. The Hindu thinks that in quarrelling with the Muslim he is benefiting Hinduism and the Muslim thinks that in fighting a Hindu he is benefiting Islam. But each is ruining his faith.
9. The term 'religion' I am using in its broadest sense, meaning thereby self-realisation or knowledge of self.
10. No religion which is narrow and which cannot satisfy the test of reason will survive the coming reconstruction of society in which the values will have changed and character, not possession of wealth, title or birth, will be the test of rnerit.

11. Religion binds man to God and man to man.
12. Religion is not really what is grasped by the brain but by the heart.
13. Religion divorced from morality is like 'sounding brass' good for nothing but making a noise and breaking heads.
14. Belief in one God is the corner- stone of all religions.
15. The foundation of religion is restraint.
16. A religion will be tested by the purity of its adherents.
17. Religion are meant to take away our savage nature, not to let it loose.
18. Religions are different roads converging to the same point.
19. The seat of a religion is in the heart.
20. You cannot defend yourself and your converging to the same point.
21. You cannot defend yourself and your religion with the help of hooligans.
22. You may be incapable of attaining the ideal, your flesh may be weak, but do not, therefore, lower the ideal, do not irreligion your religion.
23. God there is only one; but He enables me to see Him and worship Him in stone, in an Englishman, in a traitor, if you will. For I shall not hate even a traitor. My religion takes me to that length.
24. Religion does not mean merely offering one's namaz or going to the temple. But it means knowledge of one's self and knowledge of God.
25. Man's destined purpose is to conquer old habits, to overcome the evil in him and to restore good to its rightful place. If religion does not teach us how to achieve this conquest, it teaches us nothing. (Yohannan, 2013)

For Gandhiji, religion does not mean any particular historical religion. It is that religion which underlies all religions, which brings us face to face with our Maker. Gandhiji is clear about the transcending nature of religion. Therefore, he says:

"It is not the Hindu religion which I certainly prize above all other religions, but the religion which transcends Hinduism, which changes one's very nature, which binds one indissolubly to the truth within and whichever purifies. It is the permanent element in human nature which counts no cost too great in order to find full expression and which leaves the soul utterly restless until it has found itself, known its Maker and appreciated true correspondence between the Maker and itself."

Religion was the very core of his life. He says: "I could not live for a single second without religion…I go further and say that every activity of man must be derived from his religion because religion means being bound to God, that is to say, God rules your every breath." He considered the religion as the root from which all things sprang out. Every such action will be conscious, fearless, free and having no profit-making motive. This kind of actions alone can do good for the mankind and therefore better the present condition. The whole being of Gandhiji was permeated with religious fervour and religion was the main spring of Gandhiji's activities. (Joseph, 1973)

Plurality of religions is inevitable. Gandhiji believed that in theory since there is one God, there could be only one religion. But in practice, no two persons have had the same and identical conception of God. Therefore, there will perhaps, always be different religions answering to different temperaments and climatic conditions. Gandhiji says, "religion is one tree with many branches. As branches you may say religions are many, but as tree, religion is only one." But this one Religion while it transcends particular religions, does not superssede them. According to Gandhiji, this Religion harmonises them and gives them reality. Thus religion, at its height and in its depth, is one. By this Religion, Gandhiji means a belief in God and in ordered moral government of the universe and in living according to this moral order.

For Gandhiji, man without religion is man without roots. Therefore, religion is the basis on which all life structures have to be erected, if life is to be real. According to Gandhiji, religion has to be lived every moment of one's life and therefore no man can live without religion." Whether by reason, or by instinct or by superstition, man acknowledges some sort of relationship with the Divine. Even the agnostics or atheists, who say they have nothing to do with religion, admit the moral order because they associate something good with its observance and something bad with non-observance. He compares them to "a man saying that he breathes but that he has no nose." In short, according to Gandhiji, religion is essential and necessary for man so much so religion is universal, found at all times and in all places.

After a long search after truth, Gandhiji came to certain fundamental conclusions, which are the core of his religious philosophy. The first one is that all religions are essentially one. In theory we could say that since there is only one God and religion is the relation to Him, there can be only one religion. We should remember that God is not encased in a safe to be approached only through a little hole in it, but that He is often to be approached through billions of openings by those who are humble and pure of heart. Hence, there will be many religions as there are many hearts to approach the Truth. There are no two persons having the same and identical conception of God who is beyond our reason and knowledge. So religions are different roads converging to the same point. Hence, what we need is not mere tolerance but mutual and constitutive respect as pilgrims towards the same goal. The followers of other religions are to be loved and respected as the members of one's own family. This respect for other religions is our duty because our own religion is as imperfect as others. Moreover, this attitude towards other religions will help us to assimilate what is good in them. (Gandhi, 1968)

The second characteristic is that all religions are true. Gandhiji believed that all religions are 'more or less perfect', because whatever man makes is imperfect. The perfection is attributed only to God. Gandhiji says: "My Hindu instinct tells me that all religions are more or less true. All proceed from the same God, but all are imperfect because they have come down to us through imperfect human instrumentality." Each one is right from one's own standpoint. So truth is the exclusive property of no single scripture. Gandhiji considered the scriptures not as of Divine origin but as inspired. Since they are inspired and since they lead to the Truth, they contain truth. All religions are more or less perfect in the sense that it has truth and at the same time they are imperfect. All are true since all proceed from the same God. Thus, Gandhiji concludes that all religions are true but all are imperfect.

The third characteristic is a corollary of the earlier two, as religions are one and more or less true, i.e., they are equal and command the same respect. Hence, he believed in the 'Sarvaadharma Samabhava', i.e.. having equal regard for all faiths and creeds. Gandhiji says, "For me, all the principal religions are equal in the sense that they are all true. They are supplying a felt want in the spiritual progress of humanity." When he says that all religions are true and equal, he does not necessarily mean to say that they are equally true in religious terms or that they are absolutely true. While discussing the point all religions are true, we have seen that all religions are imperfect. The equality of religions is also explained on the same basis. All religions are equal but at the same time all are imperfect. (Gandhi, 1986)

After studying different religions, Gandhiji developed a view of equimindedness to all religions. The inner codes of all religions are same but they differ in their creed and cult. While all religions are equally true, no one can claim superiority over others. Therefore, Gandhiji asks: "How can I even secretly harbour the thought that my neighbour's faith is inferior to mine and wish that he should give up his faith and embrace mine? Thus, he is against religious conversions through preaching. But he is not against the genuine religious conversion that takes place through the preaching of one's life, as the rose imparts its fragrance. Such conversions are indeed a real transformation of one's life.

All religious scriptures have laid down certain moral precepts for human life. The ethical principles of all religions are basically the same. "Religious principles and dogmas may differ, but the principles of ethics must be the same in all religions." Unless we live according to these moral precepts, we cease to be religious. According to

Gandhiji, there is no such thing as religion that overrides morality. Man for instance, cannot be untruthful, cruel and incontinent and claim to have God on his side. Gandhiji's conception of religion is called 'Ethical Religion' because the essence of religion according to him is morality, and because religion is a relation to God and to man and he held them to be synonymous. Gandhiji, though he studied more or less all the world religions and had great tolerance towards other religions, was not ready to accept any religion that is in conflict with morality. (Gujral, 1985)

The perspective of free religion:

Gandhi is best described as a pluralist, with his religious ideas emphasising the equality of all religions as expressions of Truth. His pluralism is in many ways typical of a Hindu, the faith he consistently professed. He does not justify the other faiths in terms of a Hindu worldview, but as self-sufficient expressions or responses to Truth, and neither Hinduism, nor a particular school within it, is seen as having a full grasp of Truth, but like the other religions it is a human response, through which Gandhi understands and prays to God, which is beyond it.

Gandhi is certainly pluralist with regard to the theistic religions, but when it comes to atheistic ideas he shows certain traits of an inclusivist. Buddhism and Jainism are considered to be part of Hinduism, and although he gives room for non-theistic definitions of the transcendent, himself shifting between personal and impersonal conceptions, it is doubtful how fully he appreciates the differences in philosophy. When it comes to atheism in the Western sense he appears as an inclusivist resorting to an 'anonymous believer' position to understand and incorporate moral atheists. When he recognises truth in Gora's atheist convictions, it is in terms of his own concept of Truth which sees Gora as a 'godly man'. His effort to use 'Truth is God' to avoid alienating those who struggle with God is appreciated, but challenged by Gora, who saw in it a slippery slope back to theism. In the final instance Gandhi appears to accept the more radical distinction with an attitude of respect, rather than trying to incorporate Gora back into his worldview and convert him to a religious outlook.

Religious pluralism is a philosophical position in relation to other religions, thus a part of the theology of religions. The practical correlate is found in inter-religious discourse. In a sense the two are distinct: for instance a person may hold an exclusivist position yet engage fully in dialogue with religious others on the basis of tolerance or necessity, or a pluralist may consider all religions equal and true, but have little interest in dialogue due to a lack of exposure, curiosity and motivation to engage with other people. Usually, however there is some overlap between the theological position and the practical response to other traditions and their adherents. An exclusivist position reinforces the self-sufficiency of one's own tradition and community, making dialogue unnecessary, even dangerous. Pluralism on the other hand gives a motive for dialogue with others in a shared religious journey, and such engagement with others is likely to reinforce this pluralist conviction. Alan Race therefore describes theology and dialogue as 'twin tracks'.

Bearing in mind this parallel and interlinked relation between religious pluralism and inter-faith relations, Gandhi's responses to interfaith marriage shed important light on his pluralism and practice. It asks the question how far and in what ways should religions engage with one another? Gandhi's early rejection of interfaith marriages, suggests a pluralist philosophy in which religions are self-sufficient, independently functioning paths, which it is best not to mix too closely. Marriage forms a strict boundary as to how far people of different religions can and should interact. This is therefore a limited, restricted pluralism in its implications even if affirming in theory. However, whilst inter-religious marriage remains a complex issue in view of the political and social context, as well as the influence Gandhi's unusual philosophy of marriage and sexual relations brought, by the end of his life Gandhi was supportive of interfaith marriage.

He even spells out the link between pluralism and interfaith marriage by drawing attention to the ashram vow of equality of religions and practice of multifaith worship. Gandhi's pluralist philosophy and experimentation in inter-religious living and leadership can provide a resource for couples seeking interfaith marriage and defending this against opposition. Moreover, and as I will expand on later, interfaith marriage fits into the model of interfaith relations which this research draws out in Gandhi's life: friendship and interpersonal harmony between people of different faiths. (Jolly, 2012)

Our research suggests engaging in a long-term, holistic way to form interpersonal friendships across religious traditions and commitments as a way to develop and deepen interfaith understanding, harmony and one's own commitment and insight. Gandhi's model deserves to be recognised as a valid form of interfaith dialogue and engagement.

Gandhi approached the problem of conflicting beliefs in more than one way. One-way of removing the conflict is to replace the worst interpretation of a religion by its best interpretation - the best interpretation being that which is accepted by a good follower of the religion. For example, according to him, to say that Hinduism regards cows as superior to man, or that it accepts distinctions of high and low is to make a caricature of Hinduism. If interpretation in terms of the worst aspects of a religion is replaced by interpretation in terms of its best aspects, then it will be found that all great religions spring from the same source and the fundamentals are common to them all.

This is indeed a salutary piece of advice, very often forgotten in practice. Another way is to replace the misunderstanding of a belief by understanding. For example it is a misunderstanding to think that the Buddha did not believe in God. "In my humble opinion such a belief contradicts the very central fact of Buddha's teaching. In my humble opinion the confusion has arisen over his rejection, and just rejection, of all base things that passed in his generation under the name of God." In a similar way Gandhi reinterprets the belief that Nirvana means complete extinction.

Ultimately, the greatness of a man must be measured not by the amount of adulation accorded him but by the impact of his life on others. When this yardstick is applied, Mahatma Gandhi's major place in history became a legend in his own lifetime. As a leader he was full of charisma. It is important to note that he held no position in Government and had no personal possessions either. Though many may disagree with his thoughts, no one can belittle his historical role. Though Gandhiji's Ashram experiment did not succeed fully, yet it proved that people belonging to different religions could peacefully live together, work together and pray together. Gandhiji's experiment on transreligious spirituality will ever remain a beacon light to humanity. Gandhiji's vision of Ramarajya was evolved from his religious conviction.

Though some have attempted to restrict his universal vision to the boundaries of the Hindu society, in fact Gandhiji was beyond such distorted vision. In his experiments with the Transreligious Spirituality, we see a prophetic vision of a Satya Rajya (Kingdom of Truth) where peace and harmony shall prevail. The Transreligious Spirituality will hopefully establish such a Satya Rajya, a Kingdom of the Divine Spirit, prophetically proclaiming the eternal values of love, peace and unity. The Transreuous Spirituality is indeed an authentic journey in our spiritual self-awakening. All practising believers in different religions have to get awakened to the Divine within, the Truth constantly lived from within. The challenge of bringing about such a society into reality is on the shoulders of those who are moved by such a vision, as a mission leading to action for its realisation.

Conclusion:

We have thus seen that all throughout his thought and practice, Gandhiji had been a thoroughly religious man and all his important concepts have been formed under the impact of his deep religious conviction. His religious conviction and his concept of religion were basically formed under the ideas drawn from Hinduism, but he has no less been influenced in his thought by the essential elements of other religions of the world such as Buddhism, Jainism, Christianity and Islam. Similarly, Gandhiji imbibed the true spirit of the philosophy of advaita and believed that once people are made aware of this, the rivalries between man and man, between one society and the other, between nation and nation will automatically disappear, if Gandhiji's guidance was ever needed most, it is in our modem world in which people, in spite of their great scientific and material achievements, have not been able to achieve real peace of mind. If there is a will, there is a way. The concerted will of the right thinking section of mankind is indeed indomitable. Well meaning efforts in the right direction can sustain the force of Gandhian technique of reconciliation and pave the way for an equitable solution to all the maladies that threaten the world today.

References

[1] *Dictionary of Quotations* by Connie Robertson, Wordsworth Editions, 01st-Jan. 1998, p. 137.

[2] *Collected Works of Mahatma Gandhi*, 'Homage', Vol. 1, v.

[3] *Collected Works of Mahatma Gandhi*, Vol. 63, 413.

[4] *Collected Works of Mahatma Gandhi*, 'Foreword', in *CWMG*, Vol. 90, v, Vol. 53, 485).

[5] The 'Message to America' was given on 5 April 1930 but was published in the Government-controlled *Bombay Chronicle* two days later, Collected Works of Mahatma Gandhi, v. 43, p.180.

[6] M.K. Gandhi, *An Autobiography* or *The Story of My Experiments with Truth* (Ahmedabad: Navajivan, 1927/2005), 57. The paragraph that follows deals with Gandhi's ability to view his shyness no longer as an impediment but as an advantage.

[7] MK Gandhi, *Satyagraha in South Africa, op.cit.* p. 211.

[8] *Gandhi's reply to Wybergh*, Collected Works of Mahatma Gandhi, X, p. 296.

[9] *Ibid*. 58.

[10] MK Gandhi, *Satyagraha in South Africa, op.cit.* p. 131.

[11] Ahmedabad Mill-Hands Strike, Leaflet No. 10, *CWMG*, XIV, pp. 242-43

[12] *The pledge, Young India*, 12.6.1918, *CWMG*, XIV, p. 279.

[13] *Collected Works of Mahatma Gandhi*, Publications Division, Ministry of Information and Broadcasting, Government of India, 1965, p. 332.

[14] Nanda, *In Search of Gandhi*, 141.

[15] *Message to Satyagrahi Agriculturalists, Mahadevbhani Diary Vol. IV, CWMG*, XIV, p. 349.

[16] New India, 3rd March 1919, *CWMG*, XV, p.102.

[17] M.K. Gandhi, *Autobiography*, 263-64.

[18] Harijan, 11 April 1948; cited in Bhattacharya, *Gandhi the writer*, pp. 202-03.

[19] *Collected Works of Mahatma Gandhi*, Vol. 38, pp. 11-12.

[20] *Journalist Gandhi-Selected Writings of Gandhi*, pp. *11-12*.

[21] Edward Thompson, 'Gandhi: A Character Study', *Mahatma Gandhi-Essays and Reflections*, ed. S. Radhakrishnan, pp. 290-91.

[22] "The Greatest Quotations of All-Time", by Antony St Peter, Xlibris Corporation, 28 Oct 2010, p. 393.

[23] Tharoor, India, *From Midnight to the Millennium*, 22.

[24] *Everyday Useful Quotes* by Paul G. Blacketor, Xlibris Corporation, 16 Oct 2009, p. 429.

[25] Nehru on Gandhi, views on Political Culture- by Prem Misir, Posted on October 26, 2010.

[26] *Gandhi, a biographical study*, Valiant Publications, 1948, page 63.

[27] Preface, *CWMG*, XC, p. I.

[28] *Speech at AICC meeting, Bombay, Harijan Sewak*, 12-10-40 *CWMG*, LXXIII, p. 25.

[29] *The Story of Gandhi*, Children's Book Trust, 1969, p. 3.

[30] *The Essential Writings*-by Mahatma Gandhi, Oxford University Press, 17 April 2008, p. 3.

[31] *Gandhi: The Master Communicator*-Kusum Lata Chadda.

[32] *Clothing for liberation: A communicative analysis of Gandhi's Swadeshi Revolution*-Peter Gonsalves.

[33] Emma Tarlo, *Clothes Matter, Dress and Identity in India*, (Viking Penguin India, 1997) p. 73.

[34] *Harijan* 15 April 1933, p. 4.

[35] Nehru, *An Autobiography*, pp. 37-38.

[36] Prabhu and Rao, *MMG*, 40.

[37] Nehru, *The Discovery of India*, pp. pp. 399-400.

[38] *Young India*, 8th December, 1921.

[39] *Young India*, 8th December, 1927.

[40] *Collected Works of Mahatma Gandhi*, Vol. XV pp. 495-96.

[41] *Virtuous Living: Honouring the Inescapable Natural laws*- p. 115.

[42] *Bapu's Letters to Mira*. p. 257.

[43] *Ibid*.

[44] *Gandhi's Passion: the Life and Legacy of Mahatma Gandhi*, Oxford University Press, 05 April 2001, p. 41.

[45] Thomas Weber, 'Gandhi's Salt March as Living Sermon', *Gandhi Marg*, 22(4): 423.

[46] *The Essential Writings*-by Mahatma Gandhi, Oxford University Press, 17 April 2008, p. 3.

[47] *The Encyclopaedia of Gandhian Thoughts*, All India Congress Committee (I), 1985, p. 350.

[48] *Epigrams from Gandhiji:* T-7-76.

[49] "The Greatest Quotations of All-Time", by Antony St Peter, Xlibris Corporation, 28-Oct-2010, p. 315.

[50] *Facilitator's Manual for the Class of Non-violence*, by Susan lves, peace CENTER, 01 Jan. 2007, p. 31.

[51] *Collected Works of Mahatma Gandhi*, Volume 68, p. 386.

[52] *Young India,* August 25, 1920.

[53] *Young India,* Sept 6, 1926.

[54] *Young India,* Oct. 11, 1928.

[55] *Be the change!* by Anand Krishna, Gramedia Pustaka Utama, p. 55.

[56] Bhikhu Parekh, *Gandhi,* (Oxford University Press, 1997), pp. 8-9.

[57] *Clothing for liberation*: A communicative analysis of Gandhi's Swadeshi Revolution-Peter Gonsalves.

[58] *Gandhi: The Master Communicator*-Kusum Lata Chadda.

Index

A

Accountability and Privacy, 196
Act of 1908, 34
Advani, LK, I&B Minister, 69
Advertisements, 68
  Income from-, 137, 138
Agra and Delhi, 131
Ahimsa, 9, 151, 152, 153, 193, 212, 213
Ahmedabad Workers Strike, 160
Akali Dal, 69
Akbar, MJ, Editor, 104
All India Newspapers Editors Conference, (AINEC), 45, 46, 58
Ambedkar, Dr BR, 48, 50, 110
  The Then Law Minister, 54
American
  Colonies, 20
  Constitution, 48
Amrit Bazar Patrika, 40, 44
Ancestral Religious Tradition, 208
Andhra Patrika, 40
Andhra Vani—Asrami Patrika, 40
Anglo-Indian newspapers, 41
Anti-Drought Projects in Orissa, 128
Arya Samaj, 208
Atheist, 224

B

Bar Council of India, 96
Basic Purpose of Newspaper, 127
  Public Service, 127
Beasant, Annie, 38
Bengal
  Gazette, 29, 30
  Split 1905, 33
    East and West Bengal, 33
Bentinck, Lord, 31
Bhagavat Gita, 212
Bhagavad Gita or Song Celestial, 209
Bharat Press, 53
Bhartiya Lok Dal, 68
Bhausali, 46
Bill of Rights, 21, 23
  In UK, 23
BJP, 145
Black Bill, 50
Boar War, 155
Bofors Gun Deal, 73
Bolts, William, 29, 109
  Conceived First Newspaper in India, 29
Bombay
  Chronicle, Ed. BG Harimma, 40, 44
  Samachar, 125
Brahma Samaj, 208
Brij Bhushan, 81
Brij Bhushan V State of Delhi, 52, 53
Britain, 18
British
  Administration, 189
  Colonization, 177
  Empire, 151, 155
  Imperialism, 208
  India, 43
  Indians, 130
  Judges, 149
  Newspapers, 93
  Raj, 184
  Rule, 18, 24, 36
  Rulers, 181
  South Africa, 130
Buddha, 207, 210, 216, 217, 228
  And Christ, 209
Buddhism, 207, 217, 226, 229
  And Jainism, 216

Buddhist
And Muslims, 202
Period, 131

C

Canning, Lord, Governor General, 32
Case Studies, 80, 116, 117
Bennet Coleman and Co., V Union of India, 87
Brij Bhushan v Sate of Delhi, 81
Express Newspaper V Union of India, 84
Indian Express V Union of India, 89-91
Ramjilal V State of UP, 83
Romesh Thapar V State of Madras, 80
Sakal Newspaper V Union of India, 84
Virendra V State of Punjab, 82
Casteism, 140
Censorship, 40, 61, 110
Guidelines, 61
Regulations, 61
Central Emergency Press Advisory Committee (CEPAC), 58, 59
Champaran, 154
Satyagraha, 159, 160
Charisma Gandhi, 183
Charkha, 186
Chatterjee, S, Freedom Fighter, 11
Chaukhamba, 59
China, 17, 58
Chinese Aggression, 59
Christianity, 214, 229
And Islam, 206
Civil Disobedience Movement, 42-44, 162, 176, 182, 184, 187
Colonial Rule, 18
Colonization, 157
Commercialization of
Media, 198
Press, 137, 147
Commission Members, 72
Giriraj, 72
HK Paranjepee, 72
Ishrat Ali Siddiqui, 72
Rajendra Mathur, 72
SK Mukherjee, 72
Commission on Freedom of Press, 22
Communal
Conflicts, 47
Rights, 101
Writing, 100
Communication, Modern Age of-, 17, 107
Communist Party of India, 68
Confiscation of Presses, 33
Conflict Satyagraha, 158
Congress Party, 44, 60, 73, 115
Corrupt Deals, 73
Council Head in Calcutta, 29
Criminal
Law Amendment Act, 44
Procedure Code, 56

D

Daily Telegraph, 61
Dainik Jagran, 101
Dainik Janambhumi, 101
Dandi, 154
March, 154
Declaration of Rights, 21
Defamation Bill,
1988, 73, 74, 76
1989, 115
Defamation, 32
Law in India, 75, 115
Defence of India
Act, 1951, 59, 136
Rules, 44
Delhi and Calcutta, 154
Department of Censor of Newspapers, 30
Desai, Mahadev, 164
Development Journalism, 140, 204
Diary of Mahadevbhai, 191
Dinanath, Ed. Hindustan Times, 33
Divide and Rule Policies, 181
DMK, 69
Draft Constitution, 48-50
Drafting Committee, 111
Dutch Colonizers, 155

E

East India Company, Administration of-, 29
Editorial Policy, 102

Editors Conference, 55
Edwin arundale's Light of Asia, 210, 212
Effective Communication Journalism, 200
Essence of Satyagraha, 181
Ethical
  Communication, 199
  Journalism, 164, 197
  Religion, 223, 224
  Standards, 203
  Teachings, 215
Ethics, 195, 198
European
  Convention on Human Rights, 1950, 19
  Planters, 159
Explosive
  And Substance Act, 1908, 37
  Substances Act, 35

F

Fabrics of Kashmir, 131
Features of Printed World, 18, 19
Feroze Gandhi Act, 57
Financial
  Problems (Indian Opinion), 134-135
  Times London, 61
First Royal Press Commission Report, 93
Free
  Communication, 194
  India, 191
  Press, 79, 80
    Journal of Bombay, 44, 101
  Religion, 207, 223, 224
  Society, 20
Freedom
  Fighters, 155
  Of Expression, 18-20, 73, 81, 196
  Of Press (FOP), 17-27, 29-46, 30, 32, 36, 47-77, 79-91, 93-106, 109
    And British Government, 29-46, 47-77
    And Emergency, 60, 113
    And Political Parties, 67
    And Speech, 24
    Case Studies, 79-91
    In India, 24
    In USA-UK, 20
Freedom of Speech, 22, 24, 52, 79
  And Expression, 52, 61, 70
Freedom Struggle, 109, 176, 186
Fundamental Rights, 24, 48, 49, 53, 107

G

Gagging Act, 1857, 32, 109
Gandhi Mahatma (Mohandas Karamchand), 9-12, 41, 42, 95, 103, 109, 110, 125, 130, 151-171
  A Sanatan Hindu, 205
  Believed in Vedas, 205
  Born in Vaishnava Tradition of Kathiawad, 208
  Father Karamchand Gandhi, 208
  Grandfather, Uttamchand Gandhi, 208
  Mohandas Karamchand, 173, 208
  And Media Ethics, 198
  Civil Disobedience Movement, 45
  Feroze, 58
  Flame for Free Communication, 9
  Hind Swaraj, 126
  Honest Writer, 151
  Launched Satyagraha, 11
  Leader of Satyagraha, 152
  My Experiment with Truth in Gujarati, 126
  Non-Violence Pen, 152
  Philosophy, 9
  True Orator, 151
  Wrote Biographies of Great Men and Women as Tolstoy—Raja Rammohan Roy, 132
Gandhi's
  Cannon of Journalism, 197
  Concept of Religion, 221-222
  Contribution to Religious Thought, 202
  Free Attire, 173-194
  Free Communication, 195-204
  Free Religion, 205
  Free Speech, 151-171
  Journalistic Career, 188
  Newspapers, 204
  Pluralist Philosophy, 227
  Publications of Satyagraha, 161
  Religious Philosophy, 213
  Satyagraha, 184

Teachings of Reconciliation, 230
Verbal Communication, 152
Writings, 127
Gandhian
Cap, 194
Journalism, 125-149
Language, 135
Satyagraha Journalist, 201
Trait of Positive Journalism, 149
Gandhi Mrs. Indira, 58, 60, 70, 73, 113, 114
Gandhi Rajiv, 73, 74, 76, 115
Ghose, Aurobindo, 34
Gita, 212, 215
Gokhale, Gopal Krishan, 131, 132, 158
Liberal Leader of Congress, 34
Gorey, Narayan Ganesh, Socialist Leader, Rajya Sabha, 66, 113
Gora's Atheist Conviction, 226
Goswami, PK, 70
Growth of Civilization, 20
Gutenberg, Invention of Printing Press, 17

H

Halkani, KK, 81
Hari Kishore, Ed. 35
Harijan, 10, 125, 127, 141, 142, 203
Harijan Bandu, 153
Hastings, Gen. Warren, 29
Lord, 30
Hicky, James Augustus, 29, 30, 109, 125
Printed First Paper in India, 29
Hicky's Gazette, 29
Hind Samachar, Urdu Daily, 102
Hind Swaraj, 126, 127, 152, 157
Hindu
Architect, 131
Muslim Unity, 214
Palace Architecture of Gwalior, 131
Religion, 223
Society, 229
Hinduism, 206, 207, 212, 213, 223, 224
Holy Quran, 104
House of Elders, 96
Human Rights, 20
Hutchins Commission, 1947, 94

I

Idol Worship, 206
Imperial British Empire, 175
Imperialism, 9, 163, 181
Incitement of Offences Act, 1908, 34
India,
And Pakistan, 47
Export Indian Labour, 155
India's Foreign Policy, 55
Indian
Anarchist, 126
Criminal Law, 162
Express, 69, 73, 75, 76
Journalism, 147
Mohammedan Mosque and Mausoleum, 131
National Congress, (INC), 34, 155
Newspapers, 146
Opinion, 125, 130, 132, 133, 134, 156, 157, 163, 164, 191
Objectives, 129
Penal Code, 1860, 32, 84
Press, 94, 147
Press Act, 1910, 109
Press Act, 1931, 42
Indians in South Africa, 125
Indigo Planters in Champaran, 159
Information Dissemination, 195
Inquiry Committee, 98, 100
Interfaith Marriages, 227, 228
International
Commission for Study of Communication, 20
Communication, 144
Convention on Civil and Political Rights, 19
Interpretative Journals, 138
Investigative Journalism, 100
Irwin's Version of Prophet Muhammad, 213
Islam, 213, 214, 229
Islamic Religion, 210
Iyenger, A Ramaswami, 42

J

Jainism, 207, 217, 218, 226, 229
Five Cardinal Vows, 217-219

Jallianawala Bagh Massacre, 1919, 11, 40
Jamnadas Dwarkadas of Bombay, 41
Jamnadas Bajaj Foundation, 146
Janta
  Government, 70
  Party, 68, 69
Jatti, BD, 69
Jefferson, Thomas, US President, 21
Jesus Christ, 215
Johannesburg, 154
John, Adam General, 31
Journalism, 10, 94, 96, 100, 120, 125, 137, 146, 149, 150, 164, 165, 197, 204
Journalist
  Gandhi, 163
  Writing, 151
Journalists in USA, 104
Judiciary, 55

K

Kanshi Ram
  Issue, 102, 103
  Problem, 147
Kathiawad, 208
Kesari, 35
Khadi, 140, 165, 173, 175, 176, 187
  Garments, 176
Kheda, 154
  Satyagraha, 159-160
Kickbacks, 74
Koran (Quran), 206, 214
Krishna Patrika, 40
Kunzru, HN, 95

L

Latin America, 18
Liberals and Nationalists, 34
License Raj, 184
Licensing
  Act, 23
  Of Press, 31
Lord
  Chelmsford, Viceroy, 40
  Curzon, 33
  Minto's Tenure, 30
LTTE, 145, 146

M

Macaulay's Draft Bill, 31
Madras
  Legislature, 90
  Maintenance of Public Order, 1948, 80
  Presidency, 35
Maganlal, 135
Malayala Manorama, 101
Mankekar, DR, Journalist, 144
Marxist and Leftist, 72
Mathew Commission, 73
Mathew, KK, Justice, 70
Media, 202
  Council of India, 120
  Profession, 197
Meditation of Silence, 178
Message Oriented Speeches, 151
Metcalfe's Act, 31
Mill, John Stuart, 23
Milton, 23
Ministry of Information and Broadcasting, 67
Modern Society, 9
Mohammedan Mosques, 131
Mrs. Gandhi's Election, 114
Mudhalker J, Justice, 96, 117
Mukherjee, SK, 99
Munshi, KM, 51
Muslim Vote Banks, 145
Muslims in Western Countries, 04

N

Naidu, Sarojini, 133
  Gifted Lady, 133
Narasimha Rao, PV, PM, 128
Narayan, Jaiprakash, 60, 61
National
  Integration Council, 96
  Movement, 36, 109
  News Council, 94
  Press, 33
Navajian, Gujarati Weekly, 41, 153, 163
Nayar, Kuldip, 69, 147
Nehru, Jawahar Lal, 47, 73, 80, 110, 115, 152, 184
New Technology, 119

Newspaper (Price and Page) Act, 85
Nishkam Karma, 209
Non-Cooperation, 184
  Movement, 160, 162, 163
Non-Formal Education, 119
Non-Violence, 152, 174, 175, 183, 189, 200, 201, 210
  Movement, 73, 174

O

Obscenity, 32
Offending Newspapers, 58
Oil and Natural Gas Commission, 74
Old Civilization, 17
  Chinese, 17
  Egyptian, 17
  Greco-Roman, 17
  India, 17
Old Papyrus, 17
Orange Free State, 155

P

Padyatra, 182
Paranjpee, HK, 99
Parliamentary
  Committee, 74
  Proceedings (Protection of Publication), Act, 1956, 57, 69, 113
Partition, 47
Patel, Jang Bahadur, Kurmi Community, 102
Patna High Court, 53
Patriotism, 173
Peaceful Civil Resistance, 160
Peasant Unrest in Punjab, 33
Philosophy
  And Vision Journalism, 13
  Of Advaita, 229
PIllai, Chidambaram, 35
Plague at Johannesburg, 132
Pluralism, 224, 227
Plurality of Religions, 223
Political
  Parties, 67, 68, 114
  Philosophers, 20
  Subjugation, 208
Population Control, 146
Porbandar, 208
Pradip Urdu Daily, 82
Press (Emergency Powers) Act, 1931, 53
Press (Objectionable Matter) Act, 55, 56, 94, 95, 112, 117
  Explanation, 94, 95
Press Act of 1908, 33, 109
Press Act of 1908, 1910, 41
Press Act of 1910, 36, 39, 40
Press Act of India, 32, 38, 39
  1835, 31
  1878, 109
  1935, 109
Press
  Advisory Unit of Press, 59
  And Registration of Books Act, 32
  Barons, 100
  Commission of India, 20
  Commission, 55, 56, 94
    Members Details, 55
  Commission, (First), 94-96
  Complaint Commission (PCC), 93
  Council Act, 1965, 97, 117
  Council Bill, 96, 117
  Council Functions of-, 97
  Council in USA, UK and Sweden, 93
  Council of India (PCI), 67, 70, 72, 93-106, 104, 195
    Chairman PB Sawant, 195
    Legal Powers, 99
  Emergency Powers Act, 42
  In England, 23
  Law Repeal and Amendment Act, 1922, 41
  Mobilizing Role, 80
  Ordinance of 1930, 41, 42, 110
  Regulation Bodies, 93
  Trust of India, 61, 62, 96
Prevention of Publications of Objectionable Matters Act, 69
Primary Education, 146
Princess Diamond Case, 93
Printing Press, 17
Prison Advisory Committee, 45
Profession of Journalism, 136
Prosecution of Editors and Journalists, 33

Punjab Horror, 40
Purna Swaraj, 159

Q

Quit India Movement, 42, 45

R

Racism in South Africa, 151
Radhakrishnan, S, 207
Raja Rammohun Roy's Sambad Kaumadi, 125
Rajagopalachari, the Union Home Minister, 94
Rajendra Prasad, Dr. First Indian President, 152
Raju, Chalapathi, Ed, 9
Ram Charit Manas, 208
Ramayana and Bhagawat Gita, in Gujarati, 208
Rao, Chalapathi, Journalist, 147, 148
Rao, Hari Sarvothama, 35
Regional Newspaper, 147
Registration of
  South Africa Government, 133
  The Press and Books, 1867, 36, 41
Religious
  Pluralism, 227
  Renaissance, 208
Repeal of Press Govt. of India, 66
Report of Press Council of India, 114
Revolt of American Colonies, 18
Revolution of 1857, 208
Right to Freedom of Speech, 111
Rock Temples, 131
  Ajanta, 131
Romesh Thapar and State of Madras, 52
Rowlatt Act, 11, 39
Rowlatt Bills, 162
Roy, Kalinath, 40
Russia, 18

S

Sahitya Academi, 96
Salt
  Law, 173
  March, 191
  Satyagraha, 42
Samachar Bharata, 61
Sapru, Tej Bahadur, 40
Sarkaria, Press Council Chairman, 100
Sarvodaya, 152
Satya, 151, 153
Satya And Ahimsa, 163, 164, 171
Satyagraha, 140, 152, 159-165, 171, 177, 187, 189, 200
  And Ahimsa, 193
  Of South Africa, 126
  War Without Weapon, 191
Save Hindu Agitation, 82
SC/ST, 103
Science and Technology, 202
SEBI, 145
Second Press Commission (1978-82), 70-73, 99, 114, 120, 121, 146
  Recommendations of the Commission, 71
  Terms of the Commission, 70
Sedition Writing Act, 136
Shastri, Lal Bahadur, 96
Shipping Movement, 17
Shri Warsha, 101
Sikhism, 207
Sino-Indian War, 1962, 58
Siva Subramania, 35
Smuts, 161
Social
  And Economic Development in US, 21
  Stratification, 206
Socialist Party, 68
Socio-Political Change, 180
Sonar Bangla of Calcutta, 34
South
  Africa, 10, 11, 126, 129, 130, 132, 134, 152, 155-158, 163, 189, 215
  African Indians, 133
Spanish Dominican, 18
Spiritual Development, 200
Spirituality, 205
Sri Lanka's Tamils, 145
Sri Lankan Army, 146
State of Bihar, V Shailabala Devi, 82
Struggle
  For Freedom, 9
  Of Independence, 152

Supreme Court of India, 24
Suspension of Parliamentary Proceedings Act, 1956, 66
Swadeshi Journalism, 187
Swadesmitran, 40
Swaraj, 152

T

Taj Mahal Agra, 131
Tavleen Singh, Sr. Journalist, 147
Telegraph Case, 104
Terrorist Action in Bengal, 33
The Hindu, 40, 44, 73, 76, 145
The Telegraph, 77
Theory of Absolute Rights, 48
Theosophical Societies, 208
Tilak, Bal Gangadhar, 34
Titans, 131
Tolstoy, Leo, 210
Tribune, 102
Tulsidas, 208

U

UK, 93
UN, 19, 107
  Declaration, 19, 107
UNESCO, 144
UNI, 61, 62, 96
Universal Declaration of Human Rights, 19
University Grants Commission, 96
Untouchability, 140, 158, 206
Uprising Against Imperialism, 32
Urdu-i-Moalla, 35
US, 18, 21, 22, 94
  Congress, 21
  Supreme Court Decision, 22

V

Vaishnava Sect, 208
  Founder Vallabhacharya, 208
Vaishnavaism, 208
Varna Dharma, 205
Vedas, 205
Verghese, BG, 67, 68
Viceroys, 161
  Chelmsford, 161
  Irwin, 161
  LInlithgow, 161
  Reading, 161
  Wellington, 161

W

War with Pakistan, 59
Wars and Press, 58
Washington Post, 61
West German Submarines Deal, 73
Western Civilization, 127
Wood Carving, 131
World War II, 1939, 44, 110

Y

Yadav, Mulayam Singh, 147
Yellow Journalism, 94
Yeravda, 191
Young India, 10, 12, 41, 110, 125, 127, 140, 163, 203
Yugantar of Calctta, 33